AF552473

POLICE REFORMS IN INDIA

AN ANALYTICAL STUDY

By

Dr. K. Alexander

Lecturer
Dept. of Political Science &
Public Administration
St. John's College, Anchal
University of Kerala
Thiruvananthapuram–695 034

DISCOVERY PUBLISHING HOUSE
NEW DELHI-110002

First Published-2006

ISBN 81-8356-128-4

Published by

DISCOVERY PUBLISHING HOUSE
4831/24, Ansari Road, Prahlad Street
Darya Ganj, New Delhi-110002 (India)
Phone: 23279245 • Fax: 91-11-23253475
E-mail:dphtemp@indiatimes.com

Printed at:

Amit Enterprises

Preface

Looked at from various angles, it can be seen that there is a pressing need for reforming the police in Kerala though it is not vociferously articulated or incessantly canvassed. Such an important issue cannot be delayed for long in a state like Kerala with its high-level of literacy and social and political consciousness. This study has been taken up in this background. It is admitted that it would be too sanguine a hope to expect police reforms to materialised from a research study. However, creative movements every where had their beginnings in the silent birth of an idea, an abrupt incident or even a casual spark. This book would perhaps be the much needed spark to start a burning fire, demanding police reform. This book is the revised version of my Ph.D thesis. I have earnestly tried to be neutral in collecting and interpreting the data. Let the readers decide whether I have succeeded or not.

I have received help and encouragement from several individuals and institutions in the preparation of this thesis. It is not possible to mention them by name. Dr. P.J. Alexander IPS (Retd.), Hon. Professor, Institute of Management in Government, formerly Director General of Police, Kerala, and Director, I.M.G., Trivandrum, guided my research work. My easy access to his personal library, an abundant source of literature on Administration and Management, including Police Administration, helped me in this endeavour. I have received guidance and support from him at all stages of this study. I place on record my deep sense of indebtedness and gratitude to him. In designing the Questionnaires and the analysis of data, I have received assistance from M. George. I am profoundly grateful to him. P.S. Supal, M.L.A., my former student was helpful to me at all stages of this study. I place on record. I sincere thanks to him.

I am thankful to Dr. K.M. Abraham, IAS, the Director, I.M.G. for permitting me to avail of the facilities of the institute. I am also grateful to Sri K. Mukundan, Secretary, Sri K. Jayachandran, Deputy Director and Sri P. Unnikrishnan, Public Relations Officer of the Institute for their generous help and co-operation.

I am grateful to Rev. Dr. Samuel Kattukallil, Principal, St. John's College, Anchal, who has helped, encouraged and assisted me in my research efforts. I am also thankful to Dr. G. Gopalkumar, Professor and Head, Department of Political Science, University of Kerala for the support and guidance received from him. Dr. Shaji Varkey and other members of the teaching faculty of the Department have been available for consultation and discussions at all times. I am grateful to them.

In the planning and execution of collection of data through Questionnaires from the Police Department and for statistical and related information on the police in Kerala, I have received whole-heartedly support and co-operation from the Director General of Police and officers in the Police Headquarters. The IPS officers, with whom I interacted were most helpful and encouraging. But for their co-operation, authentic data on this study would not have been easy to come by. I thank them all and hope that this study would help them in pushing through their long felt need for police reforms in the State.

The facilities of the I.M.G. Library, Legislature Library, Thiruvananthapuram, the University Library, Library of the Police Training College, of the Department of Politics, University of Kerala and the Library of St. John's College, Anchal were available to me at all times. I most sincerely thank the Librarians and staff of these Libraries. I am also grateful to the M.S.C. College Management and my colleagues in St. John's College, Anchal. M/s Phoenix Computers, Kariavattom, did the DTP and related works in time. I thank them sincerely. I am grateful to all others who helped me in this study.

My sincere thanks are also due to Discovery Publishing House, New Delhi for bringing out this volume.

Koshy Alexander

Acknowledgements

I have received help and encouragement from several individuals and institutions in the preparation of this Thesis. It is not possible to mention them by name. Dr. P.J Alexander IPS (Retd.), Hon. Professor, Institute of Management in Government, formerly Director General of Police, Kerala, and Director, I.M.G, Trivandrum, guided my research work. My easy access to his personal library, an abundant source of literature on Administration and Management, including Police Administration, helped me in this endeavour. I have received guidance and support from him at all stages of this study. I place on record my deep sense of indebtedness and gratitude to him. In designing the Questionnaires and the analysis of data I have received assistance from M. George. I am profoundly grateful to him.

I am thankful to Dr. K.M. Abraham, I.A.S., the Director, I.M.G. for permitting me to avail of the facilities of the Institute. I am also grateful to Sri K. Mukundan, Secretary, Sri K. Jayachandran, Deputy Director and Sri P. Unnikrishnan, Public Relations Officer of the Institute for their generous help and co-operation.

I am grateful to Rev. Dr. Samuel Kattukallil, Principal, St. John's College, Anchal, who has helped, encouraged and assisted me in my research efforts. I am also thankful to Dr. G. Gopakumar, Professor and Head, Department of Political Science, University of Kerala for the support and guidance received from him. Dr. Shaji Varkey and other members of the teaching faculty of the Department have been available for consultation and discussions at all times. I am grateful to them.

In the planning and execution of collection of data through Questionnaires from the Police Department and for statistical and related information on the police in Kerala, I have received whole-hearted support and co-operation from the Director General of Police and officers in the Police Headquarters. The IPS officers, with whom I interacted were most helpful and encouraging. But for their co-operation, authentic data on this study would not have been easy to come by. I thank them all and hope that this study would help them in pushing through their long felt need for police reforms in the State.

The facilities of the I.M.G. Library, Legislature Library, Thiruvananthapuram, the University Library, Library of the Police Training College of the Department of Politics, University of Kerala and the Library of St. John's College, Anchal were available to me at all times. I most sincerely thank the Librarians and staff of these Libraries. I am also grateful to the M.S.C. Colleges Management and my colleagues in St. John's College, Anchal. M/S Phoenix Computers, Kariavattom, did the DTP and related works in time. I thank them sincerely. I am grateful to all others who helped me in this study.

ALEXANDER K.

Thiruvananthapuram

16 December 2003

List of Abbreviations

A.C.P.	–	Assistant Commissioner of Police
A.D.G.P.	–	Additional Director General of Police
A.I.G.	–	Additional Inspector General
A.P.I.	–	Armed Police Inspector
A.P.S.I.	–	Armed Police Sub-Inspector
A.S.I.	–	Additional Sub-Inspector
A.S.P.	–	Assistant Superintendent of Police
B.J.P.	–	Bharatiya Janata Party
B.S.F.	–	Border Security Force
C.B.I.	–	Central Bureau of Investigation
C.I.	–	Circle Inspector
C.I.D.	–	Criminal Investigation Department
C.I.S.F.	–	Central Industrial Security Force
C.P.	–	Commissioner of Police
C.P.I. (M)	–	Communist Party of India (Marxist)
C.P.I.	–	Communist Party of India
C.R.P.F.	–	Central Reserve Police Force
C.V.C.	–	Chief Vigilance Commissioner
Cr.P.C.	–	Criminal Procedure Code
D.G.P.	–	Director General of Police
D.I.G.	–	Deputy Inspector General
D.M.	–	District Magistrate

D.O.	–	Demi Official
D.P.C.A.	–	District Police Complaints Authority
D.P.O.	–	District Police Office/Officer
D.S.P.	–	District Superintendent of Police
Dy. S.P.	–	Deputy Superintendent of Police
e-governance	–	Electronic Governance
F.C.S.	–	Fair Copy Superintendent
F.I.R.	–	First Information Report
H.C.	–	Head Constable
H.F.	–	High Frequency
I.A.S.	–	Indian Administrative Service
I.C.S.	–	Indian Civil Service
I.E. Act	–	Indian Evidence Act
I.G. and D.G.	–	Inspector General and Director General
I.G.P.	–	Inspector General of Police
I.M.G.	–	Institute of Management in Government
I.P.	–	Imperial Police
I.P.C.	–	Indian Penal Code
I.P.S	–	Indian Police Service
M.L.A.	–	Member of Legislative Assembly
M.P.	–	Member of Parliament
M.V. Act	–	Motor Vehicles Act
N.A.	–	Not Available
N.C.O.	–	Non Commissioned Officer
N.C.P.	–	Nationalist Congress Party
N.C.P.S.	–	National Commission for Police Standards
N.O.C	–	No Objection Certificate
N.P.C	–	National Police Commission
P.B.X.	–	Private Branch Exchange

P.C.	–	Police Constable
P.I.L.	–	Public Interest Litigation
P.P.A.C.	–	Police Performance and Accountability Commission
P.T.C.	–	Police Training College
POTA	–	Prevention of Terrorist Activities Act
R.I.	–	Reserve Inspector
R.S.I.	–	Reserve Sub-Inspector
R.S.P.	–	Revolutionary Socialist Party
S.Ax.	–	Sax Phone
S.C.	–	Scheduled Caste
S.H.O.	–	Station House Officer
S.I.	–	Sub-Inspector
S.L.L.	–	Special and Local Legislations
S.P.	–	Superintendent of Police
S.P.S.C.	–	State Public Service Commission
S.R.C.	–	States Re-organisation Commission
S.S.L.C.	–	Secondary School Leaving Certificate
S.T.	–	Scheduled Tribe
S.T.D.	–	Subscriber Trunk Dialing
SMART	–	Simple Moral Accountable Responsive and Transparent
U.D.F.	–	United Democratic Front
U.K	–	United Kingdom
U.P.	–	Uttar Pradesh
U.P.S.C.	–	Union Public Service Commission
U.S.A	–	United States of America
V.H.F.	–	Very High Frequency
V.I.P.	–	Very Important Person
V.V.I.P.	–	Very Very Important Person

Contents

Contents

Introduction

The police are much more than a segment in the civil administrative system. This is particularly so in a country like India where they perform a wide range of functions. They are in the news almost on a daily basis and the manner in which they exercise the powers given to them is the subject of serious debate. Their control by the political executive is another such area. There have been demands to make them accountable only to the law and to ensure that they are politically neutral.[1]

The manner in which they respond to violations of law and order, place restraints on personal freedom, prevent the occurrence of crime and detect crime, all generate debates and controversies. On the one hand they are accused of going into excesses, while on the other hand, they are accused of doing too little. Suffice it is to say that at no point of time can it be said that police action went by the book. This dilemma is related to our perception of rule of law itself. While we proclaim that "all are equal before the law", we also concede or canvass that "some are more equal than the rest".

As a result, in the enforcement of law, all are not considered equal at all time. Herein lies the basic hazard to proper policing in this country. When the laws are fairly clear about their intent and purposes, the modalities of enforcement are not hampered by considerations other than the requirements of law and when law is enforced without fear or favour, it contributes significantly to Rule of Law. Any deficiency in the process results in deficiency in police service. The role of the police in the Criminal Justice System is very crucial. They set the criminal law in motion. They prevent crime, taking advantage of the provisions of the law, investigate crime which could not be prevented as prescribed by the laws and regulations and sent the delinquent for trial. An independent prosecution agency presents the evidence against the offender before the courts. An independent judiciary acting under the mandate of the law adjudicates the case and finds him/her guilty or innocent. In the former event he/she is sentenced to undergo a period in prison hopefully for reformation and re-integration into the society. Thus, in the Criminal Justice Administration the police act in tandem with the victims, the prosecution, the community of lawyers, the criminal courts, the prisons and other penal and reformative institutions. Their function here is a part of social defence. They also maintain law and order by which the pace of normal life is assured in society. They ensure that crowds are regulated, traffic is controlled, democratic dissent is not stifled and the individual is permitted to exercise his freedoms in the society without let or hindrance.

Development and order go hand in hand. Without order, the process of development will be hindered and the fruits of development will not reach the intended. Therefore, maintenance of order is critically vital to the process of development. True development is seen as a process of social change involving far reaching shifts in the roles and power relationships of different groups.[2] The modern State is compelled to enact various laws in response to the emerging socio-economic, socio-political and socio-transformational issues. Most of these legislations are enforced through the police. As a result, the reach of police functions extends to areas hitherto outside the scope of traditional policing. Even among other enforcement agencies designed under such legislations, the police emerge the ultimate arbiter. Thus, the role of the police and the demands on them are steadily on the increase. Traditionally police functions are taken to be prevention of commission of offences against the law, preservation of order and the protection of the life and property of the people.[3] But the tasks performed by the police are much wider. "The police in this country are the instrument for enforcing the Rule of Law; they are the means by which civilized society maintains order, that people may live safely in their homes and go freely about their lawful business.

Basically their task is the maintenance of Queen's Peace, that is, the preservation of law and order. Without this there would be anarchy. Policemen like everybody else are accountable to the law. They are also the law's agents: and the uniformed policeman has for many years been recognized and accepted as the embodiment of law's authority".[4] These purposes are basically unchanging, but there are constant and continuous accretions to police duties and functions. The Indian situation offers numerous instances of such additions and accretions to police functions and duties. While the Constitution of India has put police and law and order in the State List,[5] the Union List carries a reference to other armed forces of the Union.[6] The steady expansion of the police forces under the Union Government and the continuing expansion of police functions can be discerned from the data published by the National Crime Records Bureau from time to time.[7] Publications of the Government of India, of the various States and other agencies very well reveal that the crime statistics come under a number of heads most of which were not there during the early years of the Republic. There has also been an expansion of the range of enforcement and regulative activities owing to the intervention of the courts through Public Interest Litigations (P.I.L.), under the provisions of the Criminal Procedure Code (Cr.P.C.) and the writ jurisdiction of the High Courts and Supreme Court of India. In fact, a strong contention is emerging to the effect that with regard to the investigation of crimes the police should be accountable only to the judiciary. Thus, even a broad survey of police functions and duties in this country would show that the police are not just a part of civil administration but a very important and critical component. The police have, in short, come to mean to day to be the "operative agency for ensuring the essentials of civilized life and a touchstone for testing the spirit and quality of civil administration".[8]

It has also been pointed out that the police play a formative role in political development. The two important questions that have been addressed in this context are:

How does the social and political environment affect the police? and

How do the police affect the social and political environment?[9]

"Police affect political development through the things they do, the nature of the actions they perform. These actions which are not all of a kind impinge upon society on different points. Both the nature of the activity and its point of contact with the political system affect its influence on political development".[10]

It was in the 1960s that an argument came that police affect political development significantly by what they do, how they do it, what the police are and what police do to each other.[11] "The police bear primary responsibility for maintaining stable conditions of social life. Whether they do so or not determines to a large extent the fortunes of any development effort. This is particularly obvious for economic development. In so far as the form and pace of economic development condition political enterprise, the police, by maintaining conditions compatible with economic development of whatever character, affect the form of political interaction in the future. Order and security are essential conditions of economic growth. Property must be protected, contracts upheld; peculation curtailed; the opportunity to work safeguarded, and the fruits of one's labour secured for enjoyment. The balance between order and violence, lawlessness and order, security and insecurity, is held by the police; they critically determine whether development will prosper".[12]

It has also been observed that the police may play a role in the political life of a nation by participating directly in top-level policy-making as they normally possess a preponderance of force in domestic society. There have been instances where the police have lend support to the forceful overthrow of the Government by the military or the military backed dictators. That the collapse or dismantling of a regime would lead to crime, chaos and disorder in the absence of a police force, has been proved to be true by the recent developments in Iraq.[13] The police could become one of the several important constituent groups supporting or opposing Governments and they could exercise their powers to frustrate political leadership. "Perhaps most subtle of all, police possesses an almost unlimited ability to intervene in politics and policy implementation by standing aside".[14] They can also influence politics by failing to support the implementation of policy decisions already made. They can affect political development by the patterns of political competition they allow to grow and also by the degree of disorder or violence they permit in registering democratic dissent. They regulate the vociferousness of demonstrations and disruptiveness of agitation.... A society subject to periodic outburst of violence, to ambuscades and arson in the pursuit of political ends, to civil disobedience and sabotage will surely develop in quiet a different way from a society, in which violence is rare and relations among individuals proceed on the basis of stable expectations about the means of contention.[15] It is also pointed out that the police influence political life through the exercise of administrative tasks. "They may be entrusted with administrative tasks far beyond the normal concept of police duties. They may license shops, inspect buildings, supervise fire service, issue permits, run laboratories, check immigration, issue passports, register births, run industrial plants, collect taxes, solicit for public undertakings, manage hospitals and schools, direct construction of roads and supervise public health programmes.... They may bring pressure to bear upon Civil Servants to perform as police wish or they may allow others to bring improper pressure to bear without raising a hand in protection. They hold an even tighter reign over administrations when they are granted authority to investigate administrative actions or administrative personnel. Criminal acts by Civil Servants outside their work are generally subject to police investigation.... Their access to administration becomes then almost limitless...".[16]

It has also been observed that the police influence political life by what they do generally in society and the relations they establish with the public. "Even assuming that the task of police is considered minimally as maintaining law and order and limiting criminal activity, it is a mistake to conceive of police duties as being all of one kind. Several important determinations affect their substantive actions...".[17] Bayley writes, "Sir Charles Reith... has long maintained that the establishment of Peel's police in England in 1829 brought about a fundamental re-shaping of English society. If the British people are law abiding today, he has said, it is due in overwhelming measure to the effect the 'New Police' had on attitudes toward law, crime and the responsibilities of the citizenship.... The British love of order and respect for law is the result of model behaviour on the part of the British Police in spite of appalling conditions of crime, vice, public insecurity and individual apathy, hostility and indifference to law enforcement".[18] Bayley also points out that a prime cause of lawlessness, brutality and corruption in U.S.A. is according to Reith, the law enforcement machinery itself. Although the experiences of U.K. and U.S.A. would not be sufficient to conclude that the police exercise preponderant influence on the development of political institutions and the process of political development, it has to be considered that the police in contemporary society does have the functional influence to critically affect the process of political development.

The role of the police in the conduct of elections has been pointed out as another instance where they exercise substantial influence in the political process. Bayley has wryly remarked, "If popular elections are part of politics, then with the police connivance the dead may vote and the living vote more than once".[19] In a study on "Police and Elections" with the Kerala state in focus, it has been concluded that "whenever there is police interference the election is often vitiated".[20] In a country the size of India with its millions of voters, the police which has a network unparalleled by any other department by sheer visibility and presence, can create an impact on the electoral process as well as the electoral outcome. Similarly, their presence and proximity to epicenters of crime, violence and disorder exercise as a restraint on the perpetrators of lawlessness and as an assurance of safety and security to likely victims. As Bayley wrote "Perhaps most subtle of all, police possess an almost unlimited ability to intervene in politics....".[21] It is evident that, the police do play a role in this most important democratic process and Bayley points unmistakably to the potential for good and bad during elections in police conduct. The provisions of the Representation of People's Act and consequent arrangements emanating from them primarily by the Election Commission have kept the police out of the polling booth. But, they are never far away. They are not within of course, but they are neither without. "Most studies on police and the electoral process give credit to the police for the peaceful and orderly management of elections".[22] While the police justifiably complain that their role is the most important step in the political process is not acknowledged in full, nevertheless they make "the little man walking into a little booth with a little pencil marking a little cross on a little bit of paper", possible. The frequent elections and by-elections do indeed strain police resources to the maximum. But, as in the neighbouring country, the army is not called upon to oversee the electoral process because police neutrality is not suspect, though there are instances exposing aberrations. Pre-poll and post-poll arrangements further create tense law and order situations and lead to registration of a series of First Information Reports. The police perform a balancing act, a healing touch also during these tensed phases by accommodating the demands of all serious contestants for space in wooing the voters, sustaining their loyalties and in herding them to the polling booths. The police, therefore, justifiably claim that they make it possible for the masses to march to the tunes of a different drummer. Thus, the core of the democratic process is seen leaning heavily on police professionalism, for its fulfillment. In short, it can be seen that the police is much more than a cog in the administrative wheel of the State. It is in fact, a very important segment of the administrative structure.

The basic structure of the police in India can be traced back to the Police Act of 1861. The basic criminal legislations are also similarly ancient—the Indian Penal Code (I.P.C.) was enacted in 1861, the Indian Evidence Act (I.E. Act) in 1872 and the original Criminal Procedure Code (Cr.P.C.) in 1898. It was revised later in 1973. The Police Act of 1861 was on the recommendations of the Police Commission of 1860. The territories held by the East India Company had come under the British Crown after the Indian mutiny of 1857 and there were serious efforts towards homogenisation of the criminal laws and regulations. The Princely states were nudged to introduce the criminal laws that were made applicable to the British Presidencies. There were no significant moves to reform the police in India while the country was under the Crown except by the formation of the 1902 Police Commission known as the 'Fraser Commission'. The recommendations of the Commission and the dissenting note by the Maharaja of Durbhanga continue to provide interesting insights into the British perspective regarding maintenance of order and control of crime.[23] By then, however, members of the Indian Imperial Police (I.P.) were taking over most of the senior positions in the police hierarchy. They were also being inducted into the Princely states as heads of the police departments to provide the much-needed co-ordination with the rest of India. Throughout the period of national struggle for freedom, the police and regulatory departments were clearly on the side of their British masters which did not endear them too much with the Indian people.

However, after the attainment of political freedom, when the Constitution of India was framed the two covenanted services—the Indian Civil Service (I.C.S.) and the Indian Imperial Police—were retained to ensure continuity in administration and were christened as the Indian Administrative Service (I.A.S.) and the Indian Police Service (I.P.S).[24] There were no structural changes with regard to the criminal law and administration when the states were reorganized on the basis of the linguistic formula and new states came into being with new police cadres. These new states increasingly felt the need to reform and reorganize their police. A number of states appointed Police Reorganization/Police Reform Commissions. The states were enabled to do so by virtue of the distribution of powers between the Union and States where police and law and order found a place in Part-II—State list. The Terms of Reference of these Commissions and the highlights of their recommendations are being discussed elsewhere. Suffice it is to say that the state envisaged under the Constitution was at odds with the existing administrative structure, successors to the steel frame with limited objectives, almost equivalent to that of a police state. Collection of revenue and maintenance of law and order were the main considerations of the domestic policy of the pre-independent state. The Preamble of the Constitution, however, committed itself to ensuring social justice to the people of India followed by political and economic justice. The State also promised that it will be secular and democratic.[25] The long list of basic freedoms in Part-III and the philosophical base of the Indian State in Part-IV gave clear indications that the State in India is bound to be a responsive State. With an independent judiciary reading into the Constitution a mandate for "Judicial Review" went about enlarging the scope of Fundamental Rights given in Part-III and whittling away at curbs and restraints to the basic freedoms and basic rights. The emergence of Public Interest Litigations (P.I.L.) was another enabling development. Thus, from the faint contours of a Welfare State etched in the Preamble and Part-III and Part-IV, the State that emerged out of the pages of the Constitution was one that went far beyond the goals even of a

Welfare State. Planning and development added further dimensions. The task of development was also assigned to the bureaucracy. In addition, in the broad area of political development also there were strains, pulls and pressures. Thus, the State in India came under enormous pressures. However, except for a brief spell when basic democratic freedoms were denied under the emergency provisions of the Constitution, the State was able to safeguard both the form and content of parliamentary democracy. The public disapproval of the conduct of the police and the other regulatory agencies during this period found its expression in the setting up of the Shah Commission of Enquiry and also the appointment of the National Police Commission (N.P.C.).[26] Both these responses, when analysed with the benefit of hindsight were ad hoc and not serious efforts to rectify the susceptibility of the system to distortions. It may be recalled here that there have been a number of attempts at administrative reforms which produced very little qualitative changes.[27] A reasonably pragmatic response would have been to make serious attempts at the different stages of the transformation of the Indian State, to reform and to realigning the administrative system and the police sub-system to ensure smooth realization of the goals and objectives of State policies and to obviate institutions of governance becoming dysfunctional. In short, police reform, which means reform of the Criminal Justice Administration, ought to have received much more serious attention from the political leadership.[28]

At the dawn of the independence the population of India was 3611 lakhs. The strength of the police was 3.5 lakhs. The total number of cognizable crimes was 649728. A decadal study would put these figures as shown below.[29]

Year	*Population in Lakhs*	*Strength of Police in Lakhs*	*Number of Cognizable Crime*
1961	4392	N.A.	625651
1971	5482	7.07	952581
1981	6833	8.98	1385757
1991	8463	11.53	1678375
2000	10021	13.00	1771084

The most important question is whether such a burgeoning number in population, in police strength and in cognizable crime can be managed with the structures, enactments and equipments inherited by the police in India from the colonial administration with its limited objectives of governance. It is evident that there was a lamentable mismatch between the State as conceived in the 1950 Constitution and the police as designed by the 1861 Police Act.[30]

The country also saw violent and militant movements, challenges to the very concept of democratic dissent, by well orchestrated mass upsurges paralysing national life, by trade unions calling for country-wide strikes and disparate forces upsetting regional administration.[31] These developments made traditional police response obsolete. The solution chosen by the administration was primarily enhancing the strength of armed police and para-military forces. In fact, the State is often accused of transforming itself as a counter terrorist organisation violating the basic norms of police response and human rights.[32] Instead of structuring appropriate institutional responses[33] the State tinkered and toyed with the police structure without opting for purposive police reforms.

Terrorism also made its dire impact on the Indian State. Sadly, its response was enactment of harsher criminal laws. This was obviously an attempt to treat the symptoms rather than the disease. There was, thus in the first 50 years of the Republic itself, very strong and serious compulsions for reforming the police and re-writing, the basic police enactments. It could be therefore called a period of missed opportunities.

It can be seen that, where Police Commissions were appointed by various states and in 1977 by the Centre itself, with the barest of exceptions, the efforts fell short of the needs of the time and the needs of the country. The Terms of Reference of the 1902-03 Police Commission is important in this context.[34]

(i) "Whether the organisation, training, strength and pay of the different ranks of the district police, both superior and subordinate foot and mounted, whether on ordinary duty or in the reserve, are adequate to secure the preservation of the public peace and the proper investigation and detection of crime, and if not, what changes are required in them,

respectively in each province with regard to its local conditions, in order to attain these objects;

(ii) Whether existing arrangements secure that crime is fully reported or require to be supplemented in any way: and in particular, whether the village officers and the rural police in each province are efficient aids to the district police in the matter of reporting crime, and if not, how the relations between the former and the latter can (subject to the condition that the rural police in each province must not be enrolled under the Police Act) be improved.

(iii) Whether the system of investigating offences now enforce in each province, the object being to provide for the full investigation of all serious crime while avoiding interference by the police in trivial matters, is capable of improvement, and if so, in what manner; and whether the institution of fully organized Criminal Investigation Departments, either Imperial or Provincial, is recommended.

(iv) Whether the form of statistical returns now adopted is satisfactory or capable of improvement, and whether the use to which such returns are now put as tests of police working is appropriate or not.

Whether the general supervision exercised by the Magistracy over the police, and the control of superior officers (including inspectors) over the investigation of crime are adequate to prevent oppression on the part of the subordinate police; and, if not, how they can be made so.

(vi) Whether the existing organisation of the railway police, its operation as between provinces and states, and its connection with the district police are in a satisfactory conditions and, if not, what improvements can be effected; and

(vii) Whether the career at present offered to natives in the police in each province is sufficiently attractive to induce the proper stamp of men to enter it; and, if not, what steps can be taken to remedy this evil consistently with recognized measure of necessity for European control in the district charges."

One of the earliest Police Commissions appointed by the states after re-organisation was the Kerala Police Re-organisation Committee constituted on 15 January 1959, for the reorganization of the police with the following Terms of Reference.[35]

To enquire and report on:

(i) The role of the police in the Welfare State;

(ii) Whether the existing provisions of law are adequate to help, realize and secure fulfilment of the objectives laid down in the Directive Principles of the Constitution and the Public aspirations, realised thereby and in particular in the sphere of employer-employee, landlord-tenant and capital-labour relations;

(iii) The duties of the police in the context of:

(a) the free exercise of civil liberties and political rights of freedom of speech, of platform and association in a democracy consistent with the paramount security of the State;

(b) communal and linguistic tensions that crop up from time to time;

(c) demonstrations and agitations with or without the support of political parties;

(d) in property disputes;

(iv) Whether in view of the public criticism in recent times against firing by the police, the use of fire arms by the police should be totally excluded; and if not the nature of circumstances and the conditions under which it should be allowed.

(v) The use of the regulatory and restrictive powers under the Police Act; the security provisions under Chapter X and Sections 144 and 151 of Cr. P.C.

(vi) Operational technique of the police and the use of the following weapons:-

Lathi, tear-gas, coloured water;

(vii) Provisions regarding the handling of under-trial prisoners and accused persons in matters like hand-cuffing, treatment

of accused before production in court, facilities for getting evidence in the possession of accused;

(viii) Measures for controlling meetings, demonstrations and mobs.

(ix) Measures for improving the work of investigation and detection; the introduction of an incentive scheme, the feasibility of associating the public with the work of the police and the setting up of Police Advisory Committee for the purpose.

(x) Village police or at least associating village Panchayats, in some form, with the police;

(xi) Use of modern scientific devices to help in the work of the police as in some of the advanced countries in the West;

(xii) (a) reorganisation of the administrative set up of the police in the State including recruitment, training (both initial and in-service training) and promotion;

(b) special training for duty in emergencies like famine, fire, strike or sabotage relating to essential services or public utility services;

(c) dress and uniform;

(xiii) Women Police: Whether Women Police should be recruited, their conditions of service, specialized training for women police, in which departments of the police and for what specific purpose they should be posted;

(xiv) Police and the Public: Measures for better public relations between the police and the public;

(xv) Police and Development: How far the police could be utilized for National Development Work;

(xvi) Recreational facilities and welfare measures for the police;

(xvii) Juvenile Delinquency: Measures for controlling juvenile delinquency; special agencies for punishing such cases, Children's Courts and correctional/ Institutions;

(xviii) The setting up of Whitely Councils in the Police Department.

The West Bengal Police Commission was appointed on 10 March 1960 with the following mandate.[36] "Far-reaching changes have taken place in the State of West Bengal over the last decade touching various aspects of the life of the people and giving rise to many complicated problems in matters of administration of the Police Force of the State. A review of the needs and problems of the Police Force as well as a reorientation of administrative method and policy are considered desirable, taking due note of the outlook of the present times and the resources of the State as well". This Commission has been appointed to "enquire into the different aspects of the Police Administration in this State and submit a comprehensive report to the government".

The Terms of Reference of the Punjab Police Commission 1961-62 were as follows.[37]

(i) Whether the organisation, training and strength of the different ranks of the Police Force in the State are adequate for preventing breach of the peace, maintaining public order and investigation and detection of crime?

(ii) If the organization, training and strength of the Police Force in the State or the purposes mentioned in (i) above is not adequate then what revised norm of the requisite strength for different ranks should be fixed and what other changes and modifications are required to be made?

(iii) Whether in the light of the need for recruitment and retention of adequate number of men and women for the Police Service, the conditions of service in the Police are sufficiently attractive to induce the proper type of individuals to enter it and Report on pay, emoluments, Travelling Allowance and other allowances, pensions, promotions and other conditions of service, including their living conditions of different levels (excluding I.P./Indian Police Service).

(iv) To enquire and Report as to the nature and limits of the assistance which can be given by women in the

carrying out of the police duties, and as to what should be the status and conditions of service of women employed on such duties.

(v) Whether any reduction in the duties now allotted to the police is possible?

(vi) To examine the adequacy and suitability of the equipment provided for the police with particular reference to transport and radio facilities and to suggest as to whether there should be increase in the existing equipment in order to increase mobility and efficiency and to save man-power.

(vii) Whether in view of the public criticism in recent times against firing by the police, the use of fire arms by the police should be totally excluded and if not, the nature of the circumstances and the conditions under which, it should be allowed?

(viii) To consider the adequacy of the measures for controlling meetings, demonstrations and mobs, etc, and operational techniques of the police in the use of lathis, teargas, etc and to suggest any improvement therein.

(ix) Whether any changes or improvements by way of separation or otherwise in the functions of the police regarding (a) investigation and (b) prosecution of cases are called for?

(x) Whether it would be proper to separate completely the Investigating Agency from the Law and Order Agency and to set up for the former a specialised police force trained in the modern methods of investigation?

(xi) To examine the existing facilities for application of scientific aids to the investigation of crime, offer suggestions for further improvement and expansion in that respect and propose what further measures are needed to set up work in the direction.

(xii) Whether in view of the present volume and tendencies of traffic, the police are properly organized and equipped to ensure safety of life and property on roads?

(xiii) Whether the police force setup for rural areas is effective in the performance of the police duties in those areas and whether any changes are necessary in its strength, organisation, training and conditions of service and further, how, in the context of village Panchayats functioning all over the State, the efforts of the district and rural police and those of the village Panchayats can be integrated in tackling crime? The feasibility of substitution of Village Chaukidars by a system of beat constables may as well be examined in this context and necessary suggestions be made.

(xiv) Whether the general supervision exercised by the magistracy over the police, particularly in view of the separation of the executive and the judiciary and the control of the superior Police Officers over the investigation of crime and other police duties are on the right lines and what are the improvements needed in this behalf?

(xv) To examine the extent of public co-operation extended to the Police in reporting prevention and investigation of Crime; the handicaps that the Police have to face in consequence of its inadequacy or absence, and steps for its improvement, keeping in view the rule of law, the free exercise of civil liberties and political rights of freedom of speech, of platform and association, and the police aspirations in the light of the Directive Principles of the Constitution.

(xvi) To explore ways and means of bringing the public and police closer together.

(xvii) To examine and suggest as to what further steps should be taken in rooting out corruption in the police force and securing greater co-operation and assistance from the public in combating crime.

(xviii) To examine and make suggestions regarding any other problem or problems which come to the Commission's notice in the course of their enquiries concerning police organisation and its working in the state.

(xix) To workout the financial implications of the Commission's proposals, and to suggest the manner in which the reforms recommended by them can be enforced within the minimum possible period.

(xx) To consider and make recommendations and suggestions regarding any other matter which the government may refer to the Commission.

The Maharashtra Police Commission was appointed on 1 May 1962 with the following Terms of References.[38]

1. *Organisation, Strength and Training:* Are the present organisation strength and training of the Police Force in the armed and unarmed branches, including the women police, generally adequate for the preservation of law and order and the proper prevention, investigation and detection of crime? If not, what modifications are necessary therein?

2. *Pattern Yardsticks:* Is any revision necessary in the existing yardsticks prescribed for the strength of police stations (urban and rural), armed reserves, etc? If so, in what respects?

3. *Recruitment and Conditions of Service:* Are any changes necessary in the present mode and conditions of recruitment, discipline, promotion and other conditions to service? If so, what?

4. *Ancillary Police Services:* (a) Mounted Police—Are these a useful ancillary to the police force? If so, in what manner? (b) Motor Transport Section,—Can any yardsticks be prescribed for the type and strength of vehicles for various duties? How can proper utilization of its vehicles on police duties ensured. (c) Wireless Section,—Assessment of the utility and technical efficiency of the section and whether the expenditure incurred on it is commensurate with the return. Also, suggestions if any, for its improvement.

5. *Functions and duties of the Police Force:* Are any modification necessary, and if so, what is the existing conception regarding the functions and duties of the Police Force?

6. *Equipment and Scientific Aids:* Are the existing facilities for the useful scientific aids in the investigation of crime adequate? If not, what improvements are desirable?

7. *Public Relations:* (a) What should be the role of the police in industrial and labour disputes? (b) Is there any scope for improvement in the relations between the police and the public, to ensure better response and co-operation?

8. *Procedural:* (a) Are any changes necessary in the procedural law pertaining to investigation of criminal offences by the police and their prosecution in Courts? (b) Would it be practicable and advantageous to separate the investigating staff and the law and order staff? If so, how can this be achieved? (c) Would it be practicable and advantageous to separate the police-prosecuting agency from the police department? If so, in what manner? (d) Would any modification be possible in the existing system of maintenance of registers, records etc at police stations, with a view to economise in the use of executive personnel for clerical duties? (e) How can the supervision of senior officers be rendered more effective and useful? (f) What steps are necessary to reduce delays in investigation and/or prosecution of crime?

9. *Traffic.* What improvements can be suggested for the better regulation and control of traffic, particularly in larger cities like Bombay?

10. *Village Police.* Is any change necessary in the existing pattern of the Village Police Force with reference to the needs of village policing?

11. *Anti-Corruption Measures.* What measures can be suggested for eradicating corruption in the Police Force?

12. *Objectionable Practices.* What measures are suggested for the eradication of objectionable practices in investigation?

13. *Prevention of Crime.* Are any improvements possible in the existing measures taken by the police for the prevention of crime and other anti-social activities? Would it be desirable to confer upon the police further powers in this connection?

14. *Crime Detection.* What steps can be suggested for improving the detection of offences?

15. *Prohibition Enforcement.* What are the difficulties met by the police in the successful enforcement of the prohibition laws, and what concrete measures can be devised for overcoming these?

16. *Welfare.* To what extent and on what conditions should Police amenities, welfare measures and sports activities be subsidised by government? Should contributions from non-official sources be accepted towards such activities, and, if so, under what limitations?

17. *Police Buildings.* What suggestions can be made for improving police housing (both office and residential) and expediting its construction programme?

18. *Morale and General Efficiency.* Such suggestions as the Commission may wish to make for improving the morale and efficiency of the Police Force in Maharashtra State and generally with regard to the role of the Police in Democratic Welfare State.

A Police Commission was appointed by Uttar Pradesh Government on 11 May, 1970 and the Terms of Reference were brief.[39]

(i) to examine the extent of concealment and minimisation of crimes at the police stations and to recommend measures to improve the position;

(ii) to examine the present procedure of investigation and to recommend measures to expedite investigation, to raise their standards, and to provide for effective supervision of cases before the submission of charge sheets;

(iii) to recommend measures to improve the system of prosecution of cases.

A Police Commission was appointed by the Tamil Nadu Government on 20 December 1969. Its Terms of Reference were as follows:[40]

(i) Pay and allowance of police force;

(This will be discussed at joint sittings of the Police Commission and the Pay Commission with a view to arriving at an agreed decision)

(ii) General conditions of Service, Housing and Welfare;

(iii) Powers and duties of the police force and improvement of its efficiency in relation to:

(a) Maintenance of Law and Order

(b) Prevention and detection of Crime;

(c) Control and regulation of Traffic;

(d) Collections of intelligence; and

(e) Other police duties, old and new;

(iv) Modernization of organisation and methods; investigational facilities; statistics and records; research and planning.

(v) Yardsticks of manpower and supervision as well as equipment with a special reference to transport and communications;

(vi) Qualifications and recruitment, training and placement, delegation of powers and control as well as assessment of performance and promotions;

(vii) Public relations and relationship with special sections of the community like political organizations, labour, peasantry, students, press etc, complaints and grievances against the police;

(viii) Co-ordination between the police, the Courts and magistracy, general administration department and other government departments;

(ix) Co-ordination between the police organisations of the states and the government of India; and

(x) Any other aspect of police work, which the Commission considers important.

The Terms of Reference of the Assam Police Commission constituted on 21 May 1969 were as follows.[41]

1. (a) Whether the existing organizational structure and pattern of the Police Force required any change to meet the present day needs and whether any changes are necessary in the existing conception regarding the duties and functions of the Police.

(b) Whether the strength of the Police Force in the technical and non-technical branches, both armed and unarmed, is adequate for:

(i) the preservation of law and order.

(ii) the proper prevention, investigation and detection of crime.

(iii) the prosecution of the offenders.

(iv) the collection and collation of intelligence relating to law and order and security.

(v) such other duties as the police may be required to perform in the present day administration.

2. (a) Whether any particular yardstick in respect of different ranks of the Police Force for the police stations, urban and rural, as well as for the Armed Reserves and other units can be fixed.

(b) To examine and review the existing cadre strength of the Indian Police Service in relation to the Police Administrative set up and their needs in the State.

(c) Whether greater decentralization in the control of the force is desirable and whether the system of Police Commissioner should be introduced in places like Gauhati.

3. To what extent, if any, and in what manner does the force at various level need to be increased to meet the present day responsibilities and whether it is possible to estimate the future requirements for the next ten years? Whether the

increases that are required now can be phased over a period of 4 or 5 years and what would be the financial implication of such an increase.

4. (a) Are any changes necessary in the present method and condition of recruitment, training, discipline, promotion and other conditions of service of the Police Force generally or any branch thereof.

(b) What specific measures are suggested to create in the recruits greater awareness of the functions and duties of the Police Force in a Welfare State?

(c) What are the scope for improving public behaviour, outlook and responsiveness to the need of public and to weed out corruption for the betterment of police-public relationship? It may be examined if the State Anti-Corruption Branch should continue to be under the Police as at present?

5. What should be the operational technique of the police in dispersing unlawful assembles or processions? What steps should be taken in regulating processions and meetings consistent with the fundamental rights of the people?

6. (a) Are any changes necessary in the procedural law pertaining to investigation of offences and their prosecution in Courts?

(b) Whether any changes or improvement by way to separating or otherwise the functions of the Police are necessary in:

(i) Investigation (ii) Prosecution, (iii) Maintenance of law and order and prevention of crime (iv) collection of intelligence; and (v) regulation of traffic in cities and towns.

(c) How can the supervision and inspection of senior officers be made more effective and useful?

(d) What steps are necessary to reduce delays in the investigation and/or prosecution of crimes?

(e) What steps are necessary to improve the detection of crime and at the same time to avoid the arrest of innocent persons during investigation?

(f) What measures are suggested for the eradication of objectional practices in investigation?

(g) Would any modification be possible in the existing system of maintenance of registers, records etc at Police Station, with a view to economise in the use of executive personnel for clerical duties, and whether the ministerial staff of the police offices should be a part of the Force?

7. (a) Are any improvement possible in the existing measures taken by police for the prevention of crime and other anti-social activities? Would it be desirable to confer upon the police further powers in this connection?

(b) Does the number of crimes reported to police correctly reflect the number of cognizable offences actually taking place? If a large number of such cases remain unreported what are the reason?

8. (a) What are the possibilities of greater use of scientific methods in investigation by giving proper scientific training to investigation staff and setting up specially trained and equipped units to help in investigation at the District Head Quarters?

(b) Are the facilities of transport, radio and telephone communication provided to extent available and what are the scope for increasing these facilities?

9. (a) Whether the organisation of the River Police is adequate? What should be its scope, purpose and how can it be integrated with the rest of the Police?

(b) Whether the River Police should have separate police stations like G.R.P. Stations?

10. What are the difficulties faced by police in the enforcement of the Assam Excise Act, 1910. The Liquor Prohibition Act, 1952, the Essential Commodities Act, 1955. The Motor

Vehicles Act, 1939. The Cinematography Act, 1952. The Sarais Act, 1867. The Arms Act and Rules thereunder and what concrete measures can be suggested to overcome these difficulties?

11. (a) Whether special responsibilities fall in the police in a Border State and whether adequate arrangements exist and if not, what should be done?

(b) Is the present system of working of the three agencies of the Border Security Force, Land Custom and State Police in relation to violations of the International Border by way of infiltration and smuggling etc. satisfactory.

(c) Is it necessary to invest on the Police of the Border Districts additional powers under the Customs Act?

12. What are the arrangements for collection, collation and digestion of intelligence? Are they adequate for speedy action and if not what should be done?

13. (a) What improvement can be suggested in the organisation and functioning of the V.D.O.?

(b) What changes, if any, are required in the policing of the rural areas?

14. Is the organisation and staff in the following technical units of the Police Department viz (i) A.P.R.O. (ii) Fire Service (iii) Motor Vehicles Workshops and (iv) Traffic Engineering, adequate and the lines of command suitably arranged for necessary control and supervision?

15. (a) What steps are necessary to improve police amenities, welfare measures etc as also provision of housing?

(b) What should be the machinery for the ventillation and redress of policemen's grievances?

16. Do the existing rules and principles regarding relationship between Superintendent of Police and District Magistrate call for a review?

17. Any other recommendation which the Commission may like to make in regard to the proper functioning and improvement of morale and efficiency of the police?

The above instances of Police Commissions constituted by various States are not exhaustive but only illustrative. It would be of interest here to note that the 'Royal Commission on the Police, 1962, was appointed to review the constitutional position of the police throughout Great Britain, the arrangements for their control in administration, and in particular to consider.

1. The constitution and functions of local police authorities;
2. The status and accountability of members of police forces including chief officers of police.
3. The relationship of the police with the public and the means of ensuring that complaints by the public against the police are effectively dealt with; and
4. The broad principles which should govern the remuneration of the constable, having regard to the nature and extent of police duties and responsibilities and the need to attract and retain an adequate number of recruits with proper qualifications.[42]

A significant departure from the Terms of Reference of Police Commissions can be seen from the Terms of Reference of the National Police Commission appointed on 1 November 1977.[43] To render greater clarity, the resolution No. VI-24021/36/77-GPA of the Ministry of Home Affairs is extracted below:

1. Far reaching changes have taken place in the country after the enactment of the Indian Police Act, 1861 and the setting up of the Second Police Commission of 1902, particularly during last thirty years of independence. Though a number of States have appointed Police Commissions after independence to study the problems of the police in their respective state, there has been no comprehensive review at the national level of the police system after independence despite radical changes in the political, social and economic situation in the country. A fresh examination is necessary of the role and performance of the police—both as a law enforcement agency, and as an institution to protect the rights of the citizens enshrined in the Constitution. The Government of India have therefore, decided to appoint a National Police

Commission composed of the following:

(i)	Shri Dharma Vira	Chairman
(ii)	Shri. N.K. Reddy (Retired Judge, Madras High Court)	Member
(iii)	Shri.K.P. Rustumji (Ex-I.G.P., Madhya Pradesh and Ex-Special Secretary, Home Ministry)	Member
(iv)	Shri N.S. Saxena (Ex-I.G.P. UP and Ex-DG CRP and at present, Member, UPSC)	Member
(v)	Prof. M.S. Gore (Professor, Tata Institute of Social Sciences, Bombay)	Member
(vi)	Shri C.V. Narasimhan (Presently Director CBI)	Full-time Member Secretary of the Commission (on relief from his present post)

2. The following will be the Terms of Reference of the Commission:

   (i) Re-define the role, duties, powers and responsibilities of the police with special reference to prevention and control of crime and maintenance of public order.

   (ii) Examine the development of the principles underlying the present policing system, including the method of magisterial supervision, evaluate the performance of the system, identify the basic weakness of inadequacies, and suggest appropriate changes in the system and the basic laws governing the system.

   (iii) Examine if any changes are necessary in the existing method of administration, disciplinary control and accountability.

   (iv) Inquire into the system of investigation and prosecution, the reasons for delay and failure, the use of improper methods, and the extent of their prevalence;

and suggest how the system may be modified or changed and made efficient, scientific and consistent with human dignity; and how the related laws may be suitably amended.

(v) Examine methods of maintaining crime records and statistics and suggest methods for making them uniform and systematic.

(vi) Review policing in rural areas, evaluate any new arrangements that have been made, and recommend changes that are necessary.

(vii) Examine the system of policing required in non-rural and urbanized areas including metropolitan areas, and suggest the pattern that would be the most suitable.

(viii) Examine the steps taken for modernizing law enforcement, evaluate the work of police communications, the computer network, scientific laboratories and agencies for research and development, and examine whether modernization can be speeded up; examine to what extent as a result of the modernization of police forces, streamlining of its functions and its re-structuring, it would be possible to economize in the manpower in the various areas of its activities.

(ix) Examine the nature and extent of the special responsibilities of the police towards the weaker sections of the community and suggest steps to ensure prompt action on their complaints for the safeguard of their rights and interests.

(x) Recommend measures and institutional arrangements:

(a) to prevent misuse of powers by the police, and to examine whether police behaviour, outlook, responsiveness and impartiality are maintained at the correct level, and if not the steps such as recruitment and training which should be taken to improve them.

(b) to prevent misuse of the police by administrative or executive instructions, political or other pressure, or oral orders of any type which are contrary to law;

(c) for the quick and impartial inquiry of public complaints made against the police about any misuse of police powers;

(d) for the quick redressal of grievances of police personnel and to look after their morale and welfare; and

(e) for a periodic objective evaluation of police performance in a Metropolitan area/District/State in a manner which will carry credibility before the public.

(xi) Examine the manner and extent to which police can enlist ready and willing co-operation of the public in the discharge of their social defence and law enforcement duties and suggest measures regarding the institutional arrangements to secure such cooperation and measures for the growth of healthy and friendly public-police relationship.

(xii) Examine the methods of police training, development, and career planning of officers and recommend any changes that are required at any time in their service, to modernize the outlook, and to make the leadership of the force effective and morally strong.

(xiii) Examine the nature of the problems that the police will have to face in the future, and suggest the measures necessary for dealing with them, and for keeping them under continuous study and appraisal.

(xiv) Consider and make recommendations and suggestions regarding any other matter which the Government may refer to the Commission; and

(xv) Any other matter of relevance or importance having an impact on the subject.

3. The Headquarters of the Commission will be at Delhi.

4. The Commission will devise its own procedure and may consult such advisers, as it may consider necessary for any particular purpose. It may call for such information and take such evidences it may consider necessary. Ministries and Departments of the Government of India will furnish such information and documents and other assistance as may be required by the Commission. The Government of India trust that State Governments, Union Territories Administrations, Service Associations and others concerned will extend to the Commission their fullest co-operation and assistance.

5. The Commission will make its recommendations as soon as practicable".

The cataloguing of the Terms of Reference of the various Police Commissions would not be complete without a mention of the Terms of Reference of the Kerala Police Re-organisation Commission formed by the Government of Kerala on 16 August 1982, which would appear nothing less than an anti-climax in the background of the Terms of Reference of the National Police Commission and the Terms and Reference of the first Kerala Police Re-Organisation Committee. The Terms of Reference of the Kerala Police Re-Organisation Commission-1982-86 are given below.[44]

(i) Examine how the various branches of the Police Department like the Special Brach, Crime Branch, Railway Police, Local and Armed Police etc., can be reorganised in such a way that maximum efficiency particularly in collecting intelligence, detecting crimes, and prosecution of offences can be achieved;

(ii) Examine the strength of the State Police with reference to the recommendations of the National Police Commission and/or Finance Commission and also the population and incidence of crime and the scope for modernization in the techniques adopted, and Report whether the present strength is adequate;

(iii) Examine whether the strength of the Armed Battalions should be increased so as to be self-sufficient to meet any emergency without the help of outside forces like the CRPF, BSF, etc...and if so, to what extent;

(iv) Inquire into the system of investigation and prosecution, reasons for delay and failure; and suggest how the system may be modified or changed, and made efficient, scientific and consistent with human dignity; and how the related laws may be suitably amended;

(v) Examine methods of maintaining crime records and statistics and suggest methods for making them systematic;

(vi) Review of policing in rural, non-rural and urbanised areas and suggest the pattern that would be the most suitable;

(vii) Examine the steps taken for modernizing law enforcement, evaluate the work of police communications, the computer network, scientific laboratories and agencies for research and development and examine whether modernization can be speeded up; examine to what extent, as a result of modernization of police forces, streamlining of its functions and its re-structuring it would be possible to economise in the man-power in the various areas of its activities;

(viii) Examine the nature and extent of the special responsibilities of the police towards the weaker sections of the community and suggest steps to ensure prompt action on their complaints for the safeguard of their rights and interests;

(ix) Examine the methods of police training, development, and career planning of officers and recommend any changes that are required at any time in their service to modernize the outlook, and to make the leadership of the force effective and morally strong;

(x) Examine the nature of the problem that the police may have to face in the future, and suggest the measures necessary for dealing with them, and for keeping them under continuous study and appraisal;

(xi) Consider and make recommendation and suggestions regarding any other matter which the Government may refer to the Commission; and

(xii) Any other matter of relevance or importance having an impact on the subject.

Later as per D.O. Letter No. 15248/SSA3/84/ Home dated 12 March 1984, the Home Minister informed the Chairman of the Commission to look in to some more subjects, like the welfare measures initiated in Maharashtra after the police agitation of August 1983 and welfare measures existing in Central Reserve Police Force, Border Security Force, Central Industrial Security Force and States with large Armed Police strength, Police arrangements made in the background of civil disturbances in Assam, Punjab, Haryana etc. The communication also conveyed the Home Minister's suggestion that it would be advisable for the Commission to take evidence from the public, at least on some important issues before finalizing their report.[45] The Member-Secretary has in a Note appended to the Report of the Commission brought out the utter lack of sincerity on the part of the Government and the various steps taken by the administrative department and even the police department to sideline the Kerala Police Re-organisation Commission.[46] The following extract from the Note of the Member-Secretary illuminates this point.

"On 21 June 1986 I informed the Chairman in my D.O. Letter No. 1/KPC/P.J/84 dated 21 June 1986 that the Report is ready for signature and that the convenience of the two members to sign the Report may be ascertained and communicated to me. I had also informed the Chairman through this letter that the Hon'ble Chief Minister had agreed to receive the Report as soon as it was ready and that the Report may be therefore submitted between 23 and 26 June 1986.

On 23 June 1986, in his D.O. No. Sa/10616/86 the Chairman wrote Shri Kaleeswaran intimating the convenience of the Hon'ble Chief Minister to receive the Report. On 24 June 1986 Shri Kaleeswaran wrote a reply to the Chairman. The main burden of this letter is that he thought that the Draft Report of the Commission, as approved by the Chairman of the Commission and sent to him as early as 14 March 1985, was only a 'note' for further discussion in a sitting where he could give comments and that the copy received by him was submitted to the former Home Minister and has not been returned. This letter with all other correspondence referred to in this note are appended. They speak for themselves.

6. Cost of the Commission: The expenditure incurred by the Commission on account of pay and allowances of full-time Member-Secretary, supporting staff and facilities come to approximately Rs. 1,13,111.43.

7. The details given above raise a number of questions of public importance. But I am focusing attention only on two of them.

   (i) Was there really a valid reason to post an officer of the rank of Inspector General of Police as full-time Member-Secretary, if from beginning the intention was to deny him facilities necessary for his proper functioning?

   (ii) Who is accountable for the wanton waste of public money and time and service of a senior officer which could have been better utilized in public interest?

These aspects may be considered by the appropriate authorities to prevent recurrence".

These comments speak eloquently about the need and the sincerity of purpose of the Police Re-Organisation Commission, 1982-86, itself.

A brief Survey of the Terms of Reference of the 1902 Police Commission, the Kerala Police Re-organisation Committee of 1959, the West Bengal Police Commission of 1960, the Punjab Police Commission of 1961-62, the Maharashtra Police Commission of 1962, the Tamil Nadu Police Commission of 1969, the Assam Police Commission of 1969, the Uttar Pradesh Police Commission of 1970, the National Police Commission of 1977 and the Kerala Police Re-organisation Commission of 1982-1986 would bring to light that police reform efforts were ad hoc and haphazard with rare exceptions and the efforts were aimed mostly at internal management of the "Force" rather than basic changes in structure and functions. A summing up of the police functioning in the British Provinces during the fag end of the Company's rule had found that the police every where lacked professionalism, were highhanded and corrupt. "Catching Indian criminals was very much a hit-or-miss affair ... professional... policemen were rare throughout the princely India and the large swathes of the annexed territory's arrangements for law enforcement were makeshift and based upon the imagined goodwill and energy of local grandies and village headman..... whilst the company boasted that its Government was promoting peace and individual security throughout India, it failed to create the policing apparatus necessary. Nor was there a coherent policy towards law enforcement; Macaulay's proposals for a Uniform Code of Laws for the whole sub-continent were quietly shelved in 1893".[47]

The mutiny of 1857 was a wakeup call and on the Crown taking over the Indian territories, India became part of the British Empire. What followed was an acceleration of several pending efforts like Uniform Criminal Laws, a Police Act and other basic institutions of Criminal Justice Administration. "On the annexation of the Punjab in 1849 a police force was organized somewhat on the lines of Sind Police. It consisted of two branches—a military preventive police and a civil detective police. During the time of the mutiny this force contributed greatly to the restoration and preservation of order; and comparatively large bodies of military police were raised in the other provinces of Bengal; while the Punjab force was largely increased. The heavy expenditure involved proved a serious financial burden and in 1860 the Government of India urged on the Government of Punjab the necessity for a general reorganization of the police and a reduction of the cost. The question was accordingly taken up by Sir. Robert Montgomery, who had in the previous year carried out the reform of the Police of Oudh. The necessity for reform, however, was not confined to Punjab, and in August 1860, the Government of India appointed a Commission to inquire into the whole question of Police Administration in British India to submit proposals for increasing the efficiency and reducing the excessive expenditure".[48] The next landmark was the appointment of the Indian Police Commission, 1902-03, which had a very brief Terms of Reference, mostly aimed at standardization of departmental structures and procedures for functioning. This was perhaps necessary as a review had to be made about the shape the police was assuming in the preceding forty-two years. The Commission found that a lot remained to be desired in the functioning of the Police. "The Police force is far from efficient; it is defective in training and organization; it is inadequately supervised; it is generally regarded as corrupt and oppressive; and it has utterly failed to secure the confidence and cordial cooperation of the people.[49] The reforms suggested by the Commission were not even according to them "of a revolutionary character". They do not involve a complete subversion of the present system, though they aim at its radical amendments. They consist mainly in suggestions for the maintenance and development of indigenous local institutions so as to obviate the vexatious interference of the Police in cases of very little importance and to promote the co-operation of the people with the police in those of a more serious character; for the restriction of the lowest classes of officers to discharge, under closer supervision, of those more mechanical duties for which alone they are qualified; for the conduct of investigation by trained officers drawn from the better educated and more respectable classes of the community; for inspection of police work by carefully selected and trained officers of capacity and tried integrity; for supervision and control by the best European and Native officers available and for organized and systematic action against organized and professional crime. They aim also at the removal of abuses which have been brought to light in connection with Police work, at the employment of native agency to the utmost extent possible in each province without seriously impairing the efficiency of the service; at the attraction to the service of good native officers by offering them suitable position and prospects; at the recruiting of Superior European Officers of a higher class and insisting on their coming more into touch with the people, and at the adoption on the part of the whole force of a more considerate attitude towards all classes of the community so as to secure as far as possible the confidence and cooperation of the people. The Commission are not sanguine enough to believe that their proposals, even if fully adopted, will result in the immediate removal of all causes of complaint. These reforms can in any case be only gradually introduced; and years must pass before their full effects are realized. Inferior men have to be get rid of in all ranks; and evil traditions have to be broken in the force. The attitude of the people towards the police, and public opinion in regard to unrighteousness and corruption, have to be raised. All this must be, before the objects aimed at can be satisfactorily achieved. Of this the Commission are fully aware; and the members can hardly expect themselves to see the full introduction of all the reforms they propose still less to see their full results in improved police administration. But even a generation of official life is a short period in the life of a people; and the Commission believe that, before that period expires, very substantial advantages will have resulted from reforms carried out somewhat on the principles they recommend. What is required is the definite adoption of a policy based on such principles, and determined persistence in giving it effect. The Commission are confident that the recommendations they make, if accepted and persistently enforced, will result in inestimable advantage. They are encouraged in their confidence by the result of the application of similar principles in England. The Report of the English Police Commission, presented to the Parliament in 1839, contains a melancholy picture of the State of the English Police and of the attitude of the people towards them. The principal remedies proposed in that report are very similar in aim to some of those now submitted to the Government of India; and the comparison of the State of the English Police and their relations with the people now with those of sixty years ago give great ground for hope. The Commission are encouraged also by their own experience, as well as the evidence they have received, of the great improvement in the Indian Judicial and Revenue Departments, where principles such as some of those which they advocate have been applied. The character of officers has been raised; the whole tone of the service has been improved; the confidence of the people is being more and more secured; and public opinion itself is higher in respect of the matters with which these officers deal. The Commission, therefore, make their recommendations in a hopeful spirit. They realize that they involve large expenditure but they feel that the police department, which so nearly concerns the life of the people, has hitherto been starved; that the reforms they propose are absolutely essential; and it is well worthwhile to pay for them the price required".[50]

The police in India at the dawn of freedom was that which was crafted on the basis of these recommendations. The struggle for freedom had only served to further alienate the police from the public. The death and destruction that followed the partition and migration of large numbers of people from Pakistan to India and vice versa and police failure in the maintenance of order and prevention of crime, where the police had failed to live upto people's expectations were living proof of deficiencies in the system. Like the Army, the police were also truncated by European Officers retiring and the Indian officers and men opting either to remain with India or to migrate to Pakistan. This was perhaps a moment when serious efforts should have been made to create a new Police force for a new society. But the very volatile and uncertain conditions that existed in the country could not have even considered such a suggestion. Like the Indian Administrative Service (I.A.S.) and the Indian Police Service (I.P.S.), the police force also remained the erstwhile minions of the Imperial power. The police structure remained as was designed under the 1861 Police Act. This situation was to continue for another five decades till the Indian States were re-organised on the basis of the States Re-organisation Commission's (S.R.C.) Report and new geographical areas came to be grouped as states constituted on linguistic basis.

The first among the Indian States to constitute a police re-organization committee was the State of Kerala, which has created history by electing a Communist Government into office. It was Kerala, with a Communist Government which seriously contemplated re-organising the police with a view to changing its character and making it vibe well with the emerging socio-political dispensation in the country. The Terms of Reference gives sure and direct indications regarding the steps necessary for creating a new police force. The very first chapter of the Report reads "The role of the police as guardians of law and order has undergone an important change after the attainment of independence. The Police Force in the country was organized nearly a century ago by a foreign Government and during the struggle for freedom by the people, the police as the coercive arm of the Government had to sub-serve the interest of the Government then in power. They came to be looked upon with distrust and antipathy by the people who considered them the instrument of aggression used by an alien Government. After the attainment of independence and the adoption of the Constitution greater awareness of civil liberties and rights of the people guaranteed by the Constitution changed the attitude of the public towards the police. They expect a different approach by the police towards the maintenance of law and order and want them to play a new role in a progressive and enlightened democracy. It therefore became a matter of increasing importance that the method of functioning of police which was codified in the previous regime should be examined for reorientation to enable them to function as friends and guardians of the people animated by a spirit of service towards the common people which is essential in a Welfare State".[51] The Committee was therefore asked to look into the role of the police in a Welfare State, the adequacy of the existing provisions of law, to realise and secure fulfillment of the objectives given in the Directive Principles of State Policy and to realise public aspirations engendered by those provisions. They were asked to look into the employer-employee, landlord-tenant and capital-labour relations. The Committee was also asked to look into the duties of the police in the context of the free exercise of civil liberties and political rights of freedom of speech, of platform and association in a democracy consistent with the need to safeguard the security of the State. They were also asked to look into the role of the police in the background of communal and linguistic tensions, demonstrations and agitations within or without the support of political parties, property disputes etc. The Terms of Reference also included questions on the use of regulatory and restrictive powers under the Police Act, security provisions under the Criminal Procedure Code and specifically asked whether the police would avoid using firearms at all and how demonstrations, meetings and mobs can be controlled without resort of using brute force. Another important question referred to the Commission was police training and methods of recruitment and special training for basic functions like control of crime and management of order and special training for emergencies like famine, fire, strike, sabotage etc. It also considered how the police and the resources could be utilized for national development work. In fact, police and development was a phrase coined for the first time in the Terms of Reference. The Terms of Reference also included the question whether women should be inducted in to the police force and what ought to be their training and to which department and for performing which duties they should be posted. A very important question that was mooted was the setting up of Whitely Council in the police department for resolving service questions and issues.[52]

It may be observed here that the Terms of Reference were clearly futuristic and anticipated issues and concerns relevant to the management of the police force during the present day, i.e. the first years of the 21st century and in that respect the Terms of Reference of the Kerala Police Reorganization Committee of 1959 was a path breaker. These issues are not seen addressed by any other Commission appointed in this country. It was most unfortunate that the unsettled conditions that erupted in the state known as 'Liberation Struggle' — *'Vimochana Samaram'*—did not permit the Commission to make their recommendation on these important issues which with hindsight would permit an observation that deterioration of police performance even leading to a national strike and the outpouring of complaints and criticism from the public almost on every aspect of police functioning would have been obviated if the Commission had the opportunity to make their recommendations. The short Report submitted by the Committee, which is an exercise in brevity still makes their recommendations relevant and to which reference will be made later in this study.

In sharp contrast, after two decades, when the Second Police Reorganization Commission was appointed in 1982, the Terms of Reference were bland and prosaic and a few of them were shamelessly lifted from the Terms of Reference of the National Police Commission of 1977, highlighting of the lack of genuine interest to reform the police, or to attempt to resolve issues and problems that have surfaced in the State regarding police performance. It may be recalled that the police department had suffered unprecedented convulsions during the post-emergency period throwing up a number of questions regarding the style and limits of police functioning and functional dynamics. Yet, the Terms of Reference did not bother to examine any such issue or its detrimental effect on police service. It would appear therefore, that in the period of nearly a quarter of a century the interest in reforming the police or the compulsions to take a hard look on issues and problems generated by their handling of several changes and political questions were simply not considered at all relevant or important to be subjected to a critical examination for identifying ways and means of response. How did such a flagging of interest take place with regard to the police when all-around rapid socio-political changes were upsetting the existing assumptions and structures and crying out for restructuring and reformation. This is an enigma that has confronted not only the researcher but also several outstanding thinkers and authorities as can be seen from a recent study.[53]

The Police in Kerala had as on 01 January 2003, a strength of 96 IPS officers, 827 Kerala Police Service (K.P.S.) officers and 44268 officers at lower level making a total of 45171.[54] The budget proposal for the year 2002-03 was Rs. 50731 lakhs[55] of which 800 lakhs was for modernization. The total number of First Information Reports (FIRs) registered in Kerala upto 31 December 2002 is 139154 with 104200 under the IPC and 34954 under Special and Local Legislations. With a density of population of 819 per sq. kmt[56] and a total population of 31838619, the police people ratio is one of the lowest in Kerala. The crime map of Kerala was almost insignificant in terms of serious and heinous crimes till recently. With the rapid changes taking place in transport and communications, movement of people of the state in search of employment to countries outside and a flow of labour force from as far away as Bihar to the State and a host of accompanying reasons, the crime and order scenario of the state has undergone a massive transformation. Kerala ranks first in the rate of IPC crimes in states during 2000 with an average of 306.1 while the all-India average is 176.7. Thus contributing 5.6 per cent to total IPC crimes in India. This data is best represented by the following tables and charts of the National Crime Records Bureau.[57]

Table 1.1: Rate of IPC Crimes in States during 2000

States with Crime Rate (Total IPC Crimes) above All-India average

Sl. No.	*State*	*Rate*
1.	Kerala	306.1
2.	Rajasthan	298.8
3.	Madhya Pradesh	269.8
4.	Tamil Nadu	244.3
5.	Mizoram	241.5
6.	Gujarat	238.9
7.	Karnataka	209.2
8.	Haryana	198.2
9.	Arunachal Pradesh	197.3
10.	Maharashtra	189.7

Chart 1.1

Rate of Total IPC Crimes during 2000 (States-wise) All India: 176.7

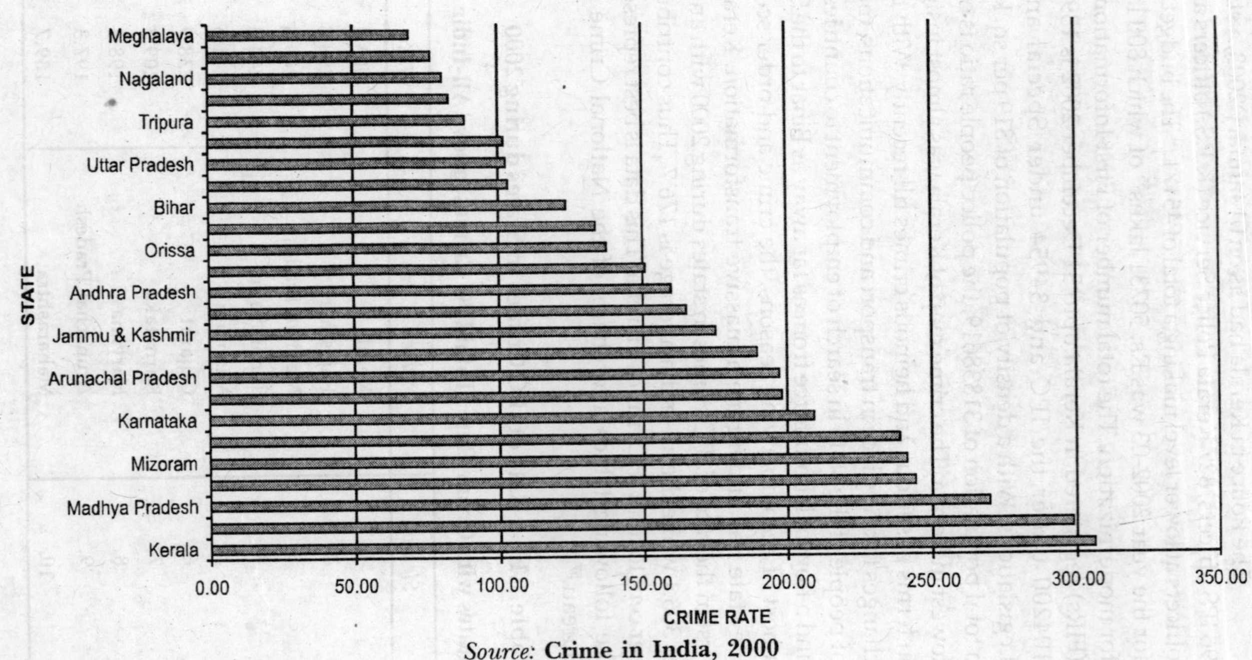

Source: Crime in India, 2000

Chart 1.2

State-wise Percentage Contribution to Total IPC Crimes during 2000

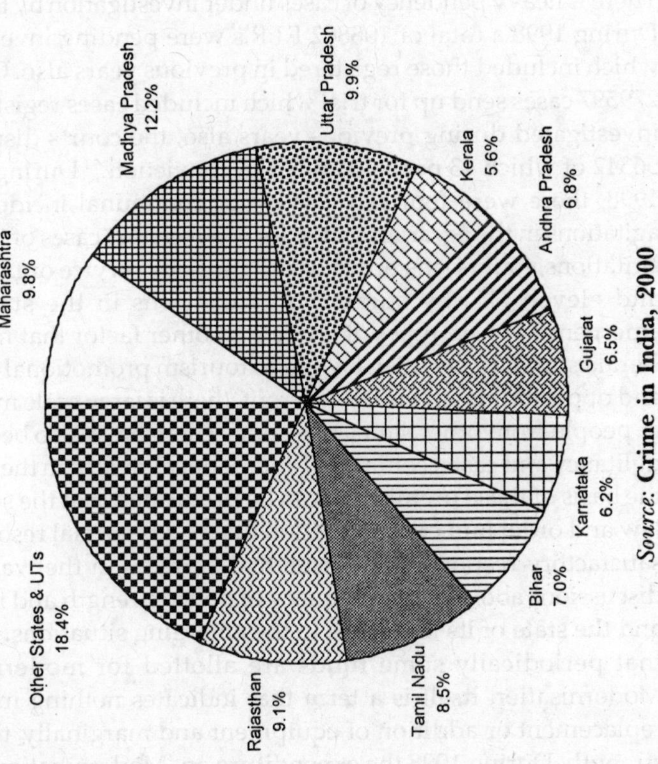

Source: **Crime in India, 2000**

The broad picture regarding crime and law and order in the state is interesting from a number of angles. Data published by the police department in Kerala is available only for 1998 and it was published in the year 2002: It is thus about half a decade behind. However, when this data is supplemented with the data published in Newspapers and periodicals it can be seen that almost every year the state is witnessing turbulence on the law and order front. There is heavy pendency of cases under investigation by the Police. During 1998 a total of 108802 F.I.R.s were pending investigation, which included those registered in previous years also. Out of the 279597 cases send up for trial which included cases registered and investigated during previous years also, the courts disposed off 56342 of which 43 per cent ended in conviction.[58] During the year 1998, there were fourteen (14) major communal incidents, four agitations in the agrarian sector, forty-seven (47) cases of industrial agitations, four (4) instances of agitations by service organizations and eleven (11) by student organizations in the state.[59] The emergence of new types of crime is another factor that makes the Kerala situation peculiar. Owing to tourism promotional activities and opportunities in the labour front, there is large scale movement of people from other states to Kerala. There have also been ethnic militancy and caste, communal and political rivalry in the state. On the basis of these premises, it can be predicated that the state has a law and order and crime situation that needs special resources for satisfactory response. The issue that surfaces in the wake of the discussions above is the adequacy of police strength and resources and the state of its relevance to the emerging situations. It is seen that periodically some funds are allotted for modernization. Modernisation itself is a term that indicates nothing more than replacement or addition of equipment and marginally, the police strength. During 1998 the expenditure on 'Modernization' was on purchase of vehicles, wireless and communication equipment computer accessories, etc. costing Rs. 2,20,37,111.[60] There was no plan outlay expenditure during 1997-98 and 1998-99.[61] The non-plan expenditure for 1997-98 was Rs. 2,63,43,60,000 and the same for 1998-99 was Rs. 2,86,41,50,000 just an increase of Rs. 22,97,90,000.[62] There is a confession in the Administration Report that "Pre-occupation with law and order duties affected the investigation of crimes to a certain extent".[63] There is also a lamentation that pending proposals for enhancement of police strength—both executive and ministerial—is a vexing issue. "Pendency over a long period will result in the wide disparity of police-population ratio. Mass recruitment to any category will not add well-trained officers/men to the force. Moreover, the Police Training College can accommodate only limited number of cadets for training. Periodical recruitment and training is necessary to mould an efficient police force".[64] This clearly discloses a police personnel policy that is archaic and not attuned to the demands of the day. It has already been pointed out that the structural framework of the police has its roots in enactments put on the statute book by the colonial administration over a century ago. There is also in comparison a gap in police technology both in dealing with crime and disorder. Further, experimentations which have been successfully tried elsewhere to enlist the whole-hearted support of the people have not received any serious attention in the State. It has also been pointed out earlier that the other components of the Criminal Justice System also suffer from like deficiencies and as a result are mostly dysfunctional. This situation should have alerted the political executive and also the bureaucracy to launch a serious agenda for police reform and not piecemeal modernization. It would appear that there is a conceptual confusion with regard to the needs of the police department and the nature of responses to be initiated.

These factors make an examination regarding the efficacy of police as a sub-system to cope with the emerging challenges to the management of crime and order, relevant. Yet, there is not a whisper regarding any serious attempt to reform the police to make them adequately well organized to provide security of life and property and basic freedoms and human rights to the people of the state. This study attempts to discuss the issue in its different facets.

Statement of the Problem

The functioning of the police in Kerala shows a sense of distrust and antipathy among the people about the department. There is a wide gap between the perceptions of the people about the police and their performance. To fill this gap, timely reforms are inevitable.

Since the formation of the State of Kerala on 1 November 1956, attempts to reform the police have not been many, barring two. The first attempt in this regard was the appointment of the 'Kerala Police Re-organization Committee' of 1959. The latter, the Kerala Police Re-organisation Commission of 1982-86 was close on the heels of the 'National Police Commission' 1977-81. Other efforts have been internal ad hoc and piecemeal either on the initiative of the Head of the Department or the political executive. In brief, no serious attempt has been made to evaluate the performance of the police, identify deficiencies, strength and weakness and introduce necessary and desirable changes so as to enable the police to march in tune with the demands on them by a people with egalitarian expectations.

Hypotheses

1. In spite of the Reports of various committees/ commissions on police reforms, no serious or well-considered effort has been made to implement the recommendations.
2. Instead of reforming the police, what the State Government has attempted so far is piecemeal modernization.
3. As clientele the people by and large are not satisfied with the performance of the police.

Objectives of the Study

The objectives of the study are:

(1) To examine the attempts made to reform the police in Kerala;

(2) To analyse the important reforms suggested for the structure and functions of police system by various commissions in Kerala;

(3) To assess how many of the suggested reforms have been effectively implemented so far;

(4) To identify the areas so far reformed consequent to the recommendations; and

(5) To identify the areas which require urgent reforms and the directions of future reforms.

Scope and Relevance

This is a pioneering study. The reform efforts on the police in Kerala have not been subjected to any academic study yet. Apart from the studies by the Kerala Police Reorganization Committee of 1959 and the Kerala Police Reorganization Commission, 1982-86, there have not been any serious studies by the Department or the Government. It would appear that the need and directions of police reforms have been always regarded as a wider issue and as a result, there, has not been any serious debate on this question in the State Legislature either. The usually shrill public reaction to crime and law and order issues, as well as police delinquencies and police violation of Human Rights make it apparent that the public are by and large not satisfied with the police as they are. There have been severely castigating comments on police investigation and conduct of police officers in the investigation of serious cases.[65] Police handling of law and order issues have also come for serious criticism. The Aadivasi struggle at Muthanga is a recent incident.[66] A simple question to be raised at this stage is why there is no clamour for reforming a deficient police sub-system. It is the silence of the beneficiaries or the clientele of police service that is most baffling. Looked at from all these points, it can be seen that there is a pressing need for reforming the police in Kerala, which has to be effectively articulated. A recent study 'Policing India in the New Millennium' has suggested making police reform a people's agenda and to enlist the support of the people for canvassing the case for police reforms. There is also a suggestion that instead of waiting for reforms to be initiated by the political executive, the police themselves may initiate a reform movement by starting to clean up their own Augean stables. In any case, there is the need for a catalytic agent to transform the latent demand for police reform in society and to ignite a self-starting reform process. This study has been taken up in this background and it is hoped that the fall out of the present study could give some momentum to the demand for police reforms.

The present study examines the various attempts made in the state of Kerala as well as by the central government at reforming the police. An analysis of the Terms of Reference and recommendations of the various commissions for police reforms has been made with the help of secondary data. It is followed by a micro-level study of six districts in Kerala from where data has been collected from the public and also the police personnel. The researcher felt such a study was essential to identify the areas so far reformed and the need and directions of future reforms.

It is admitted that, it would be too sanguine a hope to expect police reforms to materialise from a research study. The researcher has no such illusions. But his interaction with a representative group of police personnel at the different levels and the public drawn from various segments convinced him that there is a strong demand for reforming the police, although it is not vociferously articulated or incessantly canvassed. Further, as a social scientist, the researcher is convinced that while a swallow does not make a summer, creative movements everywhere had their beginnings in the silent birth of an idea, an abrupt incident or even a casual spark. Therefore, he nurses a basic belief that such an important issue like police reform in a state like Kerala with its high level of literacy and social and political consciousness cannot be delayed for long. This study could perhaps be the much-needed spark to start a burning fire, demanding police reforms.

Methodology

The methodology adopted for this study is a combination of empirical, historical and analytical methods. Both primary and secondary data were collected and utilized for the study. For the background Chapters, historical and analytical methods were used to collect and analyse secondary data from books, newspapers and journals. However, the major part of the data has been generated by using the interview method with the aid of questionnaires. For analyzing the efforts at reforming the Kerala police consequent to the recommendations of various commissions, and for identifying the areas that demand urgent reforms and the need and directions of future reforms, two field surveys using pre-tested questionnaires were conducted among the public and the police personnel. The members of the public were categorized into fourteen (14) groups and their responses were elicited. Since the state is divided into two police zones, the northern zone with the headquarters at Kozhikode and the southern zone with headquarters at Trivandrum, survey was conducted among the fourteen (14) categories in three (3) districts in each zone to make the analysis representative of the whole state. The districts of Kannur, Kozhikode and Thrissur were selected from the northern zone and Ernakulam, Kollam and Thiruvananthapuram from the southern zone. These districts were selected at random to represent the former princely states of Travancore, Cochin and the district of Malabar of the Madras Presidency. Thus in all, samples were collected from a total of six districts in the state. In each district survey was conducted among the fourteen (14) categories of the public under the jurisdiction of one rural police station and one urban police station. A total of seven hundred and fifty (750) samples were collected in all from the public.

For the purpose of data collection, the police personnel serving in the state were categorized into three (3) groups and three (3) separate questionnaires were used to elicit responses from them-first for the top management (IPS officers), second for the middle management (S.P., Dy. S.P., C.I.) and the third for the field formations (S.I.s, A.S.I.s, H.C.s. and P.C.s). Questionnaires were mailed to all the IPS officers servicing in the state. But only fifty (50) officers returned the questionnaires filled up and thus we have only fifty (50) samples from the first category. One hundred and fifty (150) samples were collected from the second category at the rate of twenty-five (25) samples from each district from which responses were elicited from the public and three hundred (300) samples were collected from the third category at the rate of fifty samples from each district from which data was collected from the public. The questionnaires employed for eliciting data from the respondents are:

- II (i) — Questionnaire used for eliciting responses from the public.
- II (ii) — Questionnaire used for the collecting data from the police personnel in the field formations.
- II (iii) — Questionnaire used to elicit responses from the police personnel at the middle management.

II (iv) — Questionnaire used for collecting data from the Senior Management (IPS officers).

An analysis of the Reports of the various state and national police commissions was also made for the study.

Limitations of the Study

There is paucity of published material on police reforms. In the state of Kerala the Reports of the Kerala Police Re-organisation Commission, 1982-86, have not been published. The belated publication of official documents and thus restricted access to such documents have been major limitations. Insufficiency of published works on the origin, growth and development of the police sub-system in Kerala has also been a major limitation. The conclusions drawn from the secondary data have been collated with primary data from the public as well as police personnel. However, the study is not free from the inherent limitations involved in the selection of samples and collection of data, though utmost care and adequate attention have been paid to make the study scientific.

Structure of the Study

The study is divided into seven chapters. The Introductory Chapter is the first Chapter. Chapter-II deals with the 'Police in Kerala—A Historical Approach'. 'Kerala Police—A Functional Analysis' is the content of the III Chapter. Chapter IV is 'A Survey of Police Reforms in Kerala. Police Reforms—Need and Directions' is the content of the V and VI Chapters—Chapter V dealing with 'Public Perceptions' and Chapter-VI with 'Police Perceptions'. The Suggestions that surfaced on police reforms during the course of the study are discussed in the concluding chapter, Chapter VII.

Survey of Literature

Identifying published material on 'Police Reforms' was a laborious task, since discussions and debates on police reforms have been appearing in the media, the various publications by Universities and academic bodies, debates in the State Legislatures and the Parliament, Reports of the various Judicial Commissions, publications by senior officers under training in the National Police Academy and researchers in police science subjects. However, the present study has a smaller canvas, that of Kerala State and necessarily it limits the survey of literature from 1 November 1956 to the present. Since police reforms have been dealt with primarily and incidentally in a variety of sources, the researcher has focused attention mainly on books and publications with Police re-organization/reform/modernization as the central theme; though he has taken the advantage of every available source of relevant information.

This survey of literature should necessarily start with the Report of the Kerala Police Re-organization Committee of 1959. The Government of Kerala had appointed a Committee for the re-organization of the State Police on 15 January 1959.[67] While appointing the Committee, the Government emphasized the need for a fundamental transformation in the role of the police with the attainment of political independence and the emergence of a democratic system based on adult suffrage inspired by the objective of the steady uplift of the common people.[68] This was perhaps a pioneering attempt among the States in India after the re-organization of the States on linguistic basis to study and report on the functioning of the police system. The Committee had been given an excellent Terms of Reference, to study and report on eighteen items, which is discussed in Chapter I. However, the political turmoil, which ultimately led to the dismissal of the Government and the imposition of President's rule under Article 356 of the Constitution, did not permit the Committee to make a detailed study of all the items in the Terms of Reference. The new Government asked the Committee to expedite its work and submit the Report urgently and that the Committee may confine itself to eight out of the eighteen items referred to the Committee in the original Terms of Reference.[69] This compelled the Committee to submit only a brief report. They examined the role of the police in a Welfare State, the adequacy of the law relating to employer-employee, landlord-tenant and capital-labour relations, the duties of the police in the context of the free exercise of civil liberties, communal and linguistic tensions, demonstrations and agitations, property disputes, use of fire arms, lathi, tear-gas and coloured water and measures for controlling meetings, demonstrations and mobs. The Report provides a basic understanding about the police and the problems they have to tackle in the State.

For an understanding of the police systems which existed in Travancore and Cochin, the Travancore State Manual[70] and the Cochin State Manual[71] were of considerable assistance. The Manual of William Logan of Malabar district gives a picture of the traditional police system there and its development under the Britishers as part of the Madras Presidency,[72] David H. Bayley, with his seminal work 'Police and Political Development in India' stirred up a creative ferment among the police officers as well as the academics. While he did not address police reform itself, his conclusions on the role the police play in society were compulsive enough to challenge an examination of the existing structures for reforms and reconstruction.[73] Following the example set by the state of Kerala, several other States had constituted police commissions to study and Report on the problems of police administration.[74] The Reports which, identified the problems confronted by the police and the recommendations are available for reference and many of them have dealt with issues and put forward recommendations which have some relevance to the state of Kerala. The Report of the National Police Commission of 1977, published during the period of 1979-81 in 8 volumes is a perennial source of interest.[75] Constituted first time in Independent India, the Commission had in it some of the best minds, which studied and analyzed police problems. With a former Indian Civil Service (ICS) officer Dharma Vira as the Chairman, the Commission was appointed to make a fresh examination of the role and performance of the police—both as a law enforcement agency, and as an institution to protect the rights of the citizens enshrined in the Constitution. The 1902 Police Commission known as "the Fraser Commission" was the immediate precursor of the National Police Commission of 1977.[76]

The Committee on Police Training under M.S. Gore as Chairman and M. Gopalan, the then I.G. of Kerala as one of its members, had made a comprehensive examination of recruitment, training and human resource development in the police.[77] This Report has the distinction of being at least partially implemented in most of the States, quite an unusual experience in police annals. However, training including design of curriculum, inclusion of new disciplines, teaching aids, all remain stuck on the recommendations of this Report for the police in India. The Kerala Police Re-organization Commission appointed by the Government of Kerala on 16 August[78] 1982 and reconstituted in 1984 was given an elaborate Terms of Reference many items of which were studied and reported by the Kerala Police Re-organization Committee of 1959 and the National Police Commission of 1977. The Commission submitted two Reports—first in 1984 and the final in 1986—with a revealing and bold minute by the Member-Secretary exposing the insincere approach of the concerned towards police reforms. Of the voluminous material produced by the Central Police Training College and later by its successor National Police Academy one paper—'Police Commissions, the Gap Between Recommendations and their Implementation[79]—stands out as it traces the tragic story of failed attempts to reform the police in Tamil Nadu, Maharashtra, Delhi and Kerala. A prolific author with about 50 titles is James Vadakkumcherry of the teaching faculty of the Police Training College, Thiruvananthapuram. He has filled a vast void in Police literature by writing practically on any and every subject of police concern. Though, he has not directly addressed police reforms, it cannot be gainsaid that his writings did not draw attention to the deficiencies and handicaps of the police sub-system. He is often compared with S.K. Ghosh of Orissa, a retired police officer, who has similarly enriched the literature on police by his numerous publications. 'Indian Police: A Developmental Approach' by P.D. Sharma[80] is a successor to D.H. Bayley's classic work on the Police in India. A number of books have appeared as sequel. One of the most illuminating study on the Police in India, an audit of their performance during the last 50 years is "Policing India in the New Millennium"[81] edited by P.J. Alexander, the supervising teacher of the present study. Fifty-seven distinguished scholars and authors, both from the academia and the services, have contributed Papers to this "great work of love involving enormous scholarship and labour...." as described by V.R. Lakshminarayanan, former Director General of Police, Tamil Nadu.[82] The book was produced with the objective of hastening police reforms with the support of the people. Justice K.T. Thomas, formerly of the Supreme Court of India has written a scholarly Foreword to this book: 'Police Administration' edited by T.N. Chaturvedi published on the occasion of the silver jubilee celebrations of the Indian Institute of Public Administration in 1978[83] has also been made use of by the researcher. It is a collection of 23 papers written by eminent authorities on almost all aspects of policing including the need for police reforms. The Indian Journal of Public Administration has published a special number on 'Towards Good Governance' in 1998,[84] which examines how good governance is dependent on the police for the promotion of Human Rights and the maintenance of law and order. Another special issue 'IT and Indian Administration'[85] identifies certain areas of policing where computer can be used. The researcher has also made full use of the various publications by the Indian Institute of Public Administration particularly the Journals and the list of references. Of special mention are Journals containing papers on "Challenges for Police in the 21st Century"[86] and the 'Police and Corruption', An Empirical Exploration.[87] Of the large number of books on the police, only a few devote direct attention to police reforms, although practically every work on the police is ultimately a call for reforming the police. Of these, 'Police: the Human Face'[88] by Remesh Chandra Dikshit, the former Director General of Police, Uttar Pradesh, is a recent study which also cries for police reform.

It is proverbial that police statistics are notorious for what they conceal rather than they disclose. The Kerala situation is not qualitatively different. But what confound the situation is the irregular publication of the data. The Annual Administration Report of the police department, which is a reliable window to take a peep into both the mechanics of the department and its functional dynamics is not published regularly or in time.[89] It is needless to say that it reduces the utility of the documents both for the administration and for the academic world. With the boons of Information Technology consciously lapped up and assimilated into the corpus of the police system, it is a wonder why such delays are permitted to occur. Yet, in the absence of more reliable material, researchers are dependent on this belated publication—The Annual Administration Report. This researcher also used the Annual Administration Reports for the available periods. 'Crime In India', published every year by the National Crime Records Bureau, Ministry of Home Affairs, New Delhi, provides with statistics related to crime, strength of the police, number of cases disposed of by the police and the courts and the number of pending cases in courts, expenditure, infrastructure, etc. of the police in India. The researcher has consulted this authentic document for this study.

This survey of literature has not been confined to those on police reforms in Kerala, as it would have made the scope of the survey rather small and limited. Instead, the survey has touched upon areas which are germane to the questions examined. While the survey has been exhaustive with regard to the literature on police reforms, it has been selective with regard to those not directly related to police reforms. Such a selection has been made in view of the unique or special nature of some publications. The Madras Police is seen to have brought out a publication titled 'The History of the Madras Police'[90] on the occasion of their centenary in 1959. It may be recalled that while experiments were conducted in different Presidencies of the Empire, it was in the Madras Presidency that these experiments took a more definite shape. The evolution of the Police in India with a brief reference to the Police in pre-British India can be seen in 'To Guard My People'—Percivel Griffiths.[91] He has dealt with the police system in India during the Hindu period, Mughal period and the British period starting with the development of police and criminal administration in the three Presidencies. The two centuries of experiment in Madras, Bombay and Bengal are also traced with the development of the police forces and the various regulations and enactments in these areas. A very short paper on the 'History of the Kerala Police'[92] by M.K. Joseph, one of the early entrants to the IPS in the Kerala cadre is seen included in a souvenir published in 1961 on the occasion of the centenary celebration of the Kerala police. A descriptive history of the Kerala police in Malayalam is 'Kerala Police Nootandukalilude' by K. Ramesan Nair, a former member of the subordinate service of the Kerala police. A number of monographs have been published by senior IPS officers undergoing training in the Central Police Training College, Mount Abu and later in the National Police Academy, Hyderabad. Under the Bureau of Police Research and Development, Ministry of Home Affairs, in-depth studies and research are conducted on various subjects of importance to policing and two among them considerably helped this researcher viz. 'Top Management in the Police: Case Study of a State Police Organization'[93] by Kuldeep Mathur and Mohit Bhattacharya and 'Organization and System of Policing of

Medium Size Cities'[94] by Mohit Bhattacharya. Every year the Bureau of Police Research and Development organizes Police Science Congress and the papers published for the Congress touch upon various aspects of police management, crime and related areas. The quarterly journal "Indian Police" published by the Intelligence Bureau, New Delhi, also contains papers on various aspects of policing in India. There are also publications brought out by the Institute of Criminology and Forensic Science, New Delhi, and various State police organisations.[95] Over and above, these publications, the print media and the electronic media, everyday carry news, comments and features on the police in this country which are an inexhaustible store of information on practically every aspect of policing in this country. Though, they are invariably critical and paint the police rather too black, the discerning researcher by sifting and panning can locate data and information which would not be available elsewhere.

REFERENCES

1. Government of India, *Report of the National Police Commission*, Vol. VIII, New Delhi, 1981, p.1.
2. *Indian Journal of Political Science*, Vol.4, No.2, June, 1979, p.107.
3. Government of Great Britain, *Report of the Royal Commission on the Police*, London, 1962, p. 21.
4. *Ibid*.
5. Article 246, List II, VII Schedule, *Constitution of India*, 1950.
6. Article 246, List I of the Union List, VII Schedule, *Constitution of India*, 1950.
7. *Crime in India*, National Crime Records Bureau, New Delhi, Ministry of Home Affairs.
8. John Coatman, *Police*, London, Oxford University Press, 1959.
9. David H. Bayley., *Police and Political Development in India*, New Jersey Princeton University Press, 1969, p. 15.
10. *Ibid*.
11. *Ibid*.
12. *Ibid*., p. 17.
13. U.S. forces in control of Baghdad must not be able to prevent looting or retaliatory crime and have been struggling to bring order in spite of its military might See, *The Hindu*, 18 April, 2003.

14. Bayley, op.cit., p. 17.
15. *Ibid.*, p. 18.
16. *Ibid.*, p. 19.
17. *Ibid.*
18. *Ibid.*, pp. 13-14.
19. *Ibid.*
20. P.J. Alexander, *Police and Elections in India*, Thiruvananthapuram, Indian Institute of Police Studies, 1989.
21. David H. Bayley, op.cit., p. 17.
22. See P.J.Alexander, *Police and Elections in India*, Thiruvananthapuram, Indian Institute of Police Studies, 1989. Also see: B.N. Gautam, "Police and Electoral Offences", *Sardar Vallabhai Patel National Police Academy Magazine*, Hyderabad, January-June, 1990, Vol. 42, No.1.
23. Government of India, *Report of the Indian Police Commission, 1902-03*, Simla, Central Printing Press, 1903.
24. Sardar Vallabhai Patel, *Debates in the Constituent Assembly*, Vol. VIII, 1985.
25. Though the phrases 'Socialist' and 'Secular' made entry thorough the 42nd amendment, the State as conceived under the 1950 Constitution had very strong and steady underpinnings of socialism as can be seen from part-III of the Constitution.
26. Government of India, Ministry of Home Affairs, Resolution No. VI-24021/36/77-G.PA-I-New Delhi, 15 November 1977 (Shah Commission).
27. A large number of committees were appointed at the national as well as the state levels to Study and Report on Administrative Reforms. To mention a few—*Gopala Swamy Ayyangar Committee*, 1949, *A.D. Gorwala Committee*, 1950, *Paul H. Appleby Committee*, 1953, *K. Santhanam Committee*, 1962, *Administrative Reforms Commission*, 1966. Kerala had three administrative reforms committees—The *E.M. Sankaran Namboodirippad Committee*, 1957, *M.K.Vellodi Commission*, 1965 and the *E.K.Nayanar Committee* of 1997.
28. The recommendations of the National Police Commission suffered neglected and gradual atrophy because it dawned on someone at the centre that police and law and order, being State subjects, the Center's initiative in appointing the National Police Commission was *ab initio* Absurd-see, P.J. Alexander, "Police Reform Perspectives"-(Mimeo), Thiruvananthapuram, *Institute of Management in Government*, 1988.
29. *Crime in India-2000*, National Crime Records Bureau, New Delhi, Ministry of Home Affairs, Vol. 48, p.13.

30. *The National Police Commission* in its VIII Report on pages 43 to 48 has given a Model Police Act. This Model Police Act is Today 23 years old.
31. See the liberation struggle in Kerala in 1959 and the mass movement under Jayaprakash Narayan in the early 1970s.
32. See: the *Reports of Amnesty International* and Various Non-Government Organizations on gross violations of Human Rights in Punjab, Jammu and Kashmir, etc.
33. See the Response of the Government in United Kingdom the Irish Republican Army and the terrorism in Ireland.
34. Government of India, Report of the Indian Police Commission, 1902-03, op.cit., pp. 1-2.
35. Government of Kerala, *Report of the Kerala Police Re-organisation Committee*, Thiruvananthapuram,_1959, pp. 2-3.
36. Government of West Bengal, *Report of the West-Bengal Police Commission*, Calcutta, 1960-61, p. 16.
37. Government of Punjab, *Report of the Punjab Police Commission*, Chandigarh, 1961-62 Appendix-1.
38. Government of Maharashtra, *Report of the Maharashtra Police Commission*, Bombay, 1964, p.169.
39. Government of Uttar Pradesh, *Report of the Uttar Pradesh Police Commission*, Lucknow, 1970-71, p. 1.
40. Government of Tamil Nadu, *Report of the Tamil Nadu Police Commission*, Madras 1971, Annexure-1.1, Vol. 2.
41. Government of Assam, *Report of the Assam Police Commission*, Tezpur, 1971, p. 800.
42. Government of Great Britain, *Report of the Royal Commission on the Police*, London, 1962.
43. Government of India, *Report of the National Police Commission*, New Delhi, 1977.
44. Government of Kerala, *Report of the Kerala Police Re-organisation Commission*, 1984.
45. *Ibid.*, p. 8.
46. The full text of the note by the Member Secretary is appended in Appendix-1.
47. Lawrence James Raj, *The Making and Unmaking of British India*, London, Abacus, 1997.
48. *Report of the Indian Police Commission*, op.cit., p. 10.
49. *Ibid.*, p. 150.
50. *Ibid.*, pp. 150-51.

51. Government of Kerala, *Report of the Kerala Police Re-organization Committee*, op.cit., p. 12.

52. The Terms of Reference in its entirety can be seen in pp.17-19 of Chapter I.

53. See: P.J. Alexander (ed), *Policing India in the New Millennium*, New Delhi, Allied Publishers, 2002.

54. Data provided by Police Headquarters and the State Crime Records Bureau, Pattom, Thiruvananthapuram.

55. Government of Kerala, *Annual Budget Summary*, 2002-03, p. 7.

56. *Malayala Manorama Year Book*, 2003.

57. *Crime in India 2000*, op.cit., p. 34.

58. Government of Kerala, *Annual Administration Report of the Kerala Police*, 1998, III.

59. *Ibid.*, pp. 57, 64.

60. *Ibid.*, p.120.

61. *Ibid.*

62. *Ibid.*

63. *Ibid.*, p.121.

64. *Ibid.*

65. Judgement by the Honorable High Court of Kerala in the Idamalayar Case and in the Prevention of Corruption Act in which R. Balakrishnan Pillai and others were accused see: *The Hindu*, 01 November, 2003.

66. See: *The Hindu*, 24 February, 2003.

67. G.O. (Ms) No. 71/59/Home dated 15, January, 1959.

68. Government of Kerala, *Report of the Kerala Police Re-organization Committee*, 1959, p. 5.

69. G.O. (Ms) No.78/Home (A) dated 19 November, 1959.

70. T.K. Velupillai, *The Travancore State Manual*, Vol. 4, Thiruvananthapuram, 1940.

71. C. Achutha Menon, *The Cochin State Manual*, Ernakulam, Cochin Government Press, 1911.

72. William Logan, *Malabar*, Superintendent, Government Press, Madras, 1951.

73. David H. Bayley. op.cit.

74. *West Bengal Police Commission*, 1960-61, *Punjab Police Commission*, 1961-62, *Maharashtra Police Commission*, 1964, *Delhi Police Commission*, 1966-68, *Uttar Pradesh Police Commission*, 1970-71, *Assam Police Commission*, 1971, *Tamil Nadu Police Commission*, 1971, etc.

75. Government of India, *Report of the National Police Commission*, op.cit.

76. Government of India, *Report of the Indian Police Commission*, op.cit.

77. Government of India, *Report of the Gore Committee*, Government of India Press, Shimla, 1974.

78. G.O. (M.S) No. 217/82/GAD., dated 30 July, 1982.

79. *Police Commissions, The Gap Between Recommendations and their Implementation* (Mimeo), Hyderabad, Sardar Vallabhai Patel National Police Academy, 1976.

80. P.D. Sharma, "Indian Police: A Developmental Approach", Unpublished Ph.D. Thesis, New Delhi, 1977.

81. P.J. Alexander (ed). *Policing India in the New Millennium*, op.cit.

82. V.R. Lakshminarayanan "Issues in Policing", *The Hindu*, 29 October, 2002.

83. T.N. Chaturvedi (ed). "Police Administration", *Indian Journal of Public Administration*, Vol. XXIV. No.1, New Delhi, Indian Institute of Public Administration, 1978.

84. T.N. Chaturvedi (ed), "Good Governance", *Indian Journal of Public Administration*, July-September, Vol. XLIV, No.3, New Delhi, Indian Institute of Public Administration, 1988.

85. T.N. Chaturvedi, (ed), "IT and Indian Administration", *Indian Journal of Public Administration*, July-September, Vol. XLVI, No. 3, New Delhi, Indian Institute of Public Administration, 2000.

86. Y.S Jafa, "Challenges for Police in the 21st Century", *Indian Journal of Public Administration*, January-March, Vol. XLVII, No.1, New Delhi, Indian Institute of Public Administration, 2001.

87. K.K. Sharma, "The Police and the Corruption—An Empirical Exploration", *Indian Journal of Public Administration*, April-June Vol. XLVII, No. 2, New Delhi, Indian Institute of Public Administration, 2002.

88. R.C. Dikshit, *Police: The Human Face*, New Delhi, Gyan Publishing House, 2000.

89. The latest Annual Administration Report of the Police Department in Kerala of 1998 was published in 2002.

90. *"The History of the Madras Police Centenary, 1859-1959"*, Madras, B.N.K. Press,1959.

91. Percivel Griffiths, *To Guard My People—The History of the Indian Police*, London, Ernest Ben Ltd., 1971.

92. M.K. Joseph, "A Brief History of the Kerala Police", Kerala Police Centenary Celebrations Souvenir, Thiruvananthapuram, 1961.

93. K. Ramesan Nair, *Kerala Police Nootandukalilude,* Trivandrum, Valsa Printers, 1985.

94. Kuldeep Mathur & Mohit Bhattacharya, *Top Management in the Police: Case Study of a State Police Organization*, New Delhi, The Indian Institute of Public Administration, 1976.

95. Mohit Bhattacharya, *Organization and System of Policing of Medium Size Cities*, New Delhi, Indian Institute of Public Administration.

Police in Kerala

A Historical Approach

The origin and development of police administration in any society is directly linked with the origin and development of its political system. Kerala is not an exception and the evolution of police administration is closely connected with the development of administration in the two princely states of Travancore and Cochin and the district of Malabar. All attempts to analyse the origin and development of police in Kerala must start with an analysis of the growth of the police system in the country. This is so because of the different stages of evolution of the police in the Princely States and the Presidencies. In Kerala, the Princely States of Travancore and Cochin had their own separate systems of policing, largely drawing authority from the rulers. The Malabar region as part of the Madras Presidency came under the various experiments at developing a police system in the Presidency by the Colonial Administration.[1] After the Mutiny, when the country came under the British Crown, serious efforts were made at homogenisation and unification of the administration of the country. The Police Commission of 1860 and the Police Act of 1861 clearly demonstrate that the British Government in India aimed at giving the administration an all India character. There were also efforts to introduce the Criminal Laws legislated for the Presidencies in to the Princely States and to change existing laws to bring them on line with the Police Act and the Criminal Laws applicable in British India. There was the presence of a Political Agent or Resident in every Indian State whose primary function was to be a keen observer of the functioning of the administrative system and the exercise of power by the Monarch with the options open for intervention. We also see that in almost all Princely States the selection of Dewans was with the tacit approval of the Paramount Power. Members of the Indian Civil Service (I.C.S.) and Indian Police Service (I.P.S.)[2] were being inducted into the administration of the Princely States to facilitate the process of homogenisation and integration. Of course, this process was persuasive than coercive and as a result the development of the systems and procedures were uneven and not uniform for the whole of the country. It took the rest of the century to make the administrative systems and procedures more or less alike in the Princely States and the Presidencies.

Though the police system as we have today is the contribution of the British administration it bears hardly any resemblance with the police systems existing in the United Kingdom (U.K.). The Indian empire had a unique system of police and civil administration as can be seen from the systems that survive in Myanmar (formerly Burma), Sri Lanka (formerly Ceylon), Pakistan, Bangladesh and India.[3] While in Great Britain and in its former colony—United States of America (U.S.A.)—the police system was largely decentralized and linked with the local government administration, in the British Indian Empire and in Independent India, the police are centralized at the State level. The State has a single police department with a Head known previously as the Inspector General of Police and currently as the Inspector General and Director General of Police. He is an adviser to the Government and wields immense power and prestige. The functions of the police are listed in the Police Act, various Special and Local Legislations and the three major criminal law enactments. Bayley has identified some of the distinct structural characteristics of the police in India thus: "The Indian Police System compared to systems in other countries has three distinguishing features. First: the police are organized, maintained, and directed by the several States of the Indian Union…Second: the Indian Police System is horizontally stratified. Like Military forces, the police are organized into cadres depending upon rank…Third: the police in each state are divided vertically into an armed and unarmed branch. This is a functional division.

The unarmed police staff of the police stations, go on patrol duties and prevent and investigate crime. The armed police are employed for those duties which require the presence of constituted physical force, such as guard duties at banks and the quelling of civil disturbances.... The Indian arrangement recognizes the value of having policemen uncontaminated by arms but also recognizes that it is necessary to have ready at hand a well-trained body of police capable of responding with overwhelming force".[4]

Perhaps, far more unique an arrangement is the Indian Police Service (IPS) which is recruited and trained by the Union Government and allotted to the States. The federal principle in the Constitution has resulted in a division of powers between the States and the Union, leaving police and management of order to the States. India has also a single Judicial System with an apex court known as the Supreme Court as the ultimate authority in all matters for judicial adjudication. It hears and disposes of appeals from the State High Courts and draws power and authority directly from the Constitution. Although *prima facie* it would appear that they militate against the federal principle, it can be seen that in the last fifty years the civil administration with the I.A.S., the police system with the IPS and the single judiciary have contributed more to strengthen the federal principle and to sustain the quest for national integration—unity among diversity, than any other aspect.

A very short survey of the historical development of the police is necessary to put this study in perspective. The indigenous system of policing in India was organized on the basis of land tenure.[5] Village was the basic unit of the traditional police system. Prevention and detection of crime, ensuring the security of the village, etc. were the responsibility of the village headman who was usually assisted by a watchman and sometimes by a special police helper. "The village watchman was, when necessity arose, assisted by all the male members of his family, by the other village servants and in some case by the whole village community.[6] His duties were to keep watch at night, find out all arrivals and departures, observe all strangers and report all suspicious persons to the headman.[7] In case of a theft, the headman was required to pay from his own pocket, the value of the stolen property if he failed to recover the same.[8] This system was meant for maintaining internal order and security of the village. "External security for the village was often obtained by negotiating to pay 'Protection Money' to a threatening band or to a criminal tribe if one was resident in the area".[9] The cities and large towns, being centres of trade and communication, had a very elaborate police system. "The head of the town police administration was the 'Kotwal', a word which comes down to us in the name given in many Indian towns today for the central police station Kotwali".[10] This system of policing has continued in India unaffected by the tides of conquests and consolidation till the arrival of the Britishers. "The other great empires—Maurya, Gupta and Moghul-were content to establish contact with the autonomous villages but not to re-order policing within them".[11]

The system of village policing began to degenerate in course of time. "Extortion and oppression flourished unchecked through all gradations of the officials responsible for the maintenance of peace and order. Both village watchmen and the heads of villages, and even the higher officials, connived at crime and harboured offenders in return for a share of the booty. Their liability to restore the stolen property or make good its value was disregarded; or if this obligation was enforced, neither the property nor its value was restored to the owner. Fines were imposed when a more severe punishment was called for; and offenders who were possessed of any property could always purchase their liberty".[12] This situation compelled the Britishers to assume some role in policing. Accordingly, in 1792, the Zamindars were relieved of their police duties and the East India Company established a police force responsible to them. The Zamindars were replaced by District Magistrates and districts were divided into a number of parts and a police officer called 'daroga' was placed over each of them. "The daroga was to raise and direct a force of men known as 'Barkandazes', literally 'Lightning Throwers' because they were armed".[13] The Kotwal, the head of the town police administration, was continued and a daroga was appointed for each ward of the city. Considerable amount of reforms were introduced in the system of Criminal Justice Administration also. The cruel and partial system of trial and punishments followed by the native governments were replaced by a mild and rational system.

The reforms introduced by the Company failed to produce any qualitative change in the system. "There was a marked increase of crime everywhere: robberies and murders, accompanied by the most atrocious and deliberate cruelties were of frequent occurrence; gangs of dacoits roamed unchecked about the country; and, in the expressive native phrase, "the people did not sleep in tranquility".[14] The daroga could not effectively control the village police. Being a force organized by an alien authority it was quiet natural that, the new system could not command assistance of local people. A Special Committee was appointed by the Court of Directors of the Company in 1813 to institute an enquiry into the administration of justice and police in the Company's territories in India.[15] As recommended by the Committee, the daroga was partially abolished and the traditional method of village policing was re-established.[16] Supervisory power over the village police was given to the District Collector who could remain in touch with the law-and-order conditions through the subordinate officers of the revenue department. This system was introduced in Madras Presidency on the basis of the Regulation of 1816 and in Bombay Regulation XII of 1827. The new system was thus described by Thomas Munro "We have now in most places reverted to the old police of the country executed by village watchmen, mostly hereditary under the direction of the heads of villages, tahsildars of districts and the collector and magistrates of the province. The establishments of the tahsildars are employed without distinction either in police or revenue duties, as the occasion requires".[17] We may see here the beginning of the system of general superintendence and control of the district police by the District Magistrate (Collector) against which there has been a decades long struggle by the police. It took the National Police Commission of 1977 to remove this anomaly of combining revenue and police functions.[18] The daroga system could not be completely abolished in Bengal. Consequent to the 'Permanent Settlement' of Lord Cornwallis, there was no subordinate revenue establishment. So the collector had to rely on the daroga to keep in touch with the law-and-order situation and to supervise the village police. Hence, as a matter of necessity, a reformed version of the daroga was retained in Bengal. This partial, abolition and reform of the daroga and retreat to the traditional village policing also produced little improvement. "Crime, especially dacoity, civil unrest and insecurity continued unabated".[19]

The conquest of Sind by Sir Charles Napier in 1843 was a significant event in the history of police administration in India. Sind had neither a village police system nor a centralized revenue administration. Napier organized a regular police force directed by its own officers on the model of the Irish Constabulary. The responsibility to direct and supervise the entire police force throughout the territory was in the hands of the Inspector General of Police and in each district the Superintendent of Police who was accountable both to the Inspector General and to the Collector.[20] Perhaps the most important feature of this system was that it was a separate and self-contained organisation and its officers have no other functions to perform.[21] This new experience was adopted with slight modifications in Punjab, Bombay and Madras.

The Mutiny of 1857 was a wakeup call to the British in the sense that it helped them to fully realize the responsibilities of governing so vast a territory. This resulted in the passing of the Government of India Act, 1858, which transferred the administration of India from the Company to the Crown in Parliament. The enactment of the Code of Civil Procedure the Indian Penal Code and the Code of Criminal Procedure followed.[22] It also led to the appointment of the Police Commission of 1860 to make an exhaustive study of the police in British India and to submit proposals for increasing efficiency and reducing expenditure.

"This Commission recommended the abolition of the military police as a separate organization, and the constitution of a single homogeneous force of civil constabulary for the performance of all duties which could not properly be assigned to the military arm. To secure unity of action and identity of system the general management of the force in each province was to be entrusted to an Inspector General. The police in each district were to be under a District Superintendent, who in the large districts, would have an Assistant District Superintendent, both these officers being Europeans. The subordinate force recommended consisted of inspectors, head constables, sergeants and constables, the head constable being in charge of a police station and the Inspector of a group of stations...On the subject of the relations between the Magistracy and the Police their conclusions were that no Magistrate of lower grade than the District Magistrate should exercise any police functions, but that in the case of District Magistrate it was not expedient to deprive the police and the public of his valuable aid and supervision in the general management of the police matters. The Commission submitted a Bill, based on the Madras Police Act, to give effect to these recommendations and this was passed into law as Act V of 1861".[23] Thus, the Indian Police Act of 1861, almost on the basis of which the police force is still organized in the country, was the result of the deliberations of the Police Commission of 1860. The Act offered authoritative answers to two questions the Britishers were confronted with—the relations between the Imperial and the Rural Police and the co-ordination between the Imperial Police administration with other functions of the Imperial authority. It may be noted here that the new structures were made applicable only to British India and the Princely States remained unaffected and continued with their own systems of policing.

Another significant event in the history of Police administration in British India was the introduction of Commissionerate system in Madras, Bombay and Calcutta on the model of the London Metropolitan Police. The problems of these port cities were unique and required special treatment. Special Police Acts were passed for each city—Calcutta Police Act, 1866, Madras City Police Act, 1888 and Bombay Police Act, 1902.[24] As per the new arrangement the Commissioners were required to report directly to the provincial government and not through the Inspector General of Police. They combined in themselves the powers of the District Magistrates and the Superintendents of Police.

The functioning of the police in British India was subjected to a searching enquiry and evaluation in 1902 when Lord Curzon appointed the Indian Police Commission, 1902-03, which is commonly known as the 'Fraser Commission'. The Commission found that "The Police is far from efficient; it is defective in training and organisation; it is inadequately supervised; it is generally regarded as corrupt and oppressive; and it has utterly failed to secure the confidence and cordial co-operation of the people".[25] The Commission endorsed the organizational principles established in 1861 and did not make any recommendation for substantial organizational change.[26] Perhaps, the most important legacy of the Police Commission of 1902-03 was that it recommended the appointment of Indians at officer level in the police. "Hitherto Indians could rise only to the ranks of Inspector of Police, the senior N.C.O. position".[27] Consequent on this recommendation, a new rank of Deputy Superintendent of Police was created to accommodate Indian Officers. However, they were not made part of the Indian (Imperial) Police. It was in 1920 that the Indian (Imperial) Police was thrown open to Indians and entrance examination for the service was conducted in India as well as in England.[28]

The police systems in the Princely States did not remain long in isolation. The British were able to nudge the States to a general level of conformity to the legislations enacted and the systems devised for the British Presidencies. It has been pointed out earlier that in every Princely State there was the presence of the 'Resident' or a political agent of the British power. The appointments of Dewans needed the concurrence of the Resident/the Governor General of the British province. There was also the induction of officers from the Indian Civil Service (I.C.S.) and Indian Imperial Police (I.P.) to the State administration. Laws applicable to the British Presidencies were made applicable to the Princely States also with suitable changes to accommodate regional disparities and local conditions. In sum, though the political map of India was in two distinct colours, one of the British Empire and the other, of the Princely States, there was very strong undercurrents compelling uniformity and homogenisation. Wherever the Princes were educated, well trained and had the benefit of the counsel of a reform-minded Resident and the assistance of a progressive Dewan, the administration moved forward almost in parallel to the British administration. Thus, the police system under the British, through a process of experimentation and vicissitudes of reform and change developed as part of the civil administration.

The State of Kerala was formed on the basis of the recommendations of the States Re-organization Commission on 1 November 1956. Prior to its formation as a single integrated State, the whole region was divided into three (3) parts—two Princely States of Travancore and Cochin and the District of Malabar. As the first step in the direction of a making a united Kerala, a homeland for the Malayalam speaking people, the princely States were united together to form the Travancore-Cochin State on 1 July 1949.[29] The district of Malabar was under direct British rule as it was part of the Madras Presidency. The history of the police in Kerala is thus, the history of the administrative development of these three constituents of the State of Kerala.

In Travancore, till the end of the 17th century, feudal chieftains or 'Pramanies' enforced law, dispensed justice and collected revenue.[30] For this purpose they organised and maintained a trained, skilled and paid set of personnel and they were designated as 'Valiya Sarvadhikaryakars', 'Sarvadhikaryakars', 'Karyakars', 'Pravarthiyakars' and 'Peons'. Their training ground called 'kalaries' imparted some military training and knowledge of 'Chattavariyolas' which were the 'ordinances' embodying the law and procedure of the land.[31] This system did not work well and was abandoned with the creation of the office of 'Dewan' as the keystone of the administrative structure. For the first time in the history of Travancore, Dewan Oommini Thampi organised a police force of two hundred (200) men.[32] 'Thanas', similar to the present day police stations were established and manned by different categories of personnel designated as 'Thana Naiks', 'Mudalpers' and 'Thanadars'. Col: John Munro, who succeeded Dewan Oommini Thampi in 1814, found this system "without order or regulation and the peons scarcely possessed any knowledge of their proper duties" and concentrated on improving the police and increasing their number considerably.[33] The first Regulation concerning the police in Travancore was passed in 1834 which was followed by a second Regulation in 1847-48. The formation of Revenue Divisions during 1854-55 had effected a thorough re-organization of the police set up." Dewan Peishcars were put in charge of these divisions and were invested with powers of general control and supervision in all matters concerning Revenue, Magisterial and Police, subject to the orders of the Dewan as the Head of the administration and Chief Magistrate."[34] The police formed the staff of the Magistracy at every level. Each Taluk Magistrate had under him one police 'Naik', one to four 'Mudalpers' and a number of 'Peons'. In addition to this, "Extra Police Officers" were employed in Districts where the incidents of crime were heavy. They exercised jurisdiction over two or three Taluks and had under them a staff of 'Naiks', 'Mudalpers' and Peons and were expected to function as 'crime police' as distinguished from 'order police'. The strength of the police force at that time was forty three (43) superior officers, fifty two (52) Naiks and one thousand nine hundred and seventy (1970) Mudalpers and peons.[35] The police thus organised appear to have discharged their duties satisfactorily. However, Dewan Sheshaiah Sastri, found this system defective and wanted to re-organize the police on the pattern of the police in British India. Later, Dewan Ramiengar exposed the limitations of the existing system in his famous 'Minute' dated 31 January 1881 which also embodied the broad outlines of the proposed re-organisation.[36] In order to attract better class of men, he sought to increase the wage structure of the personnel and planned enlistment from the open market on the basis of qualifications and contemplated gradation of rank and training. For this purpose the Police Regulation II, III and IV were enacted in 1881. Of these, Regulations II and III were made, with suitable changes, the Indian Penal Code and the Code of Criminal Procedure applicable to the Travancore State. In 1882, the re-organization was completed as per Regulation IV and the force consisted of a Superintendent of Police, three (3) Assistant Superintendents of Police, forty-six (46) Inspectors, one hundred and seventy-two (172) Head Constables and one thousand five hundred and twenty-three (1523) Constables.[37] An Armed Reserve Force consisting of one hundred and forty-seven (147) men was also organised as a striking force. O.H. Bensely, a British Officer, was appointed as the first Superintendent of Police in Travancore.

The administrative set up of the police underwent further changes in 1919. The chief of the Police was designated as the Commissioner of Police and made answerable to the Government. The police force within the jurisdiction of a District Magistrate was placed under a Superintendent of Police and sub-divisions under Assistant Superintendents of Police. However, they were to function under the general control and direction of the District Magistrate. In 1938, the designation of the Head of the Department was changed from Commissioner to Inspector General of Police and the posts of one Deputy Inspector General and one Assistant Inspector General were created. Several changes were introduced in the police from 1938 to 1949 like the formation of an Intelligence Bureau, a State General Reserve and District Reserve Units, a Wireless and Motor Transport Unit, a Motor Vehicle Taxation Branch and a Women Police Wing.[38]

The earliest attempt to set up a police force in Cochin was made by the 'Hukum Nama' of 1812. The 'Hukum Nama' or 'Ordinance' provided for the organisation of a body of 'Tannadars' under a 'Tanna Naik' for each Taluk "to keep the peace of the land".[39] They were to patrol the State, prevent commission of thefts and trade in contraband goods and arrest depredators. In 1835, this force was found ineffective and hence disbanded. A new system was introduced under Regulation IV by which Tahsildars were made Police Officers, and they were to be assisted by a 'Kotwal' and 'Peons'. This force also was found inadequate to deal with the problems of the day and King Rama Varma entrusted George Gunther, the first Superintendent of Police in Cochin with the task of reorganising the police. Consequently Regulation I, popularly known as 'Puthiya Niyamam' or 'New Law' was passed in 1883. The whole force was placed under a Superintendent of Police, Inspectors were given charge of Taluks and Head Constables of Police stations.[40] In order to give training to the entrants, a Police Training School, under an experienced officer of the Madras Police was set up. To begin with, there were thirty-two (32) Police Stations.[41] This system continued without much change till 1907-08.

Several major changes were introduced in the police administration of Cochin during 1907-08. The State was divided into three (3) inspectorates for the purpose of police administration. A new class of officers called 'Sub-Inspectors' replaced the Head Constables as Station House Officers (S.H.Os). It may be pointed out here that this replacement was in conformity with the recommendation of the Indian Police Commission of 1902-03, which has recommended that Inspectors should be put in charge of circles and Sub-Inspectors in charge of police stations.[42] For use in emergencies what continued as a 'vacancy reserve' from 1883 was made into a 'Military Police' in 1904 and they were placed under a Reserve Inspector. The other important changes introduced during this period were an upward revision of the salary scales of officers and men and the establishment of a Finger Print Bureau.

In 1921, by virtue of Regulation XII, the designation of the Police Chief was changed from Superintendent of Police to Commissioner of Police. The pay scales were revised during the year and a separation was effected between the Town and Rural

Police at Thrissur, Ernakulam and Mattancherry. In 1922, a separate harbour police was organised for the Cochin harbour. In 1932, the State was divided into two police divisions—A and B with Headquarters at Ernakulam and Thrissur. The strength of the force then stood at ninety-seven (97) officers and five hundred and eighty (580) men.[43]

It can be seen that, like in Travancore, in Cochin also the organization and development of the police was mostly on the British Indian pattern.

In ancient Malabar, feudal lords called 'Naduvazhis' and 'Deshavazhis' maintained law and order. The Mysore invasion gave a serious blow to the system and it collapsed. As C.H. Innes pointed out "...after the invasion of Tippu, Malabar, especially the South, was terrorised by bands of marauding Mappilas who found a secure retreat in the jungles of Ernad and Walluvanad".[44] By this time the Britishers took over the area and organised regular police forces to stamp out these forces, under each collectorate. A force of five hundred men (500) was raised for revenue collection and stamping out subsequent rebellions.

In 1816, by virtue of the promulgation of Regulation II, this system of police was abolished. As per the Regulation, the 'Zilla Magistrate', the 'Tahsildar' and the 'Adhikari' were made the heads of the District, Taluk and Village police respectively. The new system did not provide for constables at all. Within a very short period the utter inadequacy of the arrangement was exposed. In response to the series of rebellions by the Moplahs in mid-fifties a local police force with thirty-one (31) native officers, one hundred and fifty (150) men and two (2) buglers was raised under the command of two Military Officers. But the very next year Mr. Conolly, the Collector of Malabar was brutally murdered by a gang of four (4) Moplah convicts.[45] This was attributed as the utter inefficiency of the Police. It provided a convincing argument for police reform under Act XXIV of 1859. For the purposes of police administration the whole district was divided into two—North and South Malabar. Tellicherry was made the Headquarters of North Malabar and Kozhikode of South Malabar. In 1906 the police forces in these two regions consisted of one hundred and eighty-eight (188) officers and one thousand two hundred and seventy-eight (1278) men and one hundred and six (106) police stations.[46]

Another significant landmark in the history of police in Malabar was the setting up of the Malabar Special Police in 1885. The force had a very humble beginning and was raised as a special punitive force to deal with the frequent outbreak of rebellion by the Moplahs. Since it was quartered at Malappuram the force came to know as the 'Malappuram Special Police'. After the Moplah rebellion, a strength of six hundred (600) constables with the required complement of British and Indian Officers was sanctioned on 30 September 1921. This force rendered admirable service, from the date of its formation, in restoring order and ensuring security. With the re-organization of the States in 1956, they were shared by both the Madras and Kerala States.

The integration of Travancore and Cochin States also led to the integration of the police forces. The police in both the States were combined and placed under one Inspector General of Police. In order to secure uniformity, the Station House officers in the Travancore area were also designated as Sub-Inspectors. In order to hold an intermediary post between the Station House Officer and the Sub-Divisional Officer, Circle-Inspectors were appointed. Traffic, Vehicle taxation and Armed Reserve units were organised under separate Superintendents of Police. Perhaps, the most significant development of this period was the inclusion of all superior posts in the I.P.S.

The process of re-organization of the State of Kerala become complete with the merger of the district of Malabar with the Travancore-Cochin State, as recommended by the States Re-organization Commission (S.R.C.). This resulted in the formation of a new police force combining the police forces in the three regions. The Kerala Police Act (Act V of 1961) helped to evolve a common system and uniformity in the structure and functions of the police in United Kerala.

REFERENCES

1. *The History of the Madras Police,* (Centenary 1859-1959), Madras, B.N.K. press Private Ltd., 1959.
2. In Travancore and Cochin mostly British officers were heading the Police Department.
3. Percivel Griffiths, *To Guard My People: The History of the Indian Police,* London, Ernest Benn Ltd, 1971, p. 294.

4. David. H. Bayley, *Police and Political Development in India,* New Jersey, Princeton Press, 1969, pp. 35-36.
5. *Report of the Indian Police Commission*, 1902-03, Simla, Government Central Printing Office, 1903, p. 4.
6. *Ibid.*
7. *Ibid.*
8. J.C. Curry, *The Indian Police*, London, Faber and Faber, 1933, p. 19.
9. John Matthai, *Village Government in British India*, London, T. Fisher Unwin, Ltd., 1915.
10. David H. Bayley, op.cit., p. 38.
11. *Ibid.*
12. *Report of the Indian Police Commission*, 1902-03, op.cit., p. 5.
13. David H. Bayley, op.cit., p. 41.
14. *Report of the Indian Police Commission*, 1902-03, op.cit., p. 6.
15. *Ibid.*, p. 7.
16. J.C. Curry, op.cit., pp. 23-24.
17. *Report of the Indian Police Commission*, 1902-03, op.cit., p. 7.
18. See: *The Report of the National Police Commission*, Volume V, 1980.
19. David H. Bayley, op.cit., p. 43.
20. *Ibid.*, p. 44.
21. *Report of the Indian Police Commission*, 1902-03, op.cit., p. 9.
22. David H. Bayley, op.cit., p. 45.
23. *Report of the Indian Police Commission*, 1902-03, op.cit., pp. 10-11.
24. *Ibid.*, p. 65.
25. *Ibid.*, p. 150.
26. David H. Bayley, op.cit., p. 47.
27. *Ibid.*, p. 49.
28. *Ibid.*
29. R. Ramakrishnan Nair, *Social Structure and Political Development in Kerala*, Trivandrum, The Kerala Academy of Political Science, 1976, p. 184.
30. M.K. Joseph, "A Brief History of the Kerala Police", *Kerala Police Centenary Souvenir*, Thiruvananthapuram, 1961.
31. *Ibid.*, p. 5.
32. T.K. Velupillai, *The Travancore State Manual*, Vol. IV, Trivandrum, 1940, p. 105.

33. M.K.Joseph, op.cit., p. 6.
34. *Ibid.*
35. T. Madhava Rao, *Administration Report for 1866-67*, Trivandrum, Travancore Government Press, 1867.
36. T.K. Velu pillai, op.cit., p. 109.
37. M.K. Joseph, op.cit., p. 7.
38. *Ibid.*
39. *Ibid.*
40. *Ibid.*, p. 8.
41. *Ibid.*
42. See *the Report of the Indian Police Commission*, 1902-03, op.cit., p. 135.
43. M.K. Joseph, op.cit., p. 8.
44. *The History of the Madras Police*, op.cit., p. 410.
45. M.K.Joseph, op.cit., p. 9.
46. *Ibid.*

Kerala Police
A Functional Analysis

The structure and functions of the police in the different states of India are almost the same as they emanate from the same legislative source—the Indian Police Act, 1861. The criminal law trilogy and the Special and Local Legislations and the fact that the members of the IPS man all the senior positions (cadre posts) in every state have also contributed to shape this uniformity.[1] In all the states, the police department is headed by a senior IPS officer designated as Inspector General and Director General of Police. The designation Inspector General of Police is retained since the relevant legislations have not been amended to incorporate the new designation, Director General of Police. Below the Director General of Police is a hierarchy of officers—Additional Director General of Police (A.D.G.Ps.), Inspectors General of Police (I.G.Ps.), Deputy Inspector Generals of Police (D.I.G.Ps.), Superintendents of Police (S.Ps.), Deputy Superintendents of Police (Dy. S.Ps.), Circle Inspectors (C.Is), Sub-Inspectors (S.Is.), Additional Sub-Inspectors/Assistant Sub-Inspectors (A.S.Is.), Head Constables (H.Cs) and Police Constables (P.Cs.). These ranks, other than the police station staff have territorial as well as functional jurisdictions. The officers manning armed police battalions and district armed reserves have different designations—Commandant, Deputy Commandant, Assistant Commandant etc. Support organizations like the Forensic Science Laboratory, the Finger Print Bureau, the Crime Records Bureau, the Computer Centre, Communications and Motor Vehicle Units, have officers holding appropriate ranks depending upon the size of the organization but designated independently for each organization. For instance, the heads of the Forensic Science Laboratory and the Finger Print Bureau are called Directors while the head of the Motor Transport Unit is called Motor Transport Officer. Women Police Officers also have the same designations as their male counterparts occupying similar posts.

Chart 3.1

Organization of the Police Department in Kerala

Director General of Police to Constables

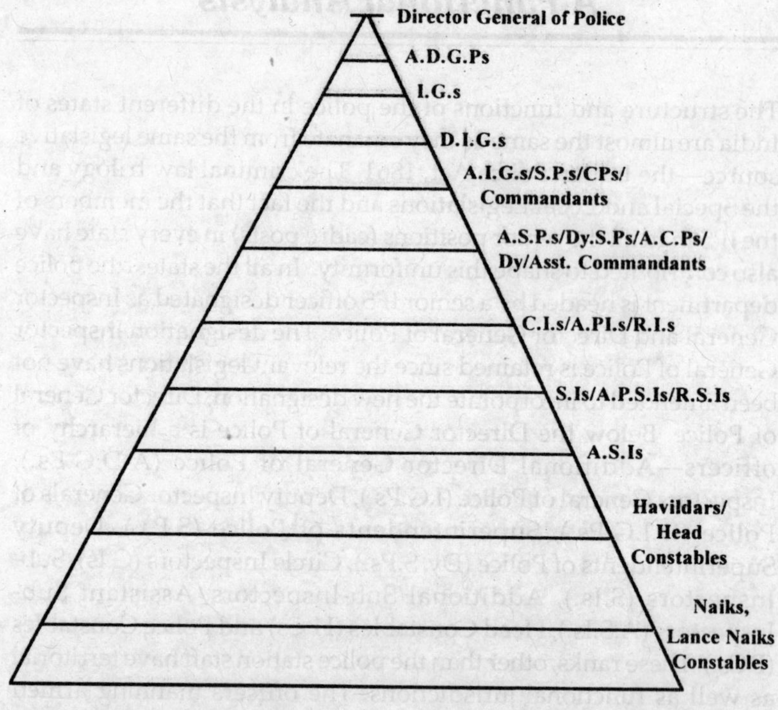

A study of the organization as represented in the Chart 3.1 shows that the police department is monolithic in character and the supervisory ranks with the Director General of Police at the apex of the organizational pyramid. The supervisory levels start with that of the Circle Inspectors with each level below being supervised by the next higher level. There are also elaborate arrangements of checks and balances. Thus, intelligence is collected by at least four (4) levels-the police stations and the District Special Branch at the District level, at the range level and at the zonal level and by the State Special Branch at the State level—and compared and collated at the level of the Additional Director General of Police, Intelligence. Similarly, investigation, of all crimes other than 'Grave Crimes' is primarily at the station level with the Circle Inspector investigating 'Grave Crimes' and supervising the investigation of the Sub-Inspector. But there are units at the disposal of the Superintendent of Police to take over the investigation of any particular case as decided by him. Cases are also taken over by the Crime Branch CID, as decided by the Director General or the Government. Occasionally, cases are also transferred to the Central Bureau of Investigation (C.B.I.), an organization under the Union Government established under the Delhi Special Police Establishment Act and on the basis of the powers given to the Union Government in List-I of the Constitution of India. Besides, the Head of the Department/the State/the Judiciary can always set-up Special Investigation Teams to investigate important cases independent of the State police agencies.[2] Control of corruption and misuse of powers is an important input of supervision and specific officers are designated as Vigilance Officers. But there is a separate organization known as the Anti-Corruption Bureau outside the police department, but manned by police personnel, to look into all matters coming within the purview of the Prevention of Corruption Act, 1988.

In every State, as has been mentioned above, the major Criminal Acts and the Police Act give the organizational outline and powers and functions of each rank. These legislations are supplemented by the Police Standing Orders or the Police Manual, being orders and instructions issued by the Head of the Department by virtue of the authority vested in him under the Police Act, from time to time. These instructions have the status of subordinate legislations. In the State, under Section 16 of the Kerala Police Act, the Head of the Department is empowered, subject to the approval of the Government, to "frame such orders and rules not inconsistent with this Act as he may deem expedient relating to the general government and distribution of the police force, the place of residence, the classification, rank and particular service and duties of the members thereof; their inspection; the description of arms, accoutrements and other necessaries to be furnished to them; to the collecting and communicating of intelligence and information; for preventing abuse or neglect; and rendering such force efficient in the discharge of all its duties".[3]

The primary functions of the Inspector General and Director General of Police have been summarized as follows:

(i) He is to serve as principal advisor to the State Government in all matters pertaining to police administration of the State...

(ii) He is to act as the administrative head of the State police organization and execute policy decisions under the directions of the State Government. He commands the line operations from the top and supervises implementation of the policy in consultation with those who formulate the policy.

(iii) He has to keep his own house in order and also keep it going in terms of daily routine work. He is responsible for internal economy and all those subjects which are necessary for the efficient handling of the security services in the State".[4]

Under section 5 of the Indian Police Act of 1861 (Act V, 1861) the Inspector General will have the full powers of a District Magistrate throughout the State.[5] He occupies a position of importance among the Heads of Departments in any State. The post carries considerable prestige. The Police Act vests in him the administration of the police throughout the State. The Inspector General and Director General of Police aids and advises the Government in formulating and implementing policies. While polices are formulated, traditionally consultations are held with the Director General of Police. In his message to the members of the Kerala Police on assuming the office of the Inspector General, a former Inspector General, M. Gopalan wrote, "It is the prerogative of Government to lay down policy and the duty of very government servant to implement the policy with utmost loyalty, correctness and competence".[6] The Inspector General and Director General provides a link between the Government and its police organization and within the department he is responsible for the general government and management of the police force. However, there have been deep inroads made in to the position of the Inspector General and Director General by the political executive, usurping his powers and by lateral contacts with officers holding positions of crucial significance. "...the political executive holds the whip hand in that the Inspector General of Police is chosen, posted, kept or transferred at his will. Even in the delegated areas, there are allegations of interference from the political executive which creates friction and disruption of normal relations. In his important functional area, it is alleged that distortions have been introduced and perpetuated".[7] The question of making the head of the police department, politically neutral and professionally independent has been therefore receiving attention in the media, among the academics, administrators and among police officers for quiet sometime. In their Report, the Kerala Study Group constituted by the State Government to assist the National Police Commission, 1977, observed as follows "Politicization of the force and weakening of the position of the Inspector General of Police cannot but damage the independence neutrality and efficiency of the force...to this end the Inspector General of Police has to be given constitutional safeguards as are available to Chairman of the State Public Service Commission. The Inspector General's post has to be made a tenure post for 5 years or till he attains the age of superannuation, whichever is earlier. Statutory safeguards alone will enable the Inspector General to stand up to political pressures in his basic functions as well as the details of day-to-day administration like postings and transfers, disciplinary action and career planning. Such an insulation of the Inspector General against political pressures will ensure that the police in a State functions as an arm of the law and not as an agent of the political party in power. The risks involved in the police in the State being reduced as a tool of the Government in power are sufficiently serious to think of statutory safeguards for the Inspector General of Police.[8] These recommendations apparently weighed with the National Police Commission, 1977, which has recommended tenure posting and other safeguards for the head of the State police department.[9] The need for such an insulation of the police organization received the imprimatur of the Apex Court which has insisted on selecting the Director of the Central Bureau of Investigation by a different process than ordinary promotion or posting and in which the Chief Vigilance Commission also plays a role.[10] This is a recommendation of the National Police Commission where no action has been taken by the State Governments and hence a priority area for reform proposals.

The Home Minister is at the apex of the police administration at the governmental level. The Chief Minister, even when he is not holding the Home Portfolio, holds a position of critical importance in the administration of the State by virtue of being the Head of Government and also owing to the functional allocations under the Rules of Business.[11] The Chief Minister normally deals with the All-India Services, the Indian Administrative Service, the Indian Police Service and the Indian Forest Service, and he can demand to see any file and can refer any issue to the Council of Ministers. The Home Secretary is the head of the administrative department in the Secretariat and he is the normal channel of communication with the Inspector General and Director General though in important matters the Chief Secretary writes directly to him. On all law and order matters the Inspector General and Director General of Police writes directly to the Chief Secretary. Relevant decisions of the Council of Ministers are communicated to him by the Chief Secretary either directly or through the Home Secretary. Extensive informal contacts also take place between the Inspector General and Director General of police and the Home Secretary and the Chief Secretary. As the Head of the Government, the Chief Minister has the right to be kept informed of all developments particularly those affecting law and order and internal security and such information is given to him by the Inspector General and Director General of Police directly or through the Chief Secretary. The Director General and Director General of police and through formal and informal channels keep the Government informed of all developments concerning the department. The Inspector General and Director General also send a number of reports to the government. Thus, it can be seen that there are limitless opportunities for personal interaction between the leadership of the police department and the political executive and also the administrative department and the Chief Secretary. This gives considerable force to the demand for appropriate reform to insulate the police leadership against interference by the political executive.

It has been pointed out above that the personnel structure of the police department is hierarchical in character and the different levels supervise both functional and territorial responsibilities. This hierarchical arrangement ensures smooth functioning of the chain of command and facilitates easy communication from the top to the bottom. The office of the Inspector General and Director General of police is known as the Police Headquarters where he has a mix of uniformed and ministerial staff to look after all functions centrally located on him. The Police Headquarters is headed by officers designated as Inspector General Administration, Deputy Inspector General Administration, Additional Inspector General (A.I.G.), and the ministerial staff headed by a Manager. There are four (4) Additional Director Generals of Police to assist the Inspector General and Director General of Police in the matter of administration by being heads of the various functional divisions in the department like Planning and Welfare, Protection of Civil Rights, Jail, Modernization, Intelligence, Crime Branch, Special Branch, etc.[12] For police administration the State of Kerala is divided into two (2) Zones, each in charge of an Inspector General of Police. They are, Northern Zone with Kozhikode as the Headquarters and Southern Zone with Headquarters at Thiruvananthapuram. Besides, the zonal Inspector General of Police with territorial jurisdiction, there are certain Inspector General with functional jurisdictions like Inspector General of Police, Crimes, Inspector General of Police, Intelligence, Inspector General of Police, Training, Inspector General of Police, Armed Police Battalion, Inspector General of Police, Headquarters, Inspector General of Police, Crime Records Bureau, etc. The Additional Director Generals of Police and Inspector Generals of Police are the senior colleagues of the Inspector General and Director General of Police and help him by controlling the organizations under them and by offering guidance and effecting supervision. The Zones are further divided into Ranges, each in charge of a Deputy Inspector General. At present there are four (4) Ranges[13] in Kerala—Kannur, Thrissur, Ernakulam and Thiruvananthapuram. In addition to the Deputy Inspector Generals heading the territorial ranges, there are certain functional areas or ranges of the department under the charge of Deputy Inspector Generals like Deputy Inspector General of Administration, Deputy Inspector General of Training, Deputy Inspector General of Armed Police Battalion, Deputy Inspector General of Crime Branch, Deputy Inspector General of Special Branch, Deputy Inspector General of Security, Deputy Inspector General of Railways etc. They function directly under the respective Inspector Generals of Police. The Deputy Inspector General functions as a connecting link between the Inspector General and the District Officer. He inspects the Districts in the Range, advises and guides the Superintendents of Police, calls for important reports and sends his Inspection notes to the Inspector General of Police.

Usually, a territorial range consists of three or more districts, each under a Superintendent of Police. A Superintendent of Police is in charge of a district and hence commonly known as the District Superintendent of Police. In Thiruvananthapuram, Ernakulam and Kozhikode, an urban-rural divide has been introduced in the police district administration. Thus, Thiruvananthapuram district is divided into a rural district known as Thiruvananthapuram Rural under a Superintendent of Police and an urban area under a Commissioner of Police. Similarly Kozhikode district has a rural area under a Superintendent of Police in charge of a district called Kozhikode Rural and an urban area under a Commissioner called Kozhikode City Police Commissioner. Ernakulam district is also divided into a rural district known as Ernakulam Rural under a Superintendent of Police and urban area called Ernakulam City under the City Police Commissioner, Ernakulam. The City Police Commissioner of Ernakulam is being conferred with powers as exercised by the Police Commissioners elsewhere.[14] However, the Commissioners in Thiruvananthapuram, Ernakulam and Kozhikode are currently holding the rank of a Superintendent of Police. The Chart 3.2 depicts a typical police organization at the district level.

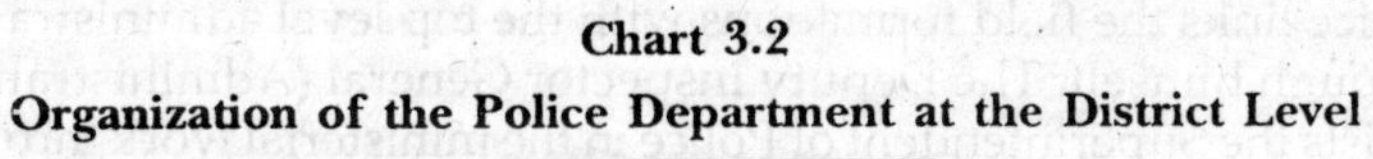

Chart 3.2

Organization of the Police Department at the District Level

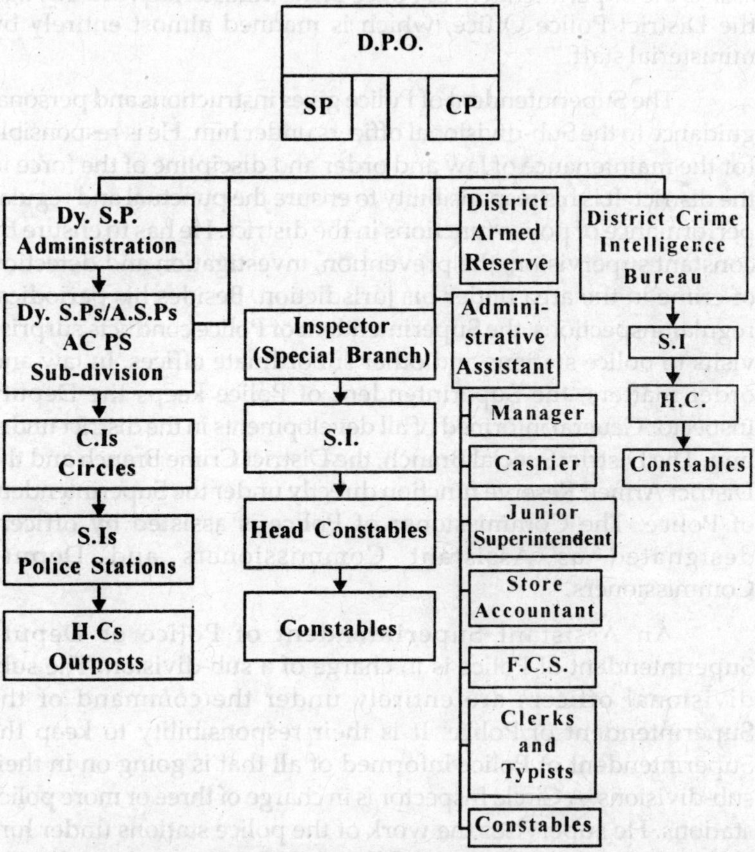

Each police district is divided into sub-divisions which are again divided into Circles and Police Stations. The number of sub-divisions, circles and police stations in a district varies in accordance with the size of the district as well as the problems of each area. A Deputy Superintendent of Police or Assistant Superintendent of Police (IPS) is in charge of a sub-division.

Usually, there are three (3) or more Circles in a Sub-division. An Inspector of Police is in charge of a Circle and has under him four or more police stations. Superintendents, Assistant or Deputy Superintendents and Circle Inspectors are wielding supervisory positions in the district police structure. Thus, a Superintendent of

Police links the field formations with the top level administration through himself. The Deputy Inspector General (Administration) assists the Superintendent of Police in the ministerial work through the District Police Office, which is manned almost entirely by ministerial staff.

The Superintendent of Police gives instructions and personal guidance to the Sub-divisional officers under him. He is responsible for the maintenance of law and order and discipline of the force in the district. It is his responsibility to ensure the punctual and regular performance of police functions in the district. He has to ensure by constant supervision, the prevention, investigation and detection of crime in the area under his jurisdiction. Besides his periodical regular inspections, the Superintendent of Police conducts surprise visits to police stations and other subordinate offices. In law and order matters, the Superintendent of Police keeps the Deputy Inspector General informed of all developments in the district under him. The District Special Branch, the District Crime Branch and the District Armed Reserve function directly under the Superintendent of Police. The Commissioner of Police is assisted by officers designated as Assistant Commissioners and Deputy Commissioners.

An Assistant Superintendent of Police or Deputy Superintendent of Police is in charge of a sub-division. The sub-divisional officers are entirely under the command of the Superintendent of Police. It is their responsibility to keep the Superintendent of Police informed of all that is going on in their sub-divisions. A Circle Inspector is in charge of three or more police stations. He supervises the work of the police stations under him and keeps the Sub-Divisional Officer and Superintendent of Police informed of the state of affairs in the circle. He also investigates important crimes.

The Police Station is a key organization of the department under the criminal law and is supervised by all higher levels. It is the base of the pyramid of police organization in the State and the most important functional unit of the department, where criminal laws get activated and power and authority flows to control crime and management of order.

Chart 3.3 gives the organization of a police station.

Chart 3.3

Police Organisation at the Police Station Level

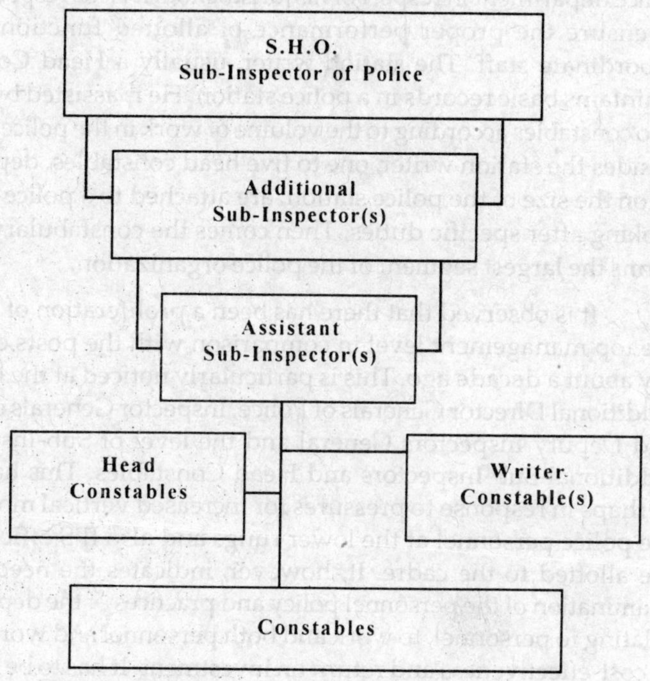

At present there are four hundred and fourteen (414) police stations and eight (8) charging stations in the State.[15] A Police station is defined as 'any post or place declared generally or specially by the State Government to be a Police Station and includes any local area specified by the State Government in this behalf'.[16] It is the primary contact point of the public with the entire police administration in the state. The Cr.P.C. calls the police station a 'Station House'. A police station is constituted by the state government with a formal Gazette notification. Usually, a Sub-Inspector of Police is in charge of thc police station, though in some important police stations a Station House Officer in higher rank like Circle Inspector or Deputy Superintendent of Police is posted.[17] The Sub-Inspector of Police is the principal investigating officer within his jurisdiction. He is primarily responsible for maintaining order and prevention and detection of crime within the limits of the police station. A Sub-Inspector is, in fact, the eyes and ears of the police department in respect of his jurisdiction. It is his responsibility to ensure the proper performance of allotted function by his subordinate staff. The station writer, usually a Head Constable maintains basic records in a police station. He is assisted by one or two constables according to the volume of work in the police station. Besides the station writer, one to five head constables, depending upon the size of the police station, are attached to a police station, looking after specific duties. Then comes the constabulary which forms the largest segment of the police organization.

It is observed that there has been a proliferation of posts at the top management level in comparison with the posts existing, say about a decade ago. This is particularly noticed at the levels of Additional Director Generals of Police, Inspector Generals of Police and Deputy Inspectors General and the level of Sub-Inspectors, Additional Sub-Inspectors and Head Constables. This has been, perhaps in response to pressures for increased vertical mobility to the police personnel at the lower rungs and also IPS officers who are allotted to the cadre. It, however, indicates the need for re-examination of the personnel policy and practices of the department relating to personnel, to work and both personnel and work linked to cost-effectiveness and return on investment. It has to be inferred that, there has not been any realistic yardstick devised to determine personnel requirements on the basis of job-demand indices. Since increase in personnel affects budget estimates and allocations, police personnel requirements have to be subjected to a serious study. While the police-population ratio and the police-crime ratio are all traditionally reliable indices, there is a section in the police leadership, who seriously suggest that quality policing has to be based on an altogether different set of indices basing people's satisfaction of police service as the first and primary concern. This introduces a new dimension to basic policy where concepts like 'Community Police', 'Neighbourhood Watch', 'Resident Association' work in tandem with the police and 'Civilian Beats' and Patrols' and 'Watch and Ward' etc. assume significance. It is evident that this is an area that needs careful study to determine the level of utilization of personnel, physical accounting of personnel on the job, productivity, customer satisfaction and very importantly, cost effectiveness and return on investment. This is certainly an area of concern for the general public and administrators.

REFERENCES

1. S.C. Misra, *State Police Organization in India*, New Delhi, Gyan Books, 1975.
2. Investigation of the Stamp Paper Scam, Maharashtra by a retired Director General of Police, K.K.Puri, is a recent instance.
3. Section 16, *The Kerala Police Act*, Cochin, Swamy Law Publishers, 2001.
4. P.D. Sharma, *Indian Police: A Developmental Approach*, New Delhi, Unpublished Ph.D. Thesis, 1977, p. 61.
5. The Kerala Police Act does not have such a provision.
6. M. Gopalan, "A Message to the Members of the Kerala Police", Trivandrum, Government Press, 24 November, 1967. Also see R. Prakasam, *Kaalathinotha Police: M. Gopalante Dauthyavum Darshanavum*, (Mal.), Trivandrum, D.C. Books, October 2003.
7. P.J. Alexander, "The Police Administration in Kerala: A Developmental Approach", Trivandrum, unpublished Ph.D. Thesis, 1979, pp. 66-67.
8. Report of the Kerala Study Group, appointed by the State Government to assist the National Police Commission, 1977, as per G.O. (Rt) 233/78/Home dated 2 February 1978, Trivandrum, (Mimeo), 1978, p. 9.
9. Report of the National Police Commission, 1977, Volume-II, 1979, pp. 30-31.
10. The search is on for a successor to the present Director of C.B.I., who is due to demit office by the end of November 2003, See *The Hindu* 23 November, 2003.
11. *Rules of Business*, Trivandrum, Government of Kerala, Superintendent, Government Press, 2002.
12. Data provided by Police Headquarters.
13. *Ibid*.
14. See *The Hindu*, 25 November 2003.
15. Data provided by Police Headquarters.
16. Section 4, *Criminal Procedure Code*.
17. The Tamil Nadu Police Commission of 1969 and the Kerala Police Re-organization Commission, 1982-86 have recommended multiple S.H.Os for police stations for delegation of powers and for fixing personal responsibility.

A Survey of Police Reforms in Kerala

The Police Commission of 1902-03 commonly known as the 'Fraser Commission' while concluding its Report had stressed the need for police reforms in these words "Inferior men have to be got rid of in all ranks, and evil traditions have to be broken in the force. The attitudes of the people towards the police, and public opinion in regard to the unrighteousness and corruption have to be raised".[1] These words very well explain the need and urgency of reforming the police for making them upright, corruption free, efficient, accountable and people-friendly. The police must be accountable to the law, to the Department and to the people. Accountability is a liability to account for proper performance of assigned tasks. In a democratic society police is accountable for its performance to the people. All activities of the police are governed by various provisions of law and each action of the police is to conform to the law of the land. So the police has an accountability to law. Finally, the police functionaries are accountable for their performance to the organisation".[2] However, it is doubtful whether the traditional mechanisms are effective to ensure this three-fold accountability except the accountability to the organisation. Due to the excessive workload and procedural problems, the Courts have never been able to fully ensure the accountability to law. As for the accountability to the department, adherence to internal standards is quite strong and no police officer feels that he is not answerable to the department. Since there is no formal method to ensure direct accountability to the people, accountability to the people is structured as accountability to the Government. Practically, accountability to the Government has come to mean willing or unwilling execution of the directives, legitimate or illegitimate, of the party in power. This has created an assumption among the people that the ruling party has the right to use the police as it wishes and it is the duty of the opposition to denounce the police as the personal police of those in power. In such a situation, the police cannot function efficiently. To earn the trust and ensure the cooperation of the people, police must be made free from partisan politics. However, the political process has to help in policing by allocating finances, ensuring public co-operation, bringing problems to the notice of the police and exposing their failures and defects. In other words, the party in power should positively contribute to policing without misusing them and the opposition should help and support the police for the good of all. This is possible when the functioning of the police becomes transparent, honest, lawful and responsive to the problems of the people for which timely reforms become imperative.

The first state in independent India to appoint a Police Commission was the State of Kerala which appointed the Kerala Police Re-organisation Committee in January 1959.[3] The State of Kerala, a motherland for the Malayalam speaking people, was formed on the Report of the State Re-organisation Commission, on 1 November, 1956. Prior to it, the area was divided into three (3) units—the Travancore, Cochin and the District of Malabar. Travancore and Cochin were princely states and Malabar was under direct British rule as it was a part of Madras Presidency. As a first step towards a united Kerala the two princely States—Travancore and Cochin were integrated to form the Travancore-Cochin state on 1 July 1949. Finally, on the basis of the principle of linguistic re-organization the district of Malabar also merged with the Travancore-Cochin State to form the state of Kerala. These three units had a record of dissimilar growth and administrative development prior to integration. This made a reform and re-structuring of the entire administration, including police administration, imperative. The Kerala Police Re-organisation Committee of 1959 was constituted in this background for the re-organization of the police with the following members.[4]

1. Sri. N.C. Chatterjee, Senior Advocate, Supreme Court, and Vice-President, Supreme Court Bar Association, New Delhi — Chairman
2. Sri. S. Mohan Kumara Mangalam, Senior Advocate, Supreme Court, Madras — Member
3. Sri. S. Guruswamy, President All India Railway Men's Federation, Madras — Member
4. Sri. P.N.K. Krishna Pillai, Personnel Manager Indian Aluminium Company, Calcutta — Member
5. Sri. M. Krishna Menon, I.P. SecretaryInspector General of Police, Trivandrum — Member-Secretary

The Committee was given an elaborate Terms of Reference, with 18 items, to study and report.[5] However, due to the removal of the ministry and the imposition of President's rule in the state, the Member-Secretary of the Commission was recalled for duty as the Inspector General of Police K. Ramanujan, who was formerly Assistant Secretary to the Committee was appointed as Secretary.[6] On 19 November 1959, the government asked the Committee to submit the Report urgently and suggested that the Committee may confine itself to items 1 to 6 and 8 of the Terms of Reference.[7] Thus, about two thirds of the items in the Terms of Reference were withdrawn from the consideration of the Committee. It was a blessing in disguise for the Committee which has recorded as follows "Due to the interruption of the work of the Committee as the result of the agitation against the Communist Government for about three months, the necessary materials could not be completely collected for the submission of a Report on all items in the Terms of Reference. The Committee, therefore, decided to confine its Report to the items mentioned as more important by the Government in the Government Order dated 19th November".[8]

Effective policing requires a close relation based on mutual help and co-operation, between the public and the police. During the freedom struggle the police force, organized by an alien regime, was used as a coercive arm to sub-serve their master's interests. Since the police were used as a willing tool to ruthlessly suppress agitations, uprisings and constitutional movements for freedom, the people developed an apathetic attitude towards them. "The police were frequently denounced as relentless prosecutors or oppressors of the weak and helpless and the tools of vested interests".[9] The dawn of independence and the adoption of a liberal democratic Constitution necessitated a fundamental transformation in the role of the police. People became more conscious of their rights and liberties guaranteed by the Constitution. The commitment of the Constitution to the concept of Welfare State and the upliftment of the common people, as declared in the Preamble as well as in the Directive Principles of State Policy, has made the perceptions of the people about the political system very high. This has created a substantial change in the expectations of the people from the police as well. "They expect a different approach by the police towards the maintenance of law and order and want them to play a new role in a progressive and enlightened democracy".[10] The changed scenario has led to a greater awareness among the people of the State of Kerala, of their basic rights and liberties. The unique features of the State like high rate of literacy, acute unemployment, lack of industries, severe pressure of population on the land etc have put more stress and strain on the police. The first elected government in the State was led by the Communist Party of India. This was one of the early experiments in constitutional government by the Communist Party and it would appear that they genuinely wanted to address some of these issues. It was in this background that the government headed by Sri. E.M. Sankaran Namboodiripad (E.M.S.) appointed the Kerala Police Re-organization Committee in January 1959.

The Committee held sittings in Delhi, Madras, Ernakulam and Trivandrum. Necessary data were collected from all Member of Parliaments, Officials of State Governments in India, the Attorney General of India, Law Officers in all the States, the Supreme Court Bar Association, Bar Councils and Bar Associations in the different States, all Members of Legislative Assembly (M.L.A.) in Kerala, important organisations of employers and workers and other distinguished persons with the help of a comprehensive questionnaire mailed to them. On 1 April 1959, the Committee held its first sitting at Delhi and examined Members of Parliament (M.P.) belonging to various political parties, retired High Court Judges, senior members of the Supreme Court Bar and trade unionists of All-India importance. The Committee in its sitting at Madras in 1959 examined the law officers of the Government including the Advocate-General of Madras, senior police officers including the Inspector-General of Police, trade unionists, senior advocates and prominent industrialists. In its sittings in Ernakulam and Trivandrum, the Committee examined the Advocate General of Kerala, the Government Pleaders, Heads of Departments including the Chief Secretary, members of State political parties including Sri V.R. Krishna Iyer, Law and Home Minister in the E.M.S. Ministry which appointed the Committee, trade unionists and important industrialists. The Committee had also examined the representatives of the Planters' Association. The Committee held its final sitting at Ernakulam between 24 and 28 December and finalized the Draft Report.

The items in the Terms of Reference on which the Committee submitted their Report are given below.

I. The Role of the Police in a Welfare State

This was Item No (1) in the Terms of Reference. After detailed study and deliberation the Committee summed up their conclusions on this item as follows.[11]

1. The objectives of the police organisation in Free India must undergo radical change. The emphasis on the negative or coercive aspect should be replaced by the realization for the need for a positive and constructive role.
2. The members of the Police Force should be given adequate training in social welfare work and they should as part of their education be trained to appreciate the temper and objectives of a democratic welfare State.
3. The primary function of the police, namely, the maintenance of law and order and the prevention and detection of crimes must be discharged. But, they must realize that in the new setup the achievement of the objectives should be effected by a method of friendly and sympathetic approach to human problems and the days of ruthless oppression are gone forever. The police must be the first servants of the public.

4. The gulf between the police and the public should be bridged by proper police-public relations and by the readiness to associate with the people and constant endeavour to deal with grievances or complaints in a sympathetic manner.

5. The police should be encouraged to participate in social welfare activities and community development work.

6. The Armed Police should have normally more time to take part in social welfare work.

7. The Taluk Police should foster greater police-public relationship by associating the public in their normal fields of activity, such as control of juvenile delinquency, traffic control, celebration of courtesy week, conduct of sports, talks in schools and youth organisations, police exhibitions, etc.

8. Sramadan or other social welfare activities should not be made compulsory and should not be made pretext for neglecting primary duties of checking and investigation of crimes and the maintenance of law and order.

9. In carrying out their duty of prevention of crime, the police should act with courtesy and firmness. Wholesale prosecutions for minor infringements of law for statistical purposes should not be resorted to. Their role should be that of mentors and instructions and warnings should be issued before such prosecutions are launched.

10. A spirit of service should be impressed on the members of the Force in Training Schools or Colleges. Development of proper police-public relations and instruction in social welfare activities should be part of the training curriculum. The pattern of instruction in training institutions has not radically altered from the days of British rule. A change should be effected to impress the police with the ideal of service to the public.

11. The Press exercises a very powerful influence on the moulding of public opinion, particularly in Kerala. Improper coverage of news often causes damage to the reputation of entire police force. A whole time Police-Public Relations Officer should function under the Inspector-General of

Police. He should arrange for prompt and regular supply of authentic information regarding the activities of the police in the State.

12. Police-public relations at the districts level should be studied constantly and improved by District Advisory Committees which will consist of local M.P.s and M.L.A.s and influential members of the public and which will coordinate the endeavours of the police and the public in maintaining peace and educating the public about police activities.

13. (a) Individual integrity of policemen is to be zealously guarded. Continued interests in the conditions of service and welfare of the police force should be maintained by the State in order to achieve the above result. Technical efficiency of the Force must be improved if it is to stand up to the strain of modern police working. The following are recommended:–

(i) Recruitment

A minimum standard of education, preferably S.S.L.C. should be insisted on for regular constabulary, other than the Armed Police.

(ii) Contentment

Conditions of service and treatment of subordinates by their own officers, by all other authorities and by leaders of the public should be such as to develop in the constables a high degree of self-respect.

(iii) Fairness and Impartiality

There should be Promotion Committees and Boards, and there should be no scope for unfairness or influence in the matter of promotions or disciplinary action and there should be neither victimization nor shielding.

(iv) Strength

The strength of the police is insufficient for effectiveness in prevention which needs more wide-spread and well-directed activity than the older method of detection and penal action.

(v) *Independence*

Independence in the exercise of authority which is very necessary to secure impartiality should be guaranteed to the members of the Force. Interference by outsiders should not be tolerated. The District Advisory Committee should take active part in securing such independence as well as in enabling Superior Officers to detect and put down corruption in the Department."

The second item in the Terms of Reference was "role of the police in the context of employer-employee relations". This was no doubt a very important issue for the Communist Government in power. In his statement regarding the police policy, the Chief Minister E.M. Sankaran Namboodiripad had specifically referred the role of the police in the law and order situation arising out of strikes and similar demonstrations resorted to by what he termed as "toiling class" as against the "owning class". The statement at the same time made it clear that the Government had no intention to weaken the role of the police in "rendering protection and assistance to the person and property of the owning classes to which they are entitled as the citizens of the State. It has been noted by the Committee that the policy statement had an adverse effect on the morale of the police and made them uncertain about their functions and powers.[12] Soon after the statement of the Chief Minister on the police policy, the police had to open fire on workers, at two places; one in a cashew nut factory at Chandanathoppe near Kollam and the other at Munnar, on plantation workers. In both these cases the strikers owed allegiance to the ruling party. Both the sections, to use the terms of the Chief Minister "the toiling class" and the "Owning class", vehemently criticized the police policy of the Government. While the employers complained that adequate protection was not given to them to enforce their fundamental rights of safety of person and property, the labour unions alleged that the police were unnecessarily interfering in their right to strike and picket. In short, the policy statement of the Chief Minister and the way in which it was implemented was the target of attack both by employers and by workmen. So it was natural that the Committee was asked to enquire and Report on the role of the police in the context of employer-employee relations.

The Committee summarized their conclusions on this subject as follows.[13]

1. In order to enable the police to tackle effectively law and order problems arising out of rival unionism in industry, steps should be taken to recognize a single bargaining agency in a bargaining unit on the following lines.

   (i) The Indian Trade Union Act should be amended as to confer additional powers on the Trade Union Registrars to supervise the expenditure of funds as well as to ensure democratic periodical election of the executive without at the same time encroaching on the independence of union functioning in an organisation.

   (ii) Only one representative union should be recognized as the sole bargaining agent in a bargaining unit.

   (iii) Where there is only one union claiming representation in a bargaining unit, that union should be compulsorily recognized.

   (iv) Where there are more than one union claiming recognition the one with the following of the majority of workers should be certified as the bargaining agent.

   (v) In case of rival claims advanced by unions for certification as sole bargaining agent, the issue should be settled by secret ballot.

   (vi) All permanent workers with a service of one year or more should have the right to vote.

   Note: These recommendations No. 5 and 6 should be tried as an experimental measure for a period of 5 years.

   (vii) Any union obtaining the majority of votes in a secret ballot should have secured at least 25 per cent of the votes of the total number of workers concerned in order to qualify for being certified as the sole collective bargaining agent.

   (viii) Any union to be qualified for being certified as the bargaining agent should have at least one year's standing.

(ix) A State Labour Relations Board should be created as a high power authority to settle the claims of unions regarding their eligibility for being certified as sole bargaining agents. That body should be authorized to conduct elections to determine the respective following of the unions wherever necessary.

(x) The State Labour Relations Board should also hear and decide disputes regarding the bargaining unit, as to whether it should be a craft, a section in a factory, an industrial unit or an industry.

(xi) Refusal to bargain with a certified representative union should be an unfair labour practice.

(xii) Other unfair labour practice and employer practices listed in the Trade Unions Amendment Act, 1947, should be included in the new law.

2. There is no need to modify or restrict the powers of owners of factory to remove goods during strike. Rare instances where such removal is mala fide in order to break a strike or to deprive the workers of their dues should be dealt with by Government by proper executive action.

3. There is no need to change the existing law under which willing workers either outsiders or persons already on the rolls of the factory, have a right to work when a strike is in progress. A code of conduct should however be evolved by which such employment during a strike is restricted to necessary minimum such as maintenance of essential services, protection of lives and property, etc.

4. There is no need for setting up any special agency to direct or advise the police about their course of action during an industrial dispute when violations of law and order take place.

The Third item in the Terms of References was the duties of the police in the context of:

(a) the free exercise of civil liberties and political rights of freedom of speech, of platform and association in a democracy consistent with paramount security of the State;

(b) communal and linguistic tensions that crop up from time to time;

(c) demonstrations and agitations with or without the support of political parties;

(d) in property disputes".

The recommendations of the Committee on this issue were as follows.[14]

1. The Government should seriously attempt to bring the political parties together to evolve a code of conduct regarding the manner in which the fundamental rights of freedom of assembly and association should be exercised, particularly regarding the manner of organisation of meetings and processions, the use of slogans, posters etc.

2. The Police Officer must regard it as his first task to win the confidence of the public in the area where he is serving. He must be looked upon by all sections of the people, as a man of integrity and impartiality possessing the confidence of all.

3. The duty of the Police Officer must be to intervene in cases of trouble long before the trouble actually erupts into violence or even danger to law and order. He must be in a position to do this by virtue of his standing among the people which would enable him to anticipate and locate trouble at its most incipient stage.

4. In order to enable the Police Officer to attain such a position in the area where he is posted, transfers must not be frequent and must be arranged in such a way as to subserve this aim.

5. Regarding the matter of enforcing ex-parte orders of courts, the police must rigorously enforce such orders, but courts should be careful about passing ex-parte orders and legislation should take into account any landlord peasant relations where there is necessity for circumscribing the power of the court to pass ex-parte orders".

The fourth, sixth and eighth items in the Terms of Reference were:

IV. "Enquire and Report on "whether in view of the public criticism in recent times against firing by the police, the use of fire arms by the police should be totally excluded; and if not the nature of circumstances and the conditions under which it should be allowed;

VI. Operational technique of the police and the use of the following weapons; Lathi, tear-gas and coloured water, and

VIII. Measure for controlling meetings, demonstrations and mobs".

The Committee considered these three items together to avoid overlapping and repetition. Their recommendations on these issues were as follows.[15]

1. Meetings and large assemblies which are gathered on the occasions of the visit of important personages and for entertainment such as festivals are generally peaceful. Their control should be effected by careful previous planning about the disposition of manpower, the division of meeting place and routes into convenient sectors, the arrangement of sufficient number of routes by pedestrians and vehicular traffic, setting up of control stations for arranging transport and disposition of forces and wide publicity by press and radio talks about the arrangements made.
2. The use of mounted police for controlling large assemblies has to be resorted to in increasing measure.
3. Political meetings and other assemblies gathered for purposes of demonstration should be studied carefully for their objectives. If they are peaceful the police should give them protection and ensure that they are not disturbed by unruly elements. In other cases the police should have useful intelligence measures to spot out trouble-mongers and send for influential leaders of the movement in order to discuss and ensure peaceful behaviour of their followers.
4. Sufficient police force should be mobilized and posted to act as a healthy check on lawlessness.

5. Unless it is impossible to control the situation, armed policemen should not be displayed in the first instance. They should be kept in reserve to be available at very short notice.
6. It is not necessary to make legal provision to ban totally the carrying of sticks or other weapons in processions. The existing provisions in law are adequate to enable preventive action in cases where feelings run high among rival sections of the public and clashes are likely to occur.
7. Lying down picketing should be handled with firmness by arrests at discretion followed by removal. Kid glove handling of such situations is looked upon as weakness and induces repetition of law violations.
8. Police should have power to arrest and remove hunger satyagraghis and have them forcibly fed if there is risk to their lives.
9. The use of coloured water or water under pressure for dispersal of unlawful assemblies is not feasible in this State.
10. Use of tear smoke is a well-known and effective method of mob dispersal. The stock position of tear smoke shell is however reported to be unsatisfactory. There should be regular changing and replacement of tear smoke shells and consideration of cost should not weigh in the matter. More tear smoke squads should be formed in each District Headquarters and training should be intensified.
11. A section of Armed Police going on bandobust duty limited to about 20 per cent should be armed with canes not more than 1" in diameter and 3ft. long. It would be possible to disperse most unlawful assemblies by a cane charge if tear smoke is not effective.
12. The lathi which is 2′8" long and 2" in diameter is a powerful weapon and should be resorted to only if a cane charge proves ineffective and use of greater force is indicated.
13. It is not possible completely to eschew the use of firearms in dispersing mobs in cases where other forms of forces have proved ineffective.

14. Force culminating in the use of fire-arms should not be resorted to for dispersing an unlawful assembly unless:

    (a) Their action causes serious damage to public or private property; or

    (b) The crowd, assembly or procession is armed with deadly weapons and there is clear and imminent danger of the deadly weapons being used; or

    (c) There are two contending groups one opposed to the other and adopting such aggressive and bellicose attitude to each other that a riot is inevitable if they are not immediately dispersed.

15. It is necessary that police detailed on duties in connection with public disorder should be armed only with .410 muskets as they are less deadly than .303 rifles.

16. The existing orders by Government and in the Police Manual which lay down that police should secure the presence of local magistrates and resort to firing only with his permission when available and the need for use of only the minimum force are adequate.

17. It is to be made very clear to the Police Force that firing should be resorted to only as a last resort, that responsible Police Officers of the area should be in a position to intervene at an earlier stage and avoid the necessity to resort to use of firearms.

18. Whenever the use of firearms by police results in loss of life there must be a judicial enquiry held if possible by a High Court Judge and definitely by a person not below the rank of a District Judge.

19. When the firing has not resulted in the loss of life there should first be an enquiry by a senior executive officer appointed by the Government and if his Report shows the need for a deeper probe, a judicial enquiry should be held".

On the use of regulatory and restrictive powers under the police Act; the security provisions and sections 144 and 151 of Criminal Procedure Code, the fifth item in the Terms of Reference, the Committee summed up its recommendation on this subject as follows.[16]

1. Section 144 should not be deleted from the Criminal Procedure Code.
2. Power to pass orders under section 144 should be confined solely to Judicial Magistrates and should be taken away from the Executive Magistrates.
3. Judicial Magistrates should be given powers to pass orders under section 144 in their houses or in places where they may happen to be at the time when the passing of such an order becomes necessary.
4. The most effective safeguard against the abuse of section 144 would be to inculcate a spirit of vigilance and independence among Judicial Magistrates so that they act purely on the basis of the material that is placed before them and appreciate that the responsibility for passing that largely rests only on them.
5. It is illegal for the Government to issue any direction either regarding the issuing or non-imposition of an order under section 144. Government may issue instructions to police about the circumstances under which an application may be made to the appropriate Magistrate, but they cannot issue any instruction to the Judicial Magistrates.
6. The resort to section 144 should be rare and only when there is a possibility of large-scale riots with the participation of considerable sections of people likely to be affected by the passing of such an order.
7. Section 30 of the Police Act should continue in force. An appeal should lie against any order of the District Superintendent of Police under section 30 of the Police Act to the District Judge who should have power to set aside or modify any order made by the Police under this section. The period for which an order can be passed under section 30 should be limited to two months.
8. The Indian Police Act should be extended to the whole of Kerala and as a consequence the redundant provisions of the Travancore-Cochin Police Act should be repealed.
9. Section 108 of the Criminal Procedure Code should be repealed".

In addition to the recommendations on the above seven items, the Committee found it necessary to comment on recruitment and training and measures for improving the quality of investigation, two items included as (XII) (a) and (IX) of the original Terms of Reference and which were later taken out of the ambit of the Committee.[17] The Committee observed that there is lack of adequate facility for training the Sub-Inspectors in the State and that the pattern of instruction in training institutions has not changed from that of the colonial period. The Committee suggested that necessary changes must be introduced in the curriculum to imbue a sense of service and a spirit of co-operation with the public among the trainees. Separation of investigation and law and order in large urban areas and the functioning of an efficient prosecuting agency independent of the police etc were suggested as measures for improving the quality of work. The Committee highlighted the necessity of trained police officers in an efficient police force and sound principles for functional division in the Department. Finally, the Committee suggested that the steps taken by the State government in pursuance of the observation of the Law Commission that the system of crime reporting is not satisfactory, as there was no agency for reporting crime in the large villages particularly in Travancore area, be examined. The Committee ended their Report with the hope that State Government would take suitable further action on their recommendations.

The next attempt at police reform in the State of Kerala was in 1982, when the 'Kerala Police Re-organisation Commission' was appointed.[18] The Terms of Reference of the Commission and further additions to the Terms of Reference are discussed in Chapter I. It is necessary to point out here that the Terms of Reference of the Kerala Police Re-organization Commission was in about half of the items identical with the Terms of Reference of the National Police Commission of 1977. This is seen pointed out by the Member-Secretary in his Note that "Of the twelve items of the Terms of Reference, items 4, 5, 6, 7, 8,9 and 10 are identical with items 4, 5, 6 and 7, 8, 9, 12 and 13 of the Terms of Reference of National Police Commission constituted by the Government of India".[19] Yet there was no attempt on the part of the Government to recast the same.

However, the Commission is seen to have taken up the issues for detailed analysis and study and made well-considered recommendations as follows.[20]

1. Increasing complexities in socio-economic development have brought forth fresh dimensions in police functions and the demands on Police service have increased. The police have a vital role in ensuring progress with order and maintenance of the social balance. Consequently, the traditional concept of policing has been transformed and there has been a steady accretion in their duties and responsibilities.
2. The Report of the Committee on Police Training (1973) emphasized the need for a new outlook and proper training for the police personnel to enable them to tackle their increasingly complex responsibilities. The National Police Commission (1977) have suggested far-reaching changes.
3. The police-population ratio in Kerala is fast changing to the disadvantage of the police organisation.
4. The crime trend in the State has been showing an upward turn as indicated by figures of cases registered under the Indian Penal Code and the Special and Local Legislations.
5. To avoid diffusion of authority and distortions in the chain of command it has to be ensured that there should be undisputed concentration of control and authority in the hands of the highest-ranking officer of the Department.
6. The new phenomenon of unionization of the force cast a heavy responsibility on senior levels who have the paramount duty of preserving the delicate balance between loyalty to the organisation and safeguarding the interests of those under their command. The importance of 'leadership by example' assume critical significance here.
7. The challenges facing the police organisation are perennial and of a constantly shifting nature. Therefore, there is need to monitor developments in all functional areas so as to initiate corrective action in time. The need for a permanent organisation for continuous evaluation of performance and prospects of the Department and for structuring appropriate and timely responses is of importance.

8. Police training, like training in other administrative contexts, has to be a continuous process in the work situation sensitizing the personnel to the goals of the administration and evolving in them a positive response to the demands by the client etc.
9. It was the need for change and improvement in police attitude and performance in the background of additional responsibilities and challenges in law enforcement they have to face, that prompted the Central Government to appoint the Committee on Police Training. Implementation of the recommendations of the Committee with necessary changes to suit the needs of the State should not be further delayed.
10. One of the principal drawbacks in the system of police training in this State lies in the difficulty in securing contented and trained instructional staff. 'Rejects' who cannot be posted elsewhere are often posted as instructors in the training institutions.
11. The first step in making available better talents for the faculty of police training institutions is to give them attractive special pay and amenities as recommended by the National Police Commission.
12. The lowest rank of instructor in in-door subjects in the Police Training College should be that of Deputy Superintendent of Police and in the Police Training School an Inspector. The record of service and performance of Circle Inspectors and Sub-Inspectors who have put in about five years of service may be assessed to determine their suitability to be empanelled as instructors. Those empanelled to be sent for a 'Training of Trainers Course' organized in the Police Training College or other institutions. One-step promotion may be given to them on being posted to the faculty, which should count for seniority in the grade. Instructional staff to be given rent-free accommodation and special pay; they are to be preferred for higher studies and training; after serving for a minimum period of three years they may be given a positing of their choice.

13. To handle police science, social science and law subjects, qualified persons from University Departments or Government Colleges may be taken on deputation.
14. The Principal, Police Training College, may be empowered to invite guest faculty and to pay honorarium at the rates existing in the Institute of Management in Government, Thiruvananthapuram.
15. There is a scale of additional staff approved by Governments for the training of constables. Such a scale of staff may be prescribed for other categories of trainees also. When a scale of staff is thus approved by Government, the Director General of Police may be empowered to post the required staff and obtain ratification from Government in due course.
16. A panel of senior officers, including those of the IPS, who have received special training or acquired expertise in select areas may be prepared and their services utilized for conducting Executive Development Programmes, in-service programmes and inter-departmental training programmes.
17. For ensuring proper training atmosphere and homogeneity in staff pattern, only Sub-Inspector cadets and equivalent ranks may be trained in Police Training College, Trivandrum. Other categories may be trained in Police Training School, Thrissur. Superintendent of Police (Training) may be vested with financial, administrative and disciplinary powers.
18. Practical training which follows induction training, should be subjected to regular monitoring and evaluation by the Principal, Police Training College.
19. Members of the faculty who prepare teaching material of acceptable standards may be suitably remunerated and such material published and periodically revised by the Police Training College.
20. Out door instructors who acquire special skills and training from Central Police and Army Training institutions in Physical Training, Unarmed Combat, Weapon and Tactics, Motor Transport, Communication, etc, may be given a 'qualification pay'.

21. Since induction training is insufficient for the different career stages, there is need for organizing frequent refresher courses or in-service courses as recommended by the Gore Committee.

22. Those in the select list should undergo a refresher course before promotion. All Police Officers, of and above the rank of Sub-Inspector of Police, should undergo some training or other once in every five years. Police Training College, on the basis of an Annual Programme Calendar, should organize ad hoc courses. Familiarization courses on Forensic Science and Medical Jurisprudence may also be organized in the Police Training College.

23. To bring about improvement in attitude and behaviour of policemen and to make such changes felt by the public, larger numbers of police personnel may be put through courses on Human Behaviour, Police Community Relations, Management of organized sections like students, workers, etc. Such courses may be organized at the District and Range Headquarters.

24. Training courses on 'observation' has to be organized especially for those who are working in the Special Branch. Courses on 'observation' may also be organized in the districts.

25. Budget provision should be made for library, publication of teaching materials and for the increased activities of the Police Training College. The financial powers of the Principal, Police Training College, should be enhanced.

26. Gadgetry and training aids should be made use of more extensively.

27. Since a new campus for the Police Training College can be found only outside the city, which may operate as a disincentive, the existing campus may be developed. A master plan may be prepared and implemented on a priority basis.

28. The system of examinations in Police Training institutions may be modified keeping in view the changes in the system in educational institutions.

29. The conduct of Departmental Tests may be entrusted with the Principal, Police Training College.

30. Police Duty Meets have to be conducted every year without fail. It will be appropriate to entrust the organisation of the meet with Deputy Inspector General of Police, Training.

31. Police training institutions should be given adequate infrastructural facilities and vehicles. The design of vehicles may be changed.

32. The Deputy Inspector General of Police, Training to be nominated as 'Training Coordinator' of the Department.

33. Viewed from the general context of law and order in the State, the present strength of Armed Police Battalions would appear to be quite adequate. Increasing the number of Battalions further, without examining the manpower needs of the Department in other important areas of functioning would therefore be unwise. With the formation of new districts, opening of more Police Stations and expansion of Special Units, perhaps there is a stronger case for strengthening the District Armed Reserves, where justified.

34. Some of the Armed Police Battalions are located in groups of companies as detachments in the Districts. This arrangement, though ad hoc and fortuitous, helps quicker deployment of personnel during emergencies with some saving in transport cost and help personnel to stay nearer home. However, dispersal of personnel in detachments takes away practically all the advantages of keeping them together in a campus of their own. Periodical re-location of detachments to headquarters and vice-versa thus becomes imperative.

35. The dispersal of Battalions in detachments and for law and order duties in districts has made closer supervision by senior officers difficult. One more post of Deputy Commandant may be created in every Battalion to assist the Commandant in managing the unit. One of the Deputy Commandants may be placed in charge of administration and the other in charge of stores and equipment, motor transport, communications and training.

36 Even Havildars get reverted for transfer to District Armed Reserves. All trained personnel are thus lost. There is need for direct recruitment to fifty per cent of the posts of Havildars. A higher educational qualification has to be prescribed for such direct recruitment.

37. A provision has now been made for recruitment to twenty-five per cent of the total strength of Armed Police Sub-Inspectors. This being a low percentage, one or two posts of Assistant Commandants in each Battalion may also be filled up by direct recruitment.

38. In a Battalion a thousand strong, the total number of officers from Commandant to A.S.Is is just 40. As the officers belong to a higher age group compared to the constables the outdoor activities are likely to suffer. Posting an active and young IPS Officer as Commandant may bring about welcome changes in such situations. Every young IPS officer should be made to do a spell of duty in a Battalion before promotion to the super-time scale as it will be an excellent opportunity to learn the art of man-management.

39. There is need for revising personnel and other records of the Battalions and to reduce scriptory work. Pay Bills, Provident Fund accounts and private fund transactions may be computerized as is done in Central Reserve Police Force and Border Security Force.

40. Records which show the movement of personnel out of the campuses for law and order duties may be maintained in every Battalion.

41. Armed Police Battalion personnel are trained and maintained for performing specific functions. They should not be wasted on duties which can be performed by other categories.

42. Deployment of Armed Police Battalion personnel to a district should not be in strength less than one platoon normally, and never in less than a section. They should be withdrawn when the need for the deployment is over.

43. Armed Police Battalion personnel on duty in a district may be deployed within the district by the Superintendent of Police. Men to be accompanied by adequate number of officers. Daily or weekly report on the activities of the personnel may be sent by the officer in charge to the Commandant and S.P., D.I.G of Police, Armed Police Battalions, to order movement of personnel under orders from Police Headquarters.
44. Armed Police Battalion personnel are deployed in Districts for months together at the risk of neglecting their training altogether. At least one company in each Battalion should be retained in Battalion Headquarters for undergoing training by rotation.
45. The recommendations of the Gore Committee regarding training of Armed Police Battalions may be fully implemented with suitable changes to meet the needs of the State.
46. The present strength of the Battalions and their location call for a centralized training institution, an Armed Police Training Centre, under a highly qualified and competent Commandant, to cater to the training needs of men and officers at all career stages.
47. Training literature and material have to be produced locally to meet training needs of the Battalions.
48. Raising a 'Technical Battalion' is likely to create administrative problems. However, it should be possible to pick up from the Battalions personnel who have had basic training in I.T.I.s or aptitude for technical jobs and to train them to handle work related to technical services.
49. The equipment, arms and gadgetry now in use with the Battalions of other States may be studied and their utility evaluated for standardization.
50. The composition of vehicles in a Battalion may be amended to include four open body trucks and four motorcycles.
51 A tear gas squad of one platoon strength may be formed in every Batialion.

52. The Battalion should have efficient wireless units. Wireless personnel and equipment to remain under the administrative and operational control of the S.P., Telecommunications, but commandants may deploy them under intimation to the S.P., Telecommunication. Change over of communication system from H.F. to V.H.F. deserves urgent attention.

53. An audit unit under a Senior Superintendent may be formed for verification of accounts and auditing of private funds of the Battalions.

54. There is need for a type design for the Battalion Campuses. The design should provide for greater security for vehicles, communication equipments, arms and ammunition.

55. The vacancies caused by transfer of personnel to District Armed Reserves can be forecast and hence timely steps to be taken for filling them up. The Madhya Pradesh Special Armed Force Battalion may be repatriated.

56. Police Headquarters may arrange to examine in detail the Report of the Working Group on motor transport as it contains a number of useful suggestions which could be considered while planning the re-organisation of the Motor Transport Unit.

57. Increased use of vehicles by Station House Officers, it would appear, has reduced police visibility. Motorcycles also may be given to Station House Officers in a few stations as an experiment aimed at increasing police visibility. Traffic Units also may be given light vehicles and motor cycles for reduction of response time and greater visibility.

58. There is scope for reducing operational cost of vehicles. Hiring of buses results in payment of huge amounts towards hire charges and therefore may be resorted to only when absolutely essential. Police heavy vehicles may be used instead.

59. To eliminate misuse, use of vehicles on payment by those who have been allotted light vehicles may be considered. Similar provisions exist in public sector and for certain levels of Government employees.

60. The practice of officers driving departmental vehicles themselves has to be stopped.

61. Police fuel stations may be opened in all District Headquarters in stages, and at Ernakulam and Kozhikode immediately and at Thrissur thereafter. This alone will help timely availability of fuel and elimination of malpractices. Fuel consumption rates of vehicles are normally high. Motor Transport Officer may conduct KMPL tests afresh and verify fuel consumption periodically.

62. The age of the fleet has to be kept low. A master plan for fleet modernization with clear condemnation and replacement policy has to be prepared for long term planning. The fleet has to be homogenous for efficient maintenance and repair. A 'spares stock' system with a minimum level of spares has to be maintained to help quick repair of vehicles. Purchase may be arranged directly from manufactures. Inventory management may be computerized.

63. District Motor Transport units must have personnel and tools for preventive maintenance and minor repairs. A mobile workshop facility may be arranged for repair and maintenance of vehicles in field offices. Central and Regional Workshops may be started for major repairs of vehicles.

64. Motor Transport Officer, Police Headquarters, may be designated Chief Motor Transport Officer and given Assistant Motor Transport Officers at Range Headquarters and Regional Workshops with delegation of powers for better coordination and speedy action. To improve promotion prospects of Drivers a few posts of A.S.I. Drivers and S.I. Drivers may be created. The present driver-vehicle ratio requires revision.

65. The financial powers of unit officers may be enhanced.

66. Technically qualified motor transport personnel may be utilized for certifying need for repairs, quality of work done, reasonableness of bills, etc. They may also inspect vehicles involved in accidents and issue required certificates.

67. Fiberglass boats may be acquired for police use.

68. There is need to expose drivers and other Motor Transport Staff to training offered by fuel marketing companies and vehicle manufactures. Training course on Driving and Maintenance may be organized for their benefit through the P.T.C.

69. There is need for barring STD facilities of telephones except in very essential cases.

70. Police Telephone exchanges may be opened in Thiruvananthapuram, Ernakulam and Kozhikode cities and in exchange for a PBX the present SAX exchange of Thiruvananthapuram city may be surrendered.

71. Electronic private telephone exchange or private telephone exchange may be considered for use in offices with concentration of officers. Police Headquarters may be linked by teleprinter with all District Headquarters. The utility of present Telex facility may be evaluated before more connections are obtained.

72. VHF communication has to be extended to all field officers and Units.

73. Well-planned structures have to be put up for Repeater Stations.

74. The requirements of wireless sets of Districts may be assessed and required numbers with ten per cent additional sets may be given. Sufficient stock of sets may be kept in Headquarters too.

75. Diversion of sets has to be discouraged. Periodical verification of equipmental efficiency may be arranged to avoid dislocation during emergencies.

76. To help efficient maintenance and inventory management, equipment may be standardized. After an ABC analysis a stock of spares and tools maybe arranged. Repair facilities in central and zonal workshops have to be expanded.

77. There is need for a Research and Development Unit, and higher level of technical supervision A qualified Engineer from Railways or Post & Telegraph Department may be taken on deputation to help planning and coordination. Qualified

Electronic and Communication Engineers may be directly recruited to Research and Development/Technical Units.

78. The functions of the Technical Committee may be widened and one of the A.I.Gs of Police made a member of the Committee in place of the Superintendent of Police, Crime Branch Criminal Investigation Department.

79. Microwave links or in its absence multi-channel VHF communication has to be planned for the State. Government have to be approached without delay.

80. The vacancies of constables, now out of the purview of the Public Service Commission, have to be filled up. The integration of mechanics and operators to be completed. To ensure uniformity in organisation, recommendations of the central study team may be implemented. Range and central workshops may be placed under Deputy Superintendents of Police (Technical) and technical personnel may be sent for training.

81. All categories of personnel may be trained in handling of VHF. In police stations all constables must be trained to operate VHF sets.

82. The syllabi of training of Police Training College, Police Training School and Armed Police Battalions should include practical lessons in handling communications equipment.

83. Messages transmitted have to be short and crisp and personnel of different categories have to be trained in the art.

84. Implementation of modernization scheme has to be reviewed periodically. Vehicle position of the unit also requires revision. Telecommunication unit may be put under the Deputy Inspector General of Police, Computer Centre, for operational efficiency when computer is on stream.

85. The main purpose for which the State Special Branch has to function is to help the Director General of Police to run the Department efficiently. It has to remain the most important and authentic channel of communication at his disposal. State Special Branch has to continue to collect intelligence regarding developing law and order situations, subject it to

analysis from the larger context and record and report events sequentially where needed. Its material has to be the basis for formal Reports and for briefing Government. It has to liaise with sister organisations. The District Special Branch may collect statistics on law and order incidents like cases registered, arrests and release made and related developments and communicate the same to the Deputy Superintendent of Police and Special Branch Control Room. The State Special Branch need not attend to these tasks but it is not advisable to divest them of the overall responsibility for the collection of intelligence, its evaluation, interpretation, communication to appropriate levels, maintenance of documents and statistics and formulation of digests and reports. It has to remain the apex intelligence agency of the State.

86. A documentation centre with sophisticated techniques for storage and retrieval of information and sections devoted to different important sectors has to be organized. Streamlining and where possible prescribing proforma for reports and periodicals may be introduced to reduce scriptory work. Steps may be taken to save manpower through use of copier machines, etc. Material on law and order and other events in other states may be collected and documented for reference.

87. The security wing has to be re-organized. Airport security and anti-hijacking measures require immediate re-organisation. Crisis management measures have to be prepared. Commando squads, bomb disposal units and fire-fighting units have to rehearse regularly to improve operational efficiency. Trained personnel should be retained for longer periods, if found suitable. The security needs of Trivandrum and Cochin airports have to be analysed and action taken on a priority basis. A unit for counter-espionage and a cell for handling communal situations are urgent requirements. There is also need for a Technical Division with the State Special Branch.

88. Training of Special Branch personnel has to be systematized. Suitable persons may be sent for training outside the State and abroad. Since collection of intelligence is the

responsibility of every police officer, periodical orientation training for the different ranks may be considered. Communications over phone by field levels to the Control Room should be confined to the bare essentials and Shorthand Reporters may be used for recording such messages. Special Branch Inspectors may be provided with residential telephones. Greater sophistication and speed may be insisted in communications.

89. The State Special Branch Control Room has to be re-organized. It may be strengthened and streamlined so as to convert it into a crisis management situation room and it must have material for assembling action groups on short notice.

90. To encourage officers to remain in the unit, attractive incentives may be offered. Field levels have to be evaluated to remove dead wood.

91. The promotion prospects of Special Branch Assistants have to be periodically evaluated to plan against stagnation. They should not be transferred out.

92. The D.I.G. of Police, C.I.D. and Railways may inspect the District Special Branch units periodically.

93. Collection of intelligence and locating and cultivating of sources must receive more attention.

94. The ultimate success of investigation depends not only on the efforts put in during the investigation but also on the efficiency with which it is prosecuted. Therefore there is need for closer co-operation between the investigating and prosecuting agencies, both during investigating stages and during trial. The N.P.C. have pointed out that on the recommendations of the Law Commission police and prosecuting agency were separated and subsequently with the coming into force of the Code of Criminal Procedure (1973) the prosecuting agency has become an independent wing of the Criminal Justice System resulting in lack of co-ordination between investigating and prosecuting agencies.

95. Successful prosecution is an important step in prevention and control of crime. Acquittal of cases in court leads to waste of effort. The concept of social cost assumes significance here. The N.P.C. have felt that there is need to evolve a new system of prosecution which would ensure coordinated functioning of both wings.

96. The weakness of prosecution is more apparent in cases tried by Magistrate's courts. The present arrangement of supervision by District Collector and the Director of Prosecution is not effective. There has to be closer supervision and qualitative improvement in supervision.

97. A post of Assistant Director of Prosecution higher in rank than that of Assistant Public Prosecutor Grade I to supervise the work of Assistant Public Prosecutors Grades I and II may be created. His services must be made available to the S.P. for consultation and advice. A post of Deputy Director of Prosecution may be created to supervise work at Range level and to be available as Legal Adviser to the Range Deputy Inspector General of Police/Deputy I.G. of Police, Crime Investigation. The Director of Prosecution may be strengthened by appointing two Deputy Directors and one Assistant Director. Assistant Directors and Assistant Public Prosecutors may be exclusively appointed for prosecution of cases like misappropriation in co-operative societies, cheating by promising NOC, economic offences, etc.

98. A senior officer from departments having large number of cases may be nominated to liaise with investigation and prosecution machinery.

99. Frequent exchange of views is required between the Director of Prosecution and Police Department at different levels. Assistant Public Prosecutors and Assistant Director of Prosecution should periodically meet Superintendent of Police and other police officers.

100. The monthly diary of Assistant Public Prosecutor must be forwarded to the Superintendent of Police.

101. Prosecutors may be associated with the investigation of cases from early stages.

102. A legal cell may be set up in the office of the D.G.P. Important decisions of High Courts and Supreme Court and instructions on defects noticed in the investigation of cases etc, may be published by the cell. It may advise the department on service and other legal matters.

103. Assistant Directors of Prosecution may attend the different courts, supervise the work of Assistant Public Prosecutors Grades I and II and prosecute important cases when so ordered by the District Collector or S.P. He may be given secretarial assistance and office accommodation in the court building itself.

104. Assistant Public Prosecutors may be briefed by head constables conversant with the facts of the case. Sub-Inspectors and Circle Inspectors may watch prosecution in courts and S.P.s and Deputy S.P.s may attend courts frequently.

105. Seminars attended by prosecution agency and investigation agency may be arranged. Familiarization courses on Forensic Science and allied disciplines as organized by the Institute of Criminology and Forensic Science may be organized through the P.T.C. for judicial officers, prosecuting officers and police officers.

106. There is need to reduce pendency. Additional courts may be provided to meet increase in workload. A legal Committee may be appointed to suggest methods for expediting disposal of cases, as suggested by N.P.C.

107. Increased use of the provisions of section 206 CrPC may be made and procedure for summary trial under section 260 CrPC may be used more extensively.

108. More Magistrates may be empowered to make summary trials and State amendments may be made to section 260 CrPC to bring more categories of offences under its purview.

109. Jurisdiction of the Magistrate's courts being linked with jurisdiction of police stations, timely notification may be issued when new police stations are opened. Cases of a police station may be posted consecutively rather than on all days in a week.

110. Receipt of records by courts from police may be acknowledged.

111. Administrative issues and problems which affect trials adversely like delay or non-service of process, failure to attend court by investigating officers, etc, may be sorted out in conferences convened by District and Sessions Judges and attended by Judicial Magistrates, Police Officers and Prosecutors.

112. Copies of records to accused may be furnished from the courts as provided in the CrPC.

113. Procedure for preferring appeal has to be simplified. Circle Inspectors and Sub-Inspectors should watch disposal of cases and ensure that opportunities to file appeals are not lost by default.

114. The prosecution system existing at present in Karnataka has many of the important features suggested above. The Director of Public Prosecution of Kerala has also suggested changes, which are more or less similar. These are appended. While attempting overhaul of the system of prosecution for greater operational efficiency and increased credibility these suggestion also may be considered".

The Commission submitted an elaborate Report in 231 pages to the Government on 31 May 1984.[21] The Report was divided into nine chapters. It reviewed the police administration in the state and dealt with training, Armed Police Battalions, Motor Transport, Tele-Communications, Special Branch and the Prosecution Agency.

The Government of Kerala re-constituted the Kerala Police Re-organization Commission in December 1984[22] to study and Report on three more items viz, Crime Record and Statistics, special responsibility of the police towards the weaker sections and police welfare.

The recommendations of the reconstituted Kerala Police Re-organisation Commission were as follows.[23]

115. "Station Crime History-Part I, has to be maintained carefully; entries in the last column to be concise and brief to the point.

116. Modus operandi classification requires revision taking into account crime trends in the State and for uniformity. Orders may be issued from Police Headquarters.

117. A New Station Crime History-Part II may be prepared for visual representation of offences against person, weaker sections, women, minorities, etc., with communal or political overtones.

118. For easy reference Computer Code Number also may be given to each subject.

119. A new Register "Part III and General Conviction Register of Offences Against Human Person" may be prescribed to record data on those convicted under chapters VIII, XI, XIV, XV, XVI and XXII of the Indian Penal Code.

120. Station Crime History-Part IV may be kept properly compiled and undated: Circular No. D5-16521/66 dated 31 March 1966 incorporating "Village Note Book" may be cancelled.

121. Subject sheet may be reduced in favour of running entries; information entered may mention law and order incidents owing to communal, agrarian and industrial causes, crime against weaker sections, violent political clashes, etc.

122. History sheets have to be re-designed to conform to data being computerized; details for identification should show easily identifiable physical peculiarities.

123. The Police Manual and Jail Manual may be amended to facilitate periodical comparison and updating of History Sheets.

124. Kerala Police Manual Rule 258 may be amended to broaden the conditions for opening suspect History Sheets.

125. Fingerprints and photographs of suspects and rowdies may also be taken; a new legislation is required to replace the 'Identification of Prisoners' Act, 1920'.

126. Fingerprints of History-sheeted suspects and rowdies may also be computerized.

127. Records which serve little purpose, like Bad Character Roll B, Handcuff Register, etc., may be cancelled.

128. Data frequently called for by Government for answering interpellation, etc., may be computerized.

129. District Crime Bureau may continue to furnish statistics on crime and criminals; Bureau requires to be strengthened.

130. Monthly Crime Review may be prepared using data available to the Police Computer Centre under the supervision of the Inspector General of Police (Crimes). This review to be the basis for the Crime Review by Police Headquarters for Government.

131. The Police computer centre may computerize data on offences against women and weaker sections, communal clashes, etc., to facilitate easy retrieval.

132. Computerization of fingerprints to be expedited; the staff earmarked for this purpose to be increased.

133. Statement for Annual Administration Report to be prepared by the Deputy Inspector General of Police, Police Computer Centre; the post of Statistical Officer may be shifted to Police Headquarters to work under Deputy Inspector General of Police (Administration).

134. Facilities of the Forensic Science Laboratory which were used to detect several cases recently have to be strengthened and the process of modernization to be accelerated.

135. For the proper management of crime and crime records, the Station House Officer should remain undisturbed for about three years; frequent transfers would only result in neglect of crime control.

136. Investigative talent can be acquired only by on the job training; workshops on investigation of different categories of crime may be organized as an interim remedial measure.

137. Training of police officers has to be frequent; crucial level of investigators to be exposed to investigation techniques more often; such training courses should be compulsory to those in the select list.

138. There is need for substantial changes in the attitude of police officers to complaints from weaker sections. Such a change

is necessary for crime prevention itself, a mandatory function of the police. Investigating officers from Kasargode and Palakkad districts, particularly, to be exposed more often to training.

139. Sections of law of offences reported under Protection of Civil Rights Act with Indian Penal Code should be altered only on the written orders of the Superintendent of Police, to avoid substitution of sections to facilitate compounding; Police Headquarters may issue directions to this effect. Cases in which section of law was so altered, currently on trial, may be taken up on revision.

140. To break the prejudice-barrier, training courses may be organized to investigating officers frequently through the Police Training College, on the model of the course organized in October 1983.

141. Superintendent of Police, Special Cell, has to be given ministerial and executive staff support.

142. Superintendent of Police, Special Cell, to receive Express Reports, Grave Crime Reports and Case Diaries of all Grave Crimes under the Protection of Civil Rights Act.

143. Primary responsibility for enforcing the Protection of Civil Rights Act may rest with the Commissioner of Police/ Superintendent of Police of Districts.

144. The Legal Advisor to the Police Department may be declared 'Special Officer' under Section 15-A(2)(ii) of the Protection of Civil Rights Act to supervise prosecution.

145. Habitual offenders under the Protection of Civil Rights Act may be History-Sheeted and security action taken wherever necessary.

146. The widened ambit of offences against weaker sections under the Indian Penal Code and Protection of Civil Rights Act and the provisions on presumption by Courts, necessitate taking precautions against unjustified prosecution, as observed by the National Police Commission.

147. In the State Advisory Committee for the Advancement of Backward Classes, the Deputy Inspector General of Police

(Protection of Civil Rights) may be made a member; in the District Advisory Committees, Superintendent of Police/ Commissioners of Police may be made Members. Proceedings of the Committees to be received by the Special Cell.

148. Welfare measures being steps to keep the force contented and in good morale, should benefit numerically large segments like constabulary and other lower subordinate levels. The educated young entrants to service deserve special attention.

149. Leave for higher studies may be liberalized; for the direct recruitment of Havildars 15 per cent of posts may be reserved for constables with higher educational qualifications; the present 10 per cent reservation for constables for enlistment as Sub-Inspectors in the General Executive may be raised to 15 per cent.

150. Educated constables with aptitude may be sponsored for skill-oriented training at government cost; those who secure such qualifications on their own may be given 'qualification pay'; their services may be utilized for technical duties during times of emergency.

151. Educated personnel with talent, regardless of rank, may be exposed to training programmes and used as a 'Core Training Team'; they may handle indoor classes and special subjects in outdoor classes in training centres.

152. The availability of funds and the number of applicants make the number of beneficiaries from the Welfare and Amenities fund small. The amount of Rs. 2000 lent to a subordinate for his marriage, etc., may be raised to Rs. 5000 in view of the present rate of inflation.

153. The family of the employees deserves greater attention for enlisting the employees undivided loyalty; many children of policemen despite handicaps show promise and therefore deserve encouragement. The merit scholarships given to children of policemen have to benefit large numbers; there should be facilities for loans for the purchase of books and for higher studies.

154. Crèche, nursery schools and primary schools may be started through the Education Department near police camps; tuition and recreation facilities offered on an experimental basis at Trivandrum proved beneficial; such ad hoc and tentative arrangements have to be institutionalized; a Committee may be set up by Director General of Police to submit detailed proposals.

155. Transport facilities may be given to school-going children of parents staying away from schools, in Camps and Lines.

156. Welfare centres/employment facilities for families of policemen may be individual and family-oriented rather than group-oriented, in view of our socio-cultural milieu; each unit may have to work out projects that can be implemented; small units of manufacturing and industrial undertakings offering part-time employment to families of policemen may succeed, in view of the status of employment and regular income they offer.

157. Recreation and entertainment facilities should include Television and Video facilities; campus plan should include a Community Hall with facilities for entertainment; the needs of Armed Reserves and Armed Police Battalion personnel here deserve special attention.

158. Games, sports and other facilities for physical relaxation should be provided in all Armed Reserve Camps.

159. In constructing quarters the needs of urban and semi-urban areas should receive special priority; type design for police station should provide 'Dormitories' also, where unmarried personnel and Armed Police detachments can be accommodated.

160. Future constructions may opt for vertical growth; quarters and office blocks have to be multi-storeyed in view of the scarcity for building space.

161. There is urgent need to help policemen without houses of their own to secure one before retirement.

162. The approach to housing has to be elastic providing for funds to build on one's own land as well as for buying a

piece of land to build on; graded installments may be tried in place of flat rates.

163. The Police Housing Co-operative Society has made excellent beginnings. It deserves to be strengthened.

164. Welfare measures to succeed should cater to the needs of most; availability of funds is important here; Government may give an one-term grant of Rs. 100 per head for building up the corpus of the fund and thereafter a matching grant of Rs. 50 per head per year; funds may be raised by holding Flag Day, Exhibition matches, etc. As the National Police Commission has suggested, grants-in-aid may be given by Central Government to State Governments at the rate of Rs. 50 lakhs to provide the corpus of the fund and thereafter Rs. 10 lakhs annually for sustaining welfare activities on a recurring basis.

165. The Police Associations may be re-organized with accent on Staff Council work.

166. Individual grievances and their resolution should remain the responsibility of supervisory levels; formal and informal arrangements may be required; besides holding 'Sabhas' Unit Heads should keep some time every week for meeting individual subordinates and to listen to their problems; they should develop and sustain an empathy towards them; such work should be rated as one of the important functions of the unit officers and should influence the assessment on them.

167. Man-management practices have to be fair; sympathy and understanding should take the place of rigidity and arbitrariness; the administration of punishment and reward system and appraisal and promotion system should not suffer from bias or prejudice.

168. Delays in settling personal claims and consequent dissatisfaction can be avoided if such papers are attended to promptly; unit officers may keep close watch on progress of action.

169. The question of delegating powers to the Administrative Assistants to sanction claims of all non-gazetted personnel may be considered.
170. Under-performers, those with personality problems and those who suffer from addiction, etc., require special attention. A "Counselling Bureau" manned by a trained 'Counsellor' may be considered to interact with such cases.
171. Women members of the force facing disabilities and career problems require 'domestic counselling'; a suitable female officer may be detailed to listen to their complaints and communicate them to higher levels; to encourage female employees to make bold in airing their grievances a "Complaint Box" may be placed where female employees work and action may be taken on anonymous and/or pseudonymous complaints too.
172. The large number of employees, occupying the lower rungs of the department, makes it necessary to appoint a 'Welfare Officer' to function from Police Headquarters; a suitable officer of the rank of Superintendent of Police of the State Cadre or a suitable person on deputation may be considered.
173. The Camp Followers merit greater sympathy; Camp Follower and Cook's allowances require revision; the number of Cooks and Water Carriers for a Company has to be doubled in view of their long working hours; Camp Followers may be brought under the Kerala Police Departmental Inquiries (Punishment and Appeal) Rules for better management".

Committees and commissions are appointed by the government for making in-depth studies of the performance of existing structures with the object of ascertaining whether they cater to the needs of the clientele and to suggest measures to improve performance in tune with the demands. With the appointment of a Commission the government commits itself to the proposition that the organization and its functional dynamics need to be re-organized or reformed. The membership of the Commission is such that the Government is enabled to secure the most credible advice and views on the issues referred to the Commission. Since the Commissions and Committees, while conducting their studies interact with the different sections of the society, their Reports provide a reliable medium for the Government on the viewpoints of the various interests. The appointment of a Commission/Committee thus ensures more objectivity, less susceptibility to pressures and a Report representing 'pooled wisdom'. But an analysis of the implementation of the recommendations made by various Commissions and Committees in India reveals that the enthusiasm shown in appointing them did not last long. This has been the fate of the Kerala Police Commission Reports also.

The Kerala Police Re-organization Committee of 1959 was asked to deal with the whole problem of police reform in a highly subjective and theoretical perspective. The Report of the Committee is a worthy document, barring some recommendations like the recommendation on the first item in the Terms of Reference, 'The role of the police in a welfare State' on which the Committee recommended that "The objectives of the police organisation in free India must undergo radical change. The emphasis on the negative or coercive aspect should be replaced by the realization for the need of a positive and constructive role" is too general and vague. The Committee's recommendations on some important items like the 'Role of the police in the context of Employer-Employee Relations' and 'Duties of the Police in the Context of Exercise of Civil Liberties' are excellent and relevant. However, the political change in the State considerably affected its implementation. The Congress-led coalition Government which came to power in March, 1960, after the mid-term elections appears to have given short shrift to the Committee's Report. Apparently, there was a general suspicion that the Committee appointed by the Communist Government, although it comprised some of the most eminent brains in the country, was leftist oriented".[24] However, many of the recommendations of the Committee prove that the members had no political biases and that the suspicion was baseless. The only recommendation which could be considered radical or revolutionary is on the ex-parte orders passed by the courts in which the Committee opined that "Legislation should take into account any landlord-peasant relation where there is necessity for circumscribing the powers of the court to pass ex-parte orders". Such radical ideas were indigestible for the Congress party leaders of that time. Consequently, the whole

Report, if implemented could have provided a sound base to work efficiently, was completely neglected and thus gathered dust in the shelves. However, several recommendations of the Committee were implemented on an ad hoc basis, and after considerable time lag".[25]

The Committee had made fifty-one (51) recommendations of which one was very vital viz. the recommendation to extend the Indian Police Act to the whole of Kerala and to repeal the redundant provisions of the Travancore-Cochin Police Act. This recommendation was given effect to by the enactment of Act V of 1961.[26] It may be seen that the State was formed on the recommendations of the States Reorganization Commission in 1956 and it took not less than five years for the Government to enact a Police Act for the whole State. Or in other words, two Police Acts—The Travancore Police Act and the Madras Police Act were in operation in the State, not an wholesome situation. Of the fourteen recommendations of the Committee on item no: (1) in the Terms of Reference, two were very specific and important—the appointment of a whole time Police-Public Relations Officer and the setting up of District Advisory Committees. Both these recommendations were implemented in 1973; a full-time police public relations officer functioning under the Inspector General of Police was appointed and District Advisory Committees consisting of local MPs and MLAs were set up. But these Committees have ceased to function for long.[27] Another important recommendation of the Committee was raising the minimum qualification of the constabulary to a pass in the S.S.L.C examination. This recommendation was only belatedly implemented. To improve greater Police-Public relation as suggested by the Committee, there has not been any concrete steps except the traditional functions like Annual Police Sports and Games, observance of Traffic weeks and conducting of seminars on the duty of the people in helping the police to prevent crime. The Committee had recommended to increase the strength of the police in proportion to the increased manpower requirements of the force. Although there have been ad hoc increases in strength from time to time, no scientific study was made on what would be an appropriate or relevant police-public ratio and consequent steps to increase police strength.

The recommendations of the Committee on item no. (ii) in the Terms of Reference viz, Employer-Employee relationship, had great relevance to the State. The State went through a vitiating spasm of agitations by organized sections of labour for improved working conditions and better remuneration. The militancy of labour unions was such that even Gherao, which was frowned upon by the Judiciary, was accepted as one of the normal idioms of labour agitation. It is relevant to point out that labour militancy and the volatile nature of labour in general along with proliferation of trade unions as back up or support organisations of various political parties led to scaring investors and driving most of the industries out of the State. The police also were discouraged from interfering in industrial disputes under a festring dispute degenerated into a law and order situation. If the recommendations of the Committee were implemented, perhaps this sad situation which has resulted in large scale unemployment of the educated in the State, could have been avoided.

The recommendations of the Committee regarding a single bargaining agency in an industry has been selectively implemented. On the whole, therefore, it has to be observed that the recommendations of the Committee would have contributed to the emergence of an entirely different industrial relations as well as work culture to the ultimate benefit of the State and its people. By discarding the recommendation which had the potential for stable labour relations, the State certainly missed an early opportunity for industrialization and drastic reduction of unemployment. What has saved the State from total chaos has been mass migration, particularly to the Gulf countries, of even unskilled labour. The human resources that was so transplanted out of the State would have qualitatively altered the financial health of the State.

With regard to the 'Role of the Police in the context of exercise of civil liberties' the Committee recommended that the frequent transfer of police officers should be avoided. But the transfer and posting policy in the State did not subscribe to this principle. True, some Heads of the Department or Police Ministers have deviated from the common practice of shuffle-at-will, but by and large transfers have been too frequent and the department has suffered in quality as a result. During the interaction of the researcher with both the public and the police personnel, transfers of police officers at the instance of political parties and transfers emerging as a source of corruption were expressed in hushed whispers, though there were some who wanted to be heard on this point. The recommendation of the Committee on the control of large assemblies by the police also has fallen on deaf ears. Unmanaged assemblies and processions disrupting vehicular traffic and normal life and business activities of the people of a locality became so prolific that the High Court of the State itself had to issue direction for restraint. Crowd management has emerged as an important function of the police everywhere and greater sophistication is seen in the techniques employed by the police forces in different countries. It is true that the recommendations of the Committee dealt primarily with the use of force or regulatory authority by the police on assemblies, processions and crowds. Yet the police department could have evolved strategies of crowd management in tune with the right to assembly given in the Constitution peacefully and without arms. The Kerala Police, as a result has been accused of over reaction or inaction and has not yet evolved an appropriate balance between democratic freedom and lawlessness.[28] It has to be therefore, pointed out that the Kerala Police again lost an opportunity to be a model in the management of large concourse of people as a result of ignoring this recommendation of the Committee. The Committee had recommended that every police firing should be followed by a judicial enquiry. This recommendation was based on a sound understanding of the role of the police and the use of force. It may be pointed out that the police are not to use force except in exceptional circumstances and that too under magisterial supervision keeping in view the theory of minimum force. The police are to protect the life, liberty and property of the people and not to take precious lives away by firing or serious bodily injury through the use of brute force. A judicial enquiry is accepted in this context to ascertain whether there has been the use of excess force. It is seen that successive governments have shied away from ordering judicial enquiries on police opening fire with heavy casualities or when there is an outcry on the police conduct of employing disproportionate force. On the recommendations under this head there have been other marginal changes like a provision in Kerala Police Act of 1961 regarding 'Management of Picketers'.

The Committee had suggested employing regulative and restrictive powers under the Police Act and Criminal Procedure Code in dealing with law and order situations. The suggestion that the power to pass order under section 144 of the Criminal Procedure Code viz., "power to issue order in urgent cases of nuisance or apprehended danger", be transferred to the judicial magistrates was a novel suggestion. However, "The Keynote of the power given under this section is directed against those who attempt to prevent the exercise of legal right by others or imperil public safety and health".[29] It is doubtful whether the purpose of the section could have been served by shifting the onus of implementing this section from the Executive to the Judiciary. The repeal of section 108 of Criminal Procedure Code also did not take place, although the provisions for security for keeping the peace and for good behaviour in Criminal Procedure Code received a second look when the code was amended in 1973. Thus, it can be seen that the first effort at police reform in Kerala State suffered fatal blows at three stages—the first when the Government which appointed the Committee had to leave office abruptly in the face of the 'Mass Upsurge' by opposition parties mostly on the alleged control of party cadres on the police administration and the so-called police policy of the Communist Government; the second when they were asked to report selectively on Seven (7) items in the Terms of Reference when the total brief was on Eighteen (18) items and the last and final blow was when the recommendations were ignored stamping it as the product of a Committee appointed by a Communist Government, which stood discredited when it was dismissed by the President of India on being satisfied that there was a failure of the constitutional machinery in the State.

As is seen concluded in a study by Senior Officers under advanced Training at Sardar Vallabhai Patel National Police Academy, Hyderabad, it can be safety concluded that "the majority of the Committee's recommendations, however, were never even subjected to scrutiny before being consigned to the dark recesses of administrative oblivion. It is rather pathetic that this was the fate of the first endeavour in independent India to take a comprehensive look at the need for police reform".[30]

The composition of the Kerala Police Reorganization Committee of 1959 was well suited for examining the issues mentioned in the Terms of Reference. The members of the Committee individually and as a group had a wealth of experience and expertise which would have enabled them to report on the Terms of Reference satisfactorily. If the Committee was, thus permitted to complete its work and submit its Report on each item of the Terms of Reference and if the Report was submitted at a time when a Government with progressive views, as the one which appointed the Committee, was in power, it would have been certain that the police in Kerala would have been put to a reform process which would have made it a 'national model'. Unfortunately both for the police in Kerala and for the Kerala State and the other states in India, it did not happen. It may be recalled again that this was a pioneering effort after the Fraser Commission of 1902-03 and after India became independent and the country was re-organised into states on linguistic basis and on the State of Kerala emerging under a political colour separate from the Congress ruled states in the rest of India. The Terms of Reference afford us a clear view of the sensitivity and concern of the state with regard to critical areas of policing. The change of government after the liberation struggle was one born out of the chaos of the mass upsurge or the 'Vimochana Samaram' which was nothing but a continuing challenge to law and order in the state. Naturally, the government could not have reformed the police as a priority agenda, in the midst of such unsettling conditions. The police response to tactics employed by the protagonists of the liberation struggle itself had generated sharply conflicting reaction in the State. In some areas they were labelled as soft and in other areas as repressive. In either case the police did not endeared itself for successfully implementing the recommendations for reform, however, tardy and inconclusive they were.

The next stage in the efforts of police reforms in the State is with the appointment of the Kerala Police Reorganization Commission of 1982. In sharp contrast to the Kerala Police Re-organisation Committee of 1959, the present Commission had members only from within the police organisation, except for one member, the Home Secretary, in charge of the administrative department and a member of the Indian Administrative Service (I.A.S.). The Commission had two Chairmen, T.A.S. Iyer the serving Director General of Police from 1982 to 1984 and on his retirement on superannuation, M.K. Joseph, the then Director General of Police from December 1984 to June 1986. It may be pointed out here that the National Police Commission, appointed by the Janata Government had submitted its Report and copies were available with the State Government. In fact, the right to association given under Volume-1 of the Report submitted on February 7, 1979, had resulted in the eruption of police strikes particularly strikes spearheaded by the paramilitary forces all over the country. The State had witnessed an army intervention to discipline the C.R.P.F. units of their Pallipuram camp and in the Cantonment. The Kerala Police also had its share of woes when a unit was quartered in the Police Training College campus and it was being assiduously courted by dissident elements to join their rank, all leading to unsavoury reports of police discipline.[31] The State also had an unusual record during the Emergency as evidenced from the results of the elections held after the lifting of Emergency. The Congress party and its allies had swept clean all the seats for Parliament and had notched seats for the State legislature obviously a favourable electoral chit to the State administration under Emergency. However, after the Emergency, the custodial death of a college student, Rajan, a suspected Naxalite, in an investigation camp at Kakkayam in Kozhikode district of the Crime Branch C.I.D rocked the State to its very foundations. In an unprecedented litigation before the High Court, the then Chief Minister had to vacate office and several senior police officers including three Indian Police Service (I.P.S.) officers were prosecuted for the crime.[32] There were also far-reaching political re-alignments within the coalition of political parties in power.[33] There were also allegations leading to strictures on senior police officers indulging in naked political activities aimed at improving the electoral prospects of some political parties.[34] On the results of the 1982 elections the Police and Home portfolio went to an younger politician who represented the Congress-A faction. In spite of all these changes, it is seen that the political leadership in the State did neither accept the National Police Commission Report nor structured a Terms of Reference which would have been an improvement on the National Police Commission Report, taking into account the special circumstances of the State. They rather aimed at re-organizing the Kerala Police than reforming it. The Terms of Reference were targeting only such areas like training, armed police battalions, motor transport, tele-communications, special branch, the prosecution agency, crime records and statistics, special responsibility of the police towards the weaker sections and police welfare. Here also the lid is blown completely by a Note, the Member-Secretary has included in the Report in which he has exposed the total lack of objectivity in the appointment of the Commission and in incurring wasteful expenditure, public money on the pretext of making the Commission study important issues when all that was intended to displace some senior officers and to confer undue career advantage to others whom the Home Minister favoured.[35] The Note of the Member Secretary is a shocking disclosure of the callousness with which the whole reform agenda was conjured up. The Member-Secretary's Note says that it was difficult for him to get the Report physically delivered to the then Home Minister and that the submission of the Report itself was made possible only when the Chief Minister took over the Home port-folio. The Report, as a result, met with a natural death. But, what is most striking from the context of the Kerala State is that a new generation political leader played such a fraud on the issue of police reforms in the State. There is no evidence to show that any of these recommendations submitted by the Kerala Police Re-organisation Commission of 1982-86 was acted upon. The Report is not yet printed and is available for perusal by the researcher by the courtesy of some Senior Officers. The Reports also have not been internally circulated, making it obvious that the recommendations would not have been taken up for implementation.

After the submission of the Reports by the National Police Commission, there was apparently a conflict of identity between the States and the Centre regarding the agency for implementation of the Reports. In the State, there was no serious effort to implement any of the recommendations. In fact, the appointment of the Kerala Police Re-organisation Commission can be seen as a diversionary tactic to obviate the need for taking up the recommendations of the National Police Commission for implementation. The cumulative result of all this is that while the 1959 Committee Report suffered a still birth the efforts both of the National Police Commission and the Kerala Police Re-organisation Commission of 1982-86 were subtly aborted.

On the recommendations of the National Police Commission there were sequel steps on the initiative of the Indian Police Service officers of Uttar Pradesh (U.P.),[36] by approaching the Apex Court for a direction for implementing the recommendations. The matter is still pending before the court. The Central Government on their initiative referred the recommendations to J.F. Ribeiro and later to K. Padmanabhayya, obviously in an effort to tone down the recommendations to minimize resistance primarily from within the civil administration.

The Ribeiro Committee submitted two Reports—the first in October 1998 and the second in March 1999. The recommendations are extracted below,[37] as any attempt to abridge them would take away sting of the damage to which the Report have been subjected. Ribeiro in his first report reported as follows.

1. "Security Commission should be set-up in each State consisting of the Minister in charge of Police as the Chairman, the Leader of the Opposition, the Chief Secretary of the State, a sitting or retired judge nominated by the Chief Justice of the State's High Court and three other non-political citizens of proven merit and integrity as members. These three citizens should be chosen by a Committee to be set-up by the Chairman of the NHRC, which has taken much interest in the establishment of this proposed institution.
2. The name of the Commission should be *"The Police Performance and Accountability Commission."* (PPAC)
3. The four non-political members of this Commission excluding the Chief Secretary, should hold office for three years after which they will be replaced by persons of equal merit chosen in the same manner.
4. The Commission will have advisory and recommendatory powers for the present. The State's DGP will be its Secretary and Convener.

5. The Commission will oversee the performance of the Police and ensure that it is accountable to the law of the land. Its functions will be as spelt out by the NPC in para 15.48 of the Report. In addition, it will ensure that no premature transfers of officers of the rank of SP and above are made without prior clearance from the Commission and that transfers are made only by the authority competent under the rules to do so.
6. Besides the Commission, a District Police Complaints Authority will be set up in each Police District as a non-statutory body to examine complaints from the public of police excesses, arbitrary arrests and detention, false implications in criminal cases, custodial violence, etc and to make appropriate recommendations to the Police Performance and Accountability Commission, as well as to the Government and to the State or National Human Rights Commission. The Principal District and Sessions Judge, the Collector of the district and the SSP should constitute this authority.
7. In every State, a Police Establishment Board should be constituted with the DGP and his four senior-most officers, borne on the IPS cadre of the State but who are immediately junior to the DGP, as members to monitor all transfers, promotions, rewards and punishments as well as other service related issues. The Board should be given the legal authority to discharge its duties by amending the relevant Rules.
8. Rules should be framed by the Government on transfers, tenures, promotions, rewards and punishments and the police authorities designated to administer these rules. Any departure from these norms and rules will be brought to the notice of the PPAC.
9. The DG of Police will be selected by the Chief Minister of the State from a panel of three names prepared by a Committee headed by the Chairman of the UPSC and consisting of the Union Home Secretary, the Director of Intelligence Bureau, the State's Chief Secretary and the State's incumbent DGP. This selection Committee may consult the CVC before

drawing up a panel. The DGP will have fixed tenure of three years. He can be removed within the period of tenure only on the recommendations of the PPAC and for specified reasons, made in writing to the Government.

10. The investigation wing of the Police will be insulated from undue pressure if the DGP is selected in the manner prescribed above and given a tenure and also if the PPAC discharges its role of overseeing police performance and ensuring accountability. All investigating officers should be specially trained in scientific methods of investigation and not utilized for law and order duties except in small rural police stations where it may not be possible to strictly demarcate the two important police functions. The investigating officers should not be shifted to law and order or other duties for five years at least." In his second Report, submitted in March 1999, Ribeiro further reported as follows:

1. "The NPC had recommended that there should be a State Security Commission at the Centre. There is no need for such an institution at the central level. In case of CBI, the Supreme Court has already given direction. The IB is an intelligence organization and the BSF and the CRPF are para-military outfits, which do not involve themselves with local politics and politicians.
2. The Central Police Committee as recommended by the NPC in its Seventh Report should be constituted.
3. The old Police Act of 1861 needs to be replaced by a new Police Act.
4. The Vohra Committee had recommended the establishment of a Nodal Cell in the Ministry of Home Affairs to deal with the problem of nexus between crime syndicates, political leaders, Government functionaries and others. It is learnt that such a cell is already operative but how far it has succeeded in its endeavour is not known to our Committee.
5. The recommendations of the Law Commission about insulating the investigative functions of the police from its law and order work should be implemented urgently.

6. The recommendations of the NPC about recruitment, training and welfare of the constabulary should be implemented.
7. The minimum educational qualifications for recruitment to the level of Constable should be Higher Secondary.
8. The NPC had recommended the reorganization of the hierarchy of the police, with an increase in the strength at middle levels of ASI/SI/Inspector to be offset by reducing numbers at the lower levels of constabulary. This would improve promotion opportunities of lower ranks. We endorse the recommendations of the NPC.
9. Every State should establish an independent Police Recruitment Board and entrust to it the task of recruitment of all non-gazetted ranks.
10. A qualitative change in the training being imparted in police training institutions is imperative to improve performance and behaviour of the police."

Thus it can be seen that the Report of the National Police Commission in eight (8) volumes produced after labourious efforts of four (4) years from 1977-1981 by a high qualitative, was reduced to just twenty (20) recommendations by Ribeiro, a gross travesty of justice to the massive efforts of the N.P.C. Reducing the Report into twenty (20) capsules was perhaps with the hope that the Government at the Centre would take the initiative at least to implement them. It may be noted that nothing was done and the buck was passed on to another Committee with a former member of the I.A.S. a bureaucrat, K. Padmanabhayya again entrusted with the task of further studying the Reports for identifying areas for implementation.

The recommendations of the Padmanabhayya Committee on Police Reform are reproduced below.[38]

1. "There should be a greater recruitment of Sub-Inspectors instead of constables. Recruitment to constabulary should be restricted till a teeth-to-tail ratio of 1 : 4 is achieved as against present ratio, which ranges from 1 : 7 to 1 : 15 in different States.
2. Constables should be recruited young. Boys/girls, who have passed 10th Standard examination and are below 19 years

in age should be eligible to appear in a common competitive qualifying examination. The successful candidates should be put through a rigorous 2-year training programme and qualify for appointment as constables only after passing a final examination.

3. The existing constabulary should be retrained to enable them to imbibe right attitudes to work. Those who do not successfully complete training should be compulsorily retired.

4. A Police Training Advisory Council should be set up at the center and in each state to advise the Home Ministers on police training matters.

5. The eligibility criteria for recruitment to the level of Sub-Inspectors should be 12th class pass and an upper age limit of 21 years. They should be recruited on the basis of a common written qualifying examination. The successful candidates must pass a final examination after undergoing a 3-year training programme. 50 per cent of vacancies of Sub-Inspectors should be filled by direct recruitment and 50 per cent reserved for promotions.

6. A constable should be classified as a 'skilled worker' in view of the skills required and risks involved in the job.

7. All promotions should be subject to completing the mandatory training programmes and passing of promotional examinations.

8. The Indian Police should adopt the philosophy of community policing. The Government of India should support this by bringing out a handbook on the subject, providing training inputs and funding pilot projects.

9. Lack of a proper tenure policy for posting of officers at different levels and arbitrary transfers have been used by politicians to control and abuse the police for their own ends. To deal with this problem, following action is required:

   (a) A body headed by the Chief Justice of the State High Court as Chairman, State Chief Secretary and an eminent public person as members should be constituted to recommend a panel of two names for appointment to the post of the Director General of Police.

(b) A Police Establishment Board consisting of DGP and three other members of the police force selected by him, should be constituted to decide transfers of all officers of the rank of Deputy Superintendent of Police and above.

(c) The minimum tenure of all officers should be 2 years.

(d) Another Committee under the Chief Secretary, with Home Secretary and the DGP as members, should be constituted to hear representations from police officers of the rank of Superintendent of Police and above alleging violation of rules in the matter of postings and transfers.

10. To deal with the problem of corruption in the police, which leads to the criminalisation of the force, the Committee has recommended a more serious enforcement of the code of conduct and simpler but more effective procedures for removing corrupt officers.

11. Since police work cannot be organized on an 8-hour shift basis, police personnel should be given a weekly off and compulsorily required to go on earned leave every year. Holiday homes may be constructed for police personnel.

12. Investigation should be separated from law and order work. In the first phase, this separation should take place at police station level in all urban areas. An Additional Superintendent of Police should be exclusively responsible for crime and investigation work.

13. Sections 25 and 26 of the Indian Evidence Act should be deleted and confessions made to police officers of the rank of Superintendent of Police and above should be made admissible in evidence.

14. Every police station should be equipped with 'investigation kits' and every sub-division should have a mobile forensic science laboratory.

15. The police leadership, through proper manpower and career planning, improved training, effective supervision and by inculcating a sense of values amongst the members of the force, can play an important role in encouraging specialization, promoting professionalism and increasing morale in the force.
16. There is an urgent need to encourage specialization in various aspects of policing.
17. In each district, there should be a crime prevention cell manned by officers who have specialized in crime prevention work.
18. To deal with cyber crime effectively, police capabilities in various areas need to be developed. Capabilities of some police institutions, like the National Police Academy in the field of training, CBI in investigation, Intelligence Bureau in cyber surveillance and the National Crime Records Bureau in cyber technology / forensics should be enhanced.
19. The present classification of offences into cognizable and non-cognizable made 150 years ago is not very relevant today. The Law Commission of India should review the entire classification and the powers of the police to investigate.
20. The concept of VIP security has been grossly, blatantly and brazenly misused. The entire concept of personal security needs a careful review and dismantling.
21. Certain offences having inter-State, national and international repercussions should be declared "federal offences" to be investigated by the Special Crimes Division of the CBI, which should function under the administrative control of the Ministry of Home Affairs.
22. Taking into account the wide ramifications of the terrorist, crime, there have to be different norms regarding the burden of proof, degree of proof and the legal procedures in regard to trial of terrorist cases. There is a need for a special and a comprehensive law to fight terrorism.
23. There should be a national counter terrorism coordinator to prepare a comprehensive counter-terrorism plan and budget.

24. A statutory independent Inspectorate of Police should be set up to carry out annual as well as thematic inspections of the police force and to report to the State government whether the police force is functioning efficiently and effectively.
25. A non-statutory District Police Complaints Authority (DPCA) should be set up with the District Magistrate as the Chairman and a senior Additional Sessions Judge, the District Superintendent of Police and an eminent citizen nominated by the DM as members. Investigations into public complaints against the police should in the first instance be done by the police department itself. Those who are not satisfied can approach the DPCA.
26. There should be a mandatory judicial inquiry into all cases of alleged rape of a woman or death of any person in police custody.
27. The Government of India should establish a permanent National Commission for Policing Standards to lay down norms and standards for all police forces on matters of common concern and to see that the State Governments set up mechanisms to enforce such standards.
28. The release of central grants for modernization or up gradation funds should be dependent upon compliance by State governments with certain basic issues, like each State having a manpower and career planning system, a transparent recruitment, promotion and transfer policy and meeting certain minimum standards for training.
29. The Police Act of 1861 should be replaced by a new Act.
30. The State Government must give high priority to the allocation of resources to the police.
31. There should be a permanent National Commission for Police Standards (NCPS) to set standards and to see that the State Governments set up mechanisms to enforce such standards.

There is need for comprehensive reforms in criminal justice administration. Public would soon lose faith in the criminal justice system unless the other components of the systems are also thoroughly overhauled simultaneously".

It may thus seen that the N.P.C. recommendations have been further distilled and reduced, and shorn of all its idealistic and theoretical backdrop. In the hands of Ribeiro and Padmanabhayya, the recommendations have been identified as those touching some aspects of police personnel policy. These recommendations bear the stamp of executive fiats and are grossly retrograde in character. The N.P.C. had recommended making the police functionally independent which meant at the district level removing the yoke of the District Magistrate an I.A.S. officer. But, it can be seen that the District Magistrate and other bureaucrats have comeback to centre stage with a vengeance. As one goes through the eight (8) volumes of the N.P.C. Report and encapsulated recommendations by Ribeiro and Padmanabhayya one feel sad that so much love's labour has been lost.

Some positive efforts to implement the recommendations of the N.P.C. were seen taken by Indrajit Gupta, while he was the Union Minister for Home in the I.K.Gujral Ministry. Some discussions on reforming the police appear to have taken place recently in Kerala, under A.K. Antony, the Chief Minister. However, there was the lingering confusion with regard to police reform and police modernization. One concrete development was the almost total de-control of the police machinery by the local leadership of the political parties in power which had created quiet a controversy in the State. Not only the opposition parties but also a faction of the party which leads the Ministry and several partners of the ruling coalition U.D.F vehemently opposed and criticized this policy of the Chief Minister.

The foregoing discussions very clearly indicate that police reform was never a serious agenda for any Government after that of E.M.S. Namboodirippad, which was the first elected government after the formation of the State of Kerala. Therefore, it can be very clearly seen that between 1902-03 and 2002-03 nearly a hundred years, police reform efforts in the State have been neither substantial nor serious and whatever changes have been brought about did not form part of national efforts. Both under the British and subsequently after 1947 under the indigenous political executive the efforts were Marginal and ad hoc.

Police Reform should be an attempt to make the police functioning less of a mystery and something that can be viewed and understood by the clientele and the public in general. It may be noted that police reform is not a static concept. What were reforms a few decades ago may not be reform measures at a subsequent stage of development. Police Reforms have to be enmeshed with the character of the State and the nature of its governance. It revolves around the attitude of the State with regard to the freedoms of the citizen, its response to redress of their injuries and generally the use to which they would employ the police organization as such. Therefore, the police have to rhyme with the goals of the State at that point of time and should be in a position to lay the ground rules for both development and order as well as individual liberty and social security. This can be achieved by a periodical revision of the legal framework, both in regard to the structure of the police as well as its functional dynamics. Changes in the Police Act, the Criminal Laws and related legislations are essential to lay down the directions for police reforms would take. What follows from this first step would be a critical look at the personnel policies, the status and adequacy of equipments and other enabling inputs. It can be both from a Plan and non-Plan point of view. Where policing and its product are taken as necessarily supportive of the development efforts of the government, no doubt, the two would be closely inter-linked. In fact, reform efforts divested of the development goals of the State would be an unproductive mismatch leading to friction and dissonance in the governing process. It is, thus, as important as changes in law and procedure. Police reforms also will have to touch upon such important aspects like rapport with the community which is set to benefit from its functioning. The relationship with other segments of the sub-system and to a greater extent its willingness to submit itself to a rigorous evaluation of its transparency, accountability and sensitivity to social cause. In the last analysis, police reforms also would mean priority assigned by the sate to social defence. The concept of police as a regulative mechanism to enforce law and order is primitive and outmoded. Policing is basically a function of social engineering. This assumption would lead us to redefine the entire verbiage of Police Reform as simply something that vibes well with peace-loving, law-abiding citizens of a society. It is his sense of satisfaction that should be taken as the most reliable parameter of acceptable police service.

REFERENCES

1. Government of India, *Report of the Indian Police Commission*, 1902-03, Simla, p. 151.
2. Government of India, *Report of the National Police Commission*, 1977 New Delhi, May 1981, Vol.VIII, p. 1.
3. G.O. (MS) No. 71/Home (A) Department, 15 January 1959.
4. Government of Kerala, *Report of the Kerala Police Re-organisation Committee*, Trivandrum, 1959, p. 1.
5. The Terms of Reference of the Kerala Police Re-organization Committee has been discussed in Chapter-I.
6. G.O. (MS) No. 595/Home (A) Department, 5 August 1959.
7. G.O. (MS) No. 787/Home (A) Department, 19 November 1959.
8. Government of Kerala, *Report of the Kerala Police Re-organization Committee*, op.cit., p. 5.
9. *Ibid*., p. 9.
10. *Ibid*., p. 1.
11. *Ibid*., pp. 22-24.
12. *Ibid*., p. 26.
13. *Ibid*., pp. 38, 39 and 47.
14. *Ibid*., p. 53.
15. *Ibid*., pp. 85-86.
16. *Ibid*., pp. 94, 95.
17. As per G.O. (MS) No. 787/Home (A), Department, 19 November, 1959.
18. G.O (MS) No. 217/82/GAD, 30 July 1982.
19. Government of Kerala, *Report of the Kerala Police Re-organization Commission*, Thiruvananthapuram, May 1984, p. 2.
20. *Ibid*., p. 104.
21. Government of Kerala, Final Report of the Kerala Police Re-organization Commission, Thiruvananthapuram, 1986, p. 1.
22. G.O (MS) No. 177/84/Home, 13 December 1982.
23. Government of Kerala, Final Report of the Kerala Police Re-organization Commission, op.cit., pp. 46-56.
24. "Police Commission: The Gap between Recommendations and their Implementation", (Mimeo), Hyderabad, Sardar Vallabhai Patel National Police Academy, 1976, p. 15.
25. *Ibid*., p. 16.

26. *Ibid*.

27. In a statement on 1 November, 2003 the present head of the police department has suggested resurrecting the committee. See: *The Hindu* 2 November, 2003.

28. The Kerala Police was charged of using massive force resorted to firing on adivasis in the Muthanga Wildlife Sanctuary in Wayanad district on 19, February, 2003.

29. P.L Maltik., *The Criminal Court Hand Book*, Lucknow, Eastern Book Company, 1992, p. 97.

30. *Police Commission: The Gap Between Recommendations and Their Implementation*, op.cit., p. 18.

31. The researchers interaction with the retired police officer who has liaisoned with the army for the operation.

32. *K.L.T. 335*, 1977, T.V. Eachara Varier vs. Secretary to the Ministry of Home Affairs and Others.

33. Two parties aligned with the L.D.F., Congress (A) and Kerala Congress (M) crossed over to the U.D.F.

34. See: 1978, *KLT/86* (Kerala Law Times) on Election Petition also see: No. XVII of 1977 decided on December 21, 1977.

35. Note of the Member-Secretary in the Final Report of the Kerala Police Re-organization Commission, 1986, pp. 109-137.

36. N.K. Singh, "Police Reforms" in *Policing India in the New Millennium*, P.J. Alexander (ed), New Delhi, Allied Publishers, 2000, p. 287.

37. Government of India, *Report of Police Performance and Accountability Committee*, New Delhi, 1999.

38. Government of India, *Report of the Padmanabhayya Committee on Police Reforms*, New Delhi, August, 2000.

Police Reforms in Kerala
Need and Directions: Public Perception

It was considered necessary to elicit the perceptions of the public regarding the need and directions of 'police reforms' through a questionnaire, since as has been pointed out earlier, there did not have in Kerala any coherent programme for police reform. It may be recalled that constituting the Kerala Police Re-organisation Committee of 1959, was a political decision by the first elected Communist Government in Kerala. It is evident from the Terms of Reference that the Government intended to examine several areas hitherto unexplored by any Committee or Commission constituted for re-organizing the police sub-system. However, the civil disturbances that engulfed the State leading to the dismissal of the Government by the President of India under Article 356 of the Constitution placed severe constraints on the Commission. It is evident from the very slim size of the Report, just 97 pages, and the limited discussions on the different issues considered by them. The second attempt in this regard was the Kerala Police Re-organisation Commission of 1982-86. It is doubtful whether there was the application of the collective political mind in either constituting the Commission or in outlining a Terms of Reference for it. The Member-Secretary himself has pointed out that part of the Terms of Reference was lifted verbatim from the Terms of Reference of the National Police Commission after that Commission had submitted the Report on those issues.[1] During discussions with several senior police officers, this researcher was told that the constitution of the

Kerala Police Re-organisation Commission was a clever ploy on the part of the then Home Minister to sideline the Director-General of Police and elevate another one of his choice. Later, there was a reversal of policy by which the Chairman and Members became part-time and the Member-Secretary became full-time as by then the displeasure of the Home Minister found a new victim in the Member-Secretary, the full-time Chairman having superannuated. It can therefore, be seen that the second exercise was in fact not a bonafide or genuine attempt at reforming the police. The Terms of Reference itself give the impression that the Government did not expect anything but very innocuous recommendations aimed at meaningless cosmetic changes. This background made it essential to elicit the perceptions of both the public and the police regarding police reforms. The responses from the police personnel are discussed in the next Chapter.

A State with a population of 3,18,38,619[2] of which 2,28,11,763[3] are qualified voters, it was considered necessary to devise a statistical formula for selecting a representative sample. In this, the researcher sought the help of experts who suggested identifying a universe of seven hundred and fifty (750) people from fourteen (14) categories in six (6) districts under two (2) police zones in Kerala. The researcher personally interviewed all the seven hundred and fifty (750) respondents. The responses arranged in tabulated form under each question is given below in Table 5.1.

Table 5.1: Personal profile of the respondents. Sample taken for analysis

District	*No. of Respondents*	*Percentage*
Kannur	124	16.53
Kozhikode	121	16.13
Thrissur	122	16.27
Ernakulam	123	16.40
Kollam	132	17.60
Thiruvananthapuram	128	17.07
Total	**750**	**100.00**

Source: Personal survey.

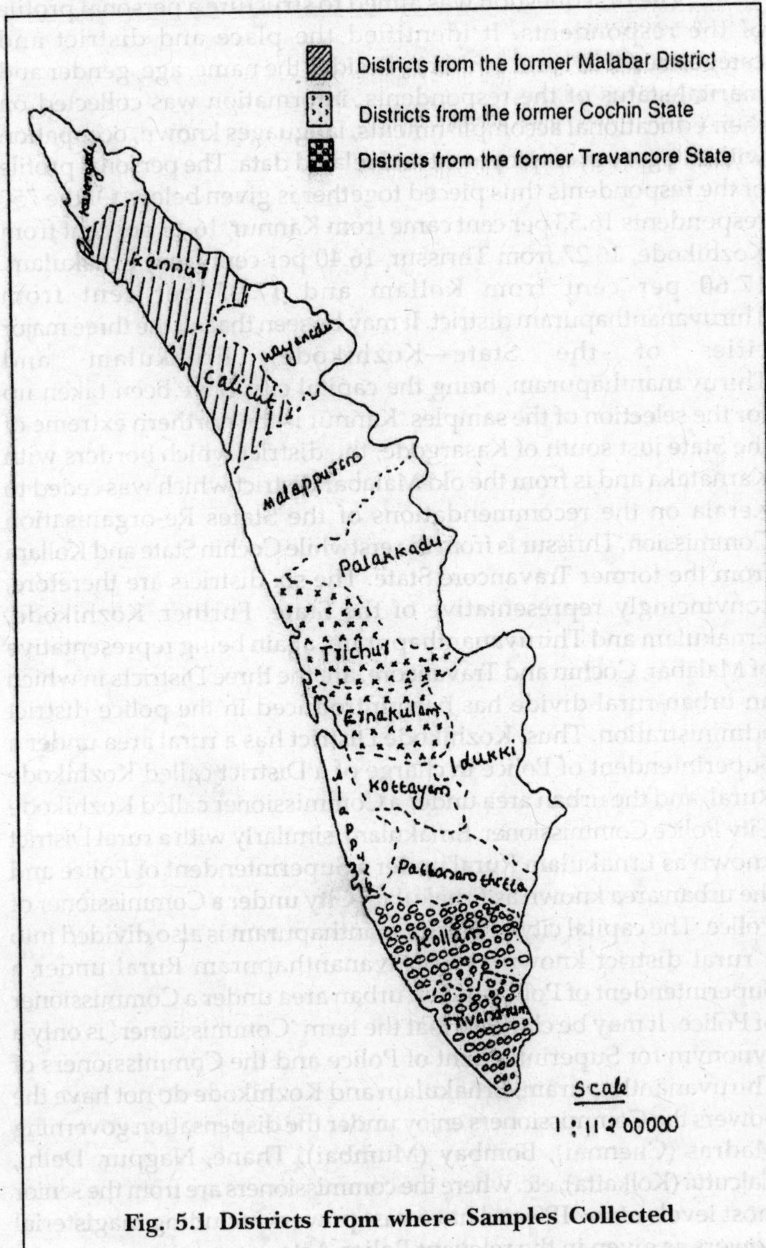

Fig. 5.1 Districts from where Samples Collected

The first question was aimed to structure a personal profile of the respondents. It identified the place and district and categorized it as rural or urban. Besides the name, age, gender and marital status of the respondents, information was collected on their educational accomplishments, languages known, occupation with category of employment and related data. The personal profile of the respondents thus pieced together is given below. Of the 750 respondents 16.53 per cent came from Kannur, 16.13 per cent from Kozhikode, 16.27 from Thrissur, 16.40 per cent from Ernakulam, 17.60 per cent from Kollam and 17.07 per cent from Thiruvananthapuram district. It may be seen that all the three major cities of the State—Kozhikode, Ernakulam and Thiruvananthapuram, being the capital city, have been taken up for the selection of the samples. Kannur is the northern extreme of the State just south of Kasargode, the district which borders with Karnataka and is from the old Malabar district which was ceded to Kerala on the recommendations of the States Re-organisation Commission. Thrissur is from the erstwhile Cochin State and Kollam from the former Travancore State. The six districts are therefore, convincingly representative of the State. Further, Kozhikode, Ernakulam and Thiruvananthapuram, again being representative of Malabar, Cochin and Travancore, are the three Districts in which an urban-rural divide has been introduced in the police district administration. Thus, Kozhikode District has a rural area under a Superintendent of Police in charge of a District called Kozhikode Rural, and the urban area under a Commissioner called Kozhikode City Police Commissioner. Ernakulam, similarly with a rural District known as Ernakulam Rural under a Superintendent of Police and the urban area known as Ernakulam City under a Commissioner of Police. The capital city of Thiruvananthapuram is also divided into a rural district known as Thiruvananthapuram Rural under a Superintendent of Police and an urban area under a Commissioner of Police. It may be clarified that the term 'Commissioner' is only a synonym for Superintendent of Police and the Commissioners of Thiruvananthapuram, Ernakulam and Kozhikode do not have the powers the Commissioners enjoy under the dispensation governing Madras (Chennai), Bombay (Mumbai), Thane, Nagpur, Delhi, Calcutta (Kolkatta), etc. where the commissioners are from the senior most levels of the IPS and have vast powers including magisterial powers as given in the relevant Police Acts.

Table 5.2: Rural-Urban distribution of the respondents

Place	*Number*	*Percentage*
Rural	374	49.87
Urban	376	50.13
Total	**750**	**100.00**

Source: Personal survey.

The rural-urban divide of the respondents are almost equal, 49.87 per cent from rural and 50.13 per cent from urban.

Table. 5.3: Age distribution of the respondents

Age	*Number*	*Percentage*
Less than 30 years	92	12.27
From 30 to 39 years	140	18.67
From 40 to 49 years	301	40.13
From 50 to 59 years	158	21.07
Above 60 years	59	7.87
Total	**750**	**100.00**

Source: Personal survey.

The respondents were found to be from five (5) age groups. Those who were less than 30 years of age and those who are above 60 years of age are comparatively smaller per cent, the first being 12.27 per cent and the latter 7.89 per cent. The largest per cent of respondents, 40.13 were in the age group of 40 to 49 years. The next higher figure 21.07 per cent were in the age group of 50 to 59 years and those who were between 30 to 39 are 18.67 per cent. Of these, males make up 86.13 per cent and females 13.87 per cent. While the sampling technique broadly suggested the number of respondents to be interviewed from each District, there was no gender distribution. Though the sex ratio of the population of Kerala is Female 1058 and male 1000,[4] there was an unexpected reticence on the part of women to come forward and express themselves on police reform and many of them pleaded either ignorance or lack of interest. As a result the female respondents were disproportionately low.

Table 5.4: Marital status

Marital status	*Number*	*Percentage*
Married	644	85.87
Unmarried	103	13.73
Widow/Widower	3	0.40
Total	**750**	**100.00**

Source: Personal survey.

The marital status of the respondents show that 85.87 per cent of respondents were married which in a way compensates for the smaller per cent of women respondents and those who were unmarried are 13.73 per cent. The number of respondents who do not have their spouses living are just 3 or 0.40 per cent.

Table. 5.5: Educational status

Level of Education	*Number*	*Percentage*
Upto SSLC	220	29.33
SSLC	38	5.07
Undergraduate	45	6.00
Graduate	120	16.00
Post-graduate	71	9.47
Professional	240	32.00
Research Degree	16	2.13
Total	**750**	**100.00**

Source: Personal survey.

The educational background of the respondents is representative of the high rate of literacy of the State. 29.33 per cent of respondents were studied upto S.S.L.C. or 10th standard, only 5.07 per cent have passed SSLC but did not go beyond, 6 per cent completed a course of college education but did not graduate, 16 per cent were graduates. 9.47 per cent of respondents were post-graduates, 32 per cent of respondents were professionals and 2.13 per cent with research degrees. It is evident that the highly educated people of Kerala do have a concern for reforming the police and they have views of their own on the issue. Among the respondents those who know Malayalam, the mother tongue, only were 37.87 per cent. Those who are conversant in both Malayalam and English come to 48.27 per cent of the respondents and those who know one more language besides Malayalam and English are 13.87 per cent.

Table. 5.6: Employment profile

Occupation	*Number*	*Percentage*
Government employee	160	21.33
Private employee	197	26.27
Self-employed	168	22.40
Unemployed	225	30.00
Total	750	**100.00**

Source: Personal survey.

The employment profile has examined whether the respondent is government employee, private employee, self-employed or unemployed and also the various categories of employment. It has been seen that 26.27 per cent of the respondents were privately employed, 22.40 per cent were self-employed, 21.33 per cent were government employed and 30 per cent of the respondents were unemployed.

Of the 750 respondents 9.33 per cent of respondents were Doctors, 9.47 per cent Engineers, 8.13 per cent Lawyers, 6.67 per cent Teachers, 6.27 per cent other Professionals, 7.67 per cent Political Activists, 5.73 per cent Trade Union Activists and 6.27 per cent Service Organisation Activists. There were 6.93 per cent students, 6.67 per cent Organised Labourers, 6.27 per cent Casual Labourers, 7.73 per cent Motor Vehicle Drivers, 6.80 per cent Businessmen and 6.13 per cent Agriculturists. It can be seen that the employment profile shows that the respondents fairly well represented the various professions.

Table 5.7: Category of employment

Category of Employment	*Number*	*Percentage*
Doctor	70	9.33
Engineer	71	9.47
Lawyer	61	8.13
Teacher	50	6.67
Other professionals	47	6.27
Political activist	57	7.60
Trade union activist	43	5.73
Service organisation activist	47	6.27
Student	52	6.93
Organised labourer	50	6.67
Casual labourer	47	6.27
Motor vehicle driver	58	7.73
Business man	51	6.80
Agriculturist	46	6.13
Total	**750**	**100.00**

Source: Personal survey.

Table 5.8: Familiarity with police organisation and police functions

	Number	*Percentage*
Quiet familiar	304	40.53
Familiar	202	26.93
Somewhat familiar	182	24.27
Not familiar	62	8.27
Total	**750**	**100.00**

Source: Personal survey.

The respondent's familiarity with police organisation makes their responses authentic. It elevates the status of the respondents from a casual observer or a passer-by to some one who has perceived the organisation critically and one who has identified the basic strength and weakness of its functional dynamics. Since the response of the samples were to form the basis for drawing appropriate deductions on the need and directions of police reforms, the question administered specifically aimed at eliciting the familiarity of the respondents with the police organisation and functions. Of the respondents 40.53 per cent were quiet familiar with the organisation and functions of the police department in Kerala. 26.93 per cent of respondents were just familiar and 24.27 per cent somewhat familiar. Only a small per cent of respondents, 8.27, have stated that they were not familiar with the police organization and functions. When those respondents who were quiet familiar, familiar and somewhat familiar added together it makes up 91.73 per cent which is quiet a high per cent of the respondents. It is therefore safe to assume that nearly 92 per cent of the respondents were familiar with the police organisation and functions.

Table 5.9: If familiar identify police functionaries at the State Level, police functionaries at the District Level and police functionaries at the Police Station Level

State level	*Number*	*Percentage*	*District level*	*Number*	*Percentage*	*Police Station level*	*Number*	*Percentage*
D.G.P	616	89.53	S.P	649	94.33	S.I	575	83.58
D.G.P I.G.P			S.P. Dy. SP	2	0.30	S.I, A.S.I	1	0.15
D.I.G	31	4.51	S.P, Comma-ndantant			S.H.O	110	15.99
D.G.P I.G.	3	0.44	Asst. Comma-ndantant	1	0.15	S.I, A.S.I H.C, P.C	2	0.30
D.G.P, A.D.G.P I.G.P, D.I.G	3	0.44	I.G, S.P	1	0.15			
Others	35	5.09	S.P, DIG Others	1 34	0.15 4.94			
Total	688	100.00	Total	688	100.00	Total	688	100.00

Source: Personal survey.

Of those respondents who claimed to have familiarity with the police organisation and functions, when it came to identifying the particular level of leadership of the police department, it is of substantial interest to find that the respondents were perceiving the department through the image of the Head of the Department or the Director General of Police (D.G.P.). This aspect of the response of the large majority of respondents point out to a very significant factor, the important position of the Head of the Department in the police structure. Deferring a discussion of this aspect, the researcher would mention that any reform aimed at the police organisation has to take into account the crucial position of the Director General of Police in the structure of the organisation and the monolithic character of the department, where the flavour of the police service and delivery system is the style of functioning of the Head of the Department. In other words, within the police structure the style of management ultimately is personal. An officer with right type of training and career exposure and the required commitment to the people of the State would be delivering the type of service that is justified under the constitutional philosophy and the basic laws governing the organisation. In fact, as has been rightly pointed out by the National Police Commission, 1977, the Head of the Police Department is central to its concept of functioning. The other functionaries at the State level are not too well known to the respondents under scoring the very high status and visibility of the Director General of Police in the scheme of things.

When it comes to the officers at the District level the most familiar face for the respondents was that of the Head of the District Police or the Superintendent of Police (S.P.). It is a striking aspect of the responses that again the police in a district is seen through the image or "personality" of the Superintendent of Police. The other functionaries were neither visible nor familiar except for a very small percentage of respondents.

The responses assume the very same pattern when they were asked to identify police functionaries at the police station level. The sub-Inspector of Police is the officer with whom the public interact at the police station level and in his absence those who is in charge of the post of Station House Officer (S.H.O). It may be seen that a vertical perception of the organisation by the respondents has clearly identified the three levels that are crucial in the police organisation; the Director General of Police (D.G.P.) or the Head of the Department, the District Superintendent of Police (S.P.) or the District Officer, the Sub-Inspector or the Station House Officer. This is an aspect of the organisation that has serious implications for any quest for reform. Conversely, a question also can be asked whether any reform effort can by-pass the other levels and those who occupy those seats. Fortunately for the police department, a person who is occupying a post does so only for a short tenure of two (2) or three (3) years, after which he is moved out to make way for another. Therefore, the recommendation of the National Police Commission, 1977, for fixity of tenure for the Head of the Department, assumes considerable significance.

A question was addressed to the respondents to elicit information on their familiarity with the laws empowering the police. Their response is given in the Table 5.10:

Table 5.10: Familiarity with the laws empowering the police

	Number	*Percentage*
Quiet familiar	291	38.80
Familiar	250	33.33
Somewhat familiar	134	17.87
Not familiar	75	10.00
Total	**750**	**100.00**

Source: Personal survey.

Only respondents or 38.80 per cent have stated that they were quiet familiar with the laws empowering the police. An almost equal number per cent 250 or (33.33) per cent of respondents have stated that they are were familiar with the laws empowering the police while 134 or 17.87 per cent of respondents have stated that they were only somewhat familiar with the laws empowering the police. These three categories make up 90 per cent as against 10 per cent of the respondents who were not at all familiar with the laws empowering the police. This data is interesting in that it indicates to some amount of uncertainty regarding the legality and authenticity of police actions. The extent of discretion at their disposal and the grey areas are virtually large and unchartered. When a member of the clientele is not in a position to understand clearly the limits of empowerment under the law by the police, it is difficult for him to cry halt when a foul is seen committed or to stop from pressuring the police to act in a particular way when they plead helplessness on account of the absence of legal backing. Either way a member of the public, who is not sure about the services which he is legitimately entitled to have, is a person who will push for more and not be contended with the police as a delivery system is authorized under law to dispense with. The germ of discontent for the public regarding police service would have its genesis in this area of indefiniteness of legality for police responses to an emerging situation. It also points out to an area where police community relations are raw and yet to be evolved and assume shape.

Table 5.11: If familiar, mention the laws under which the police function in Kerala

Laws	*Number*	*Percentage*
Kerala Police Act	658	97.48
Indian Penal Code	529	78.37
Criminal Procedure Code	511	75.70
Special Legislations like M.V. Act/Arms Act	295	43.70
Indian Evidence Act	280	41.48
Police standing orders	225	33.33
Other special and local legislation	189	28.00
Any other	000	000

Source: Personal survey.

The responses to this question leave us with no fresh insight except that those who have familiarity with the laws empowering the police also have familiarity with the basic legislations that guide their functioning. For instance, of the 89 per cent of respondents familiar with the laws empowering the police 97.48 per cent were familiar with the Kerala Police Act, 78.37 per cent with the Indian Penal Code (IPC) and 75.70 per cent with the Criminal Procedure Code (Cr.P.C). It is very interesting to find that the familiarity of the respondents with regard to the legislations empowering the police have come in a rough order of priority which is in fact a reflection of the importance of these legislations. The Kerala Police Act, outlines the contours of the police organisation, the duties and responsibilities of various ranks and the power and authority given to them to manage the life of the society. The Act also indicates areas that contribute significantly to the process of socialization and the role assigned to the police with regard to social defence and social engineering.[5] When the criminal law is set into motion by a victim, he draws support from the Criminal Procedure Code which defines a complaint, a cognizable offence, the types of trial, the powers of the courts, the powers of the Station House Officer, the powers of the police to arrest, search the person of a suspect or his residence and the whole gamut of police powers and the agencies of control namely the Judiciary, the Executive magistracy and the Police hierarchy. The IPC on the other hand defines offences and prescribes its punishments. The Criminal Procedure Code and the Indian Penal Code are enmeshed and dovetailed into the First schedule in the classification of offences in the Criminal Procedure Code.[6] It is only at the stage of trial, the legality of the investigation and the *bonafides* and correctness under the law of the various steps taken by the police are evaluated. Such an evaluation is always against the norms laid down by the Indian Evidence Act. The Indian Evidence Act like the Indian Penal Code, a pre-independence Act, makes or unmakes a police Report when its quality is measured on the touchstone of the Evidence Act. This is by and large an area of the legal practitioners both for the prosecution and against the prosecution. Therefore, the fact that 41.48 per cent of the relevant segment of the respondents have stated that they were familiar with the I.E. Act, does not qualitatively affect the data furnished under this head. In fact only 33.33 per cent have indicated that they were familiar with police standing orders and another per cent still less, 28 per cent have indicated that they were familiar with the local and special legislations. It may be pointed out here that the police standing orders are subordinate legislations and special and Local Legislations are primarily ad hoc in nature. Therefore, unless a member of the public has a specific interaction with the police, the police standing orders, special and local Legislations or the provisions of the I.E. Act would have only limited relevance for him. Viewed in this background, the responses which claim familiarity with the most important legislations appear to give the respondents more credibility.

Table 5.12: Familiarity with the functioning of a police station

	Number	*Percentage*
Quiet familiar	311	41.47
Familiar	217	28.93
Somewhat familiar	173	23.07
Not familiar	49	6.53
Total	**750**	**100.00**

Source: Personal survey.

The Police Station is the most important office in terms of service to the people in the police sub-system. In fact, the police organisation has at its base the police station and the entire edifice is built on this bedrock. Practically most other police offices are designed as the supervisory network of the police station or to function as Check and Balance. It is the police station, thus the most important cog in the wheel of the police sub-system. It is also a stage at which a person who approaches the police has his first contact with them and returns satisfied or dissatisfied. It is, thus, the most important meeting ground between the demand for police service and the supply of police service. It is here that the dream of a people-friendly police takes roots or withers away. Therefore, it was considered appropriate to ask the respondents regarding their familiarity with the police station. 6.53 per cent of the respondents were not familiar at all in the functioning of the police station; only 41.47 per cent were quiet familiar with the functioning of the police station. 52 per cent of the respondents were familiar and somewhat familiar with the functioning of the police station. These figures broadly indicate that the responses are not influenced by subjectivity, since only 41.47 per cent claimed to be quiet familiar with the functioning of a police station, and it is quiet probable that nearly 60 per cent of the responses are not those who have been influenced by their familiarity with the police grassroot level organisation. This, no doubt, enhances the quality of the service.

Table 5.13: Association with any political party

	Number	Percentage
Yes	330	44.00
No	393	52.40
No comments	27	3.60
Total	**750**	**100**

Source: Personal survey.

A question was asked regarding the association of the respondents with one or other political parties. It was necessary to ask such a question because of the love-hate relationship or the see-saw relationship between the police and the public in the State. It is very often seen that the political parties in power and their supporters invariably support the police and their response to public agitations, criticism of investigation of cases and/or other instances of interaction with the police and the people. On the other hand, those political parties in the opposition and their supporters condemn the police in practically everything they do with unconcealed enthusiasm. With frequency in change of seats is almost only for five years, the police-public relationship is subject to see-saw or the familiar love-hate syndrome. It was also necessary to find out the quality of the responses in as much as those who are supporters of a political party would be toeing their line in regard to their approach to the police. In a State where twenty-two (22) political parties and 2.28,11763[8] registered voters being wooed by each one of them and the different political parties and their support systems extend even to the village level, it would indeed be difficult to find many people who are not connected with the various political parties. Among the respondents, 44 per cent have admitted that they have connection with one or the other political party. 3.60 per cent of respondents did not want to commit themselves on this point. 52.40 per cent of respondents have candidly stated that they have no association with any political party. It may be recalled that respondents were drawn from Government employees, private employees, self-employed and others whom did not belong to any of the above three groups. It is no doubt, a feature of political propaganda and education that the police as a group of public servants and as representative of various categories of employees and police response are part of the process. Therefore, the attitude of these people about the police is likely to be coloured. But it is a matter of relief that those who have no affiliation with political parties are nearly 53 per cent of the total respondents.

Table. 5.14: If yes, mention the party/organisation

Party/Organisation	*Number*	*Percentage*
C.P.I (M)	111	33.64
Congress	91	27.58
C.P.I	51	15.45
B.J.P	50	15.15
Muslim League	14	4.24
R.S.P. (B)	5	1.52
Kerala Congress (B)	3	0.91
Janata Dal	2	0.61
Congress (S)	2	0.61
N.C.P.	1	0.30

Source: Personal survey.

The figures in the above table are the broad spectrum of association of the 44 per cent of respondents with various political parties functioning in the State. 33.64 per cent, 27.58 per cent, 15.45 per cent and 15.15 per cent of respondents have their loyalties towards the Communist Party of India (Marxist), [C.P.I. (M)], Congress (I), Communist Party of India (C.P.I.) and Bharatiya Janata Party (B.J.P.), respectively. But some other parties also have some support from the respondents ranging from 14 or 4.24 per cent to 1 or 0.30 per cent of respondents. This distribution makes the respondents to a great extent representative and it can be safely considered that the views expressed by them would be broadly representative.

Table 5.15: Have you ever come into contact with the police?

	Number	*Percentage*
Yes	611	81.47
No	138	18.40
No comments	1	0.13
Total	**750**	**100.00**

Source: Personal survey.

The respondents were asked to give their impressions on their personal interaction with the police. The views of the respondents touch upon a number of aspects regarding the police in the State. Among the total respondents 81.47 per cent have come into contact with the police in one-way or other. 18.40 per cent of the respondents however, did not have any such opportunity to form an impression through personal interaction. A very small fraction 0.13 per cent of the respondents did not have any comments to offer to this question.

Table 5.16: If yes, in what capacity?

	Number	*Percentage*
As complainant	183	29.95
As witness	107	17.51
As accused	245	40.10
All the three	38	6.22
As an advocate	29	4.75
As intermediary	5	0.81
Official	4	0.65
Total	**611**	**100.00**

Source: Personal survey.

The respondents who had contacted the police did so in a number of capacities. 29.95 per cent as complainants, 17.51 per cent as witnesses, 40.10 per cent as accused, 6.22 per cent as all the above, 4.75 per cent of the respondents have approached the police as an advocate or counsel and 0.81 per cent as intermediaries and 0.65 per cent of the respondents contacted the police in official capacity.

Table 5.17: How did you contact the police?

	Number	*Percentage*
All by yourself	391	63.99
In response to summons	127	20.79
Through intermediaries	61	10.00
Any other	32	5.22
Total	**611**	**100.00**

Source: Personal survey.

63.99 per cent of the respondents contacted the police all by themselves and 10 per cent through intermediaries. However, 20.79 per cent met the police in response to a summons issued by the court, which indicates that it was part of a legal procedure and 5.22 per cent in some other way.

Table 5.18: At what level was your contact with the police?

	Number	*Percentage*
Station Level	603	98.69
Supervisory level in the Department	48	7.86
Higher UPS	3	0.49

Source: Personal survey.

The large majority of respondents 98.69 per cent had contact with the police at the station level and a very small per cent, 7.86, had contact at the supervisory levels also in the department. Only a very small per cent, 0.49, of the respondents had contacted the higher-ups in the police department.

Rating of the respondents regarding their impression of interaction with the police was revealing (Table 5.19). 59.41 per cent of respondents rated the results of their interaction with the police as unsatisfactory while 248 or 40.59 per cent of respondents have found their interaction satisfactory. It is an important aspect of police-public interaction in the State that there is a traditional belief that generally all contacts with the police leave an unhappy impression with the public. Quiet contrary to this stereo-type

Table 5.19: Rate your experience/impression of your contact with the police. If unsatisfactory, because the police were? If satisfactory, because

Experience/Impression	*Number*	*Percentage*	*Experience/Impression*	*Number*	*Percentage*
Unsatisfactory Because	363	59.41	Satisfactory Because	248	40.59
Rude and discourteous	227	62.53	Approached through a departmental higher up	11	4.47
Brusque and impatient	163	44.90	Approached through a political worker/leader	80	32.52
Not inclined to listen and help	227	62.53	Approached through an influential person of the locality	88	35.77
Style of police work	13	3.58	Sheer weight of your personality	27	10.98
Any other	1	0.28	Previous Acquaintance with the police officer in charge	20	8.13
			Police are generally helpful and anxious to be of assistance	15	6.10
			To avoid public criticism	4	1.63
			Any other	3	1.22

Source: Personal survey.

impression, it is seen that 40.59 per cent of respondents have recorded their interaction as satisfactory. It would appear that the difference between respondents, who were satisfied and respondents who were dissatisfied is less than 20 per cent. When it is taken into account that among the contacts, there were 40.10 per cent as accused, 17.51 per cent as witness and 29.95 per cent as complainants, it would appear that the status of the respondent in relation to his position in a legal proceeding had some bearing on the impressions generated by the interaction.

The respondents were asked to point out the basis for the dissatisfaction who found the interaction unsatisfactory and for the satisfaction who found the interaction satisfactory. The respondents who encountered very rude and discourteous behaviour on the part of the police come to 62.53 per cent. 44.90 per cent of respondents found the police to be brusque and impatient, a large per cent of respondents, again 62.53 per cent found the police not inclined to listen and help. A small per cent of respondents 3.58 per cent have categorized this type of behaviour as part of the style of police work, a behavioural aberration. It is obvious that there is no concern for customer satisfaction in the idiom of police behaviour at the contact point and the police did not treat their clientele with respect, courtesy, patience or with an attitude of rendering a public service.

The opinion of the respondents who found police behaviour satisfactory is very significant in this context. It is seen that whenever a respondent approached through an influential person of the locality, political worker or leader, a departmental higher-up or through the strength of previous acquaintance with the concerned officer, they received satisfactory service from the police. In the case of 10.98 per cent of respondents such behaviour is the result of the sheer weight of their personality. These observations of the respondents are very revealing and unmistakably lead to infer that the police are by and large or generally rude and discourteous, brusque and impatient and not inclined to listen and help. Their attitude undergoes a change only when at the contact point the member of the public has a patron-saint in the form of a departmental higher up, a political worker/leader, an influential person of the locality or the rare asset of having been an acquaintance. Police station being the first point of contact, there has to be radical and substantial reform in police behaviour.[9] The initial response of the police to a great extent determines the subsequent course of events and for a victim an unpleasant encounter at the very beginning itself will have discourteous consequences. Therefore, the responses indicate that police behaviour has to be so reformed as to make it acceptable without exception. It follows that this is an area where police reform efforts assume significance.

Table 5.20: Did you have to incur any expenditure?

	Number	*Percentage*
Yes	207	33.88
No	393	64.32
No Comments	11	1.80
Total	**611**	**100.00**

Source: Personal survey.

It is generally assumed that service from public departments is without hidden costs. Wherever a member of the public has to make a payment, it normally assumes the form of remittance of a fee into the Treasury through a chalan, a Bank through a pay-in-slip or affixing a stamp or a Draft accompanying the paper concerned. The citizen has to meet his travel cost and suffer loss of remuneration while being away pursuing justice from Government functionaries. This is, perhaps, the ideal situation. It is almost a fact of life that there are hidden costs for securing service from public offices. Studies on corruption have categorized this into various payments— for action (speed money), for inaction (hush money), for tilting the balance in one's favour or tilting it to the disadvantage of another. India has come to be rated as a corrupt society. "Our democracy is based on corruption. Democracy requires political parties and political parties need funds. All our political parties collect funds in cash which is unaccounted money. Black money is the oxygen for corruptions. Corruption is the oxygen for Black Money. Therefore, our entire democracy is based on corruption... All our political parties are very vocal about the need for fighting corruption and also for providing good governance but when it comes to actual performance what we have is the highly misgoverned and corrupt country.[10] The Vohra Committee[11] had clearly indicated in 1993 that there is a criminal-politician-civil servant, nexus in this country. The 'Netha-Babu' nexus has been identified as one of the foolproof methods for civil servants to do the bidding of the political executive and yet remain not caught.[12] Mafia and Black Money have been identified as serious threats to democracy.[13] In this background, the researcher felt compelled to ask the respondents whether they had to incur an expenditure for meeting with the police officials and if so what was the amount involved and what was the ostensible explanation for the expenditure.

It can be seen from Table 5.20 that 33.88 per cent of respondents have admitted that they have to incur some expenditure. 64.32 per cent have however, stated that they did not have to incur any expenditure. We may recall here that 40.10 per cent of the respondents have gone to the police station as accused and 17.51 per cent as witnesses making a total of 58 per cent of the respondents. It is most likely that the persons who were taken to the police stations as accused or persuaded to go to the police as witnesses make up the 64.32 per cent of respondents who did not have to incur any expenditure. In the scheme of things as it exists at the ground level, the accused is often forced to spent in more to be in the good books of the police or to ward-off the malevolent influence of the police configuration. Yet, there would be a section of the accused who remain immune to a general practice of spending some money on a trip to the police office.

Table 5.21: If yes, how much?

Amount	*Number*	*Percentage*
Below Rs. 1000	170	82.13
Rs. 1000-2000	30	14.49
Above Rs. 2000	4	1.93
Do not remember	2	0.97
No comments	1	0.48
Total	**207**	**100.00**

Source: Personal survey.

To the question regarding the amount spent, 82.13 per cent of the respondents stated that it was below Rs.1000. 30 or 14.49 per cent of the respondents have stated that it was between Rs. 1000 and 2000 and 4 or 1.93 per cent have stated that it was above Rs. 2000.

Table 5.22: Specify the purpose for which the amount was spent

Purpose	*Number*	*Percentage*
As bribe/graft	146	70.53
Purchase of stationery	11	5.31
Hiring of vehicle	61	29.47
Entertaining police personnel	101	48.79
Payment of intermediary(ies)	1	0.48

Source: Personal survey.

The large majority of those who have spent money, 146 or 70.53 per cent have stated that the amount was spent as bribe/graft. A percentage as high as 101 or 48.79 per cent have said that the expenditure was incurred in entertaining the police personnel. 61 or 29.47 per cent of respondents indicated that the amount spent was for hiring vehicles. From the responses of a very small per cent 1 or 0.48, per cent it is seen that intermediaries also have to be paid.

It has to be pointed out here that the facilities of the Police department have improved through centrally supported modernization plans.[14] The pay and allowances of a constable or a sub-inspector is also not too meager.[15] In this background the revelation of the respondents that large amounts have to be spent as graft/bribe, hiring of vehicles, purchase of stationery, entertaining police personnel etc., have to be very decisively discouraged.

Table 5.23: How many times did you have to visit the police office/officer?

Number of Times	*Number*	*Percentage*
Once	77	12.60
Twice	359	58.76
Several times	175	28.64

Source: Personal survey.

It is seen from Table 5.23 that 58.76 per cent of respondents had to visit the police station at least twice and only a very small per cent 12.60, had to visit only once. The repeated visits are occasions to put pressure on the clientele to extract bribes and favours. The potential for mischief on the part of a disgruntled police officer is so vast and lethal that many of the clientele pay the amount/service demanded. The flow of money into the Criminal Justice System will, no doubt, sully the course of Justice. Therefore, freeing the police service outlets from corruption and demanding favours is an important area for reform to be concentrated.

Table 5.24: What impression do you carry about your interaction with the police?

Impression	*Number*	*Percentage*
Courteous	45	7.36
Discourteous	132	21.60
Helpful	241	39.44
Unhelpful	339	55.48
Friendly	78	12.77
Indifferent	299	48.94
Intimidating	240	39.28

Source: Personal survey.

The response to the above question has elicited very desperate answers. 55.48 per cent of respondents found the police unhelpful. 48.94 per cent found the police indifferent, 39.28 per cent intimidating and 21.60 per cent discourteous. Only 39.44 per cent found the police helpful, 12.77 per cent found the police friendly, and 7.36 per cent found them courteous. These responses are rather surprising in as much as they have come from respondents who had to visit the police office through the regular channels and undergo the harrowing experiences.

Table 5.25: Were you satisfied with the service received from the police?

Purpose	Number	Percentage
Not satisfied	367	60.07
Satisfied	235	38.46
No comments	9	1.47
Total	**611**	**100.00**

Source: Personal survey.

The large majority of respondents were not satisfied with the service they received from the police, viz. 60.07 per cent.

38.46 per cent of respondents were satisfied with the service received from the police and 1.47 per cent of respondents reserved their comments to this question.

Table 5.26: If not satisfied with the service from the police, what, according to you are the reasons?

Reasons	Number	Percentage
Inadequacy of laws	27	7.36
Inability of the police to apply law strictly	195	53.13
Political pressure	206	56.13
Indifference on the part of the police	219	59.67
Lack of proper training	183	49.86
Lack of accountability	158	43.05
Lax supervision	103	28.07

Source: Personal survey.

59.67 per cent of respondents have said that it was owing to the indifference on the part of the police that they were unsatisfactory. 56.13 per cent of respondents have said that the police service received was not satisfactory because it was subject to political pressure. 49.86 per cent of respondents have said that the police lack proper training 43.05 per cent have pointed out the lack of accountability as the reason for their dissatisfaction and 28.07 per cent pointed to the lax supervision. 53.13 per cent of respondents have stated that the reason behind the unsatisfactory service which they received from the police was the inability of the police to apply law strictly. A small per cent of respondents, 7.36, have indicated that there is inadequacy of laws to deal with particular situations and as a result the police service has become unsatisfactory. Whatever be the various reasons adduced by the respondents, the picture that emerges clearly from their answers is that police service is unsatisfactory to the large majority of its clients and that this persisting failure on the part of the police to provide satisfactory service creates a chain between the police and the community which is hard to bridge. Therefore, the task before any attempt at police reform should aim at generating greater acceptability for the police from the community and less of distrust and suspicion. This is an area of considerable import.[16]

Table 5.27: Did you approach any agency to redress your grievances about the police?

	Number	*Percentage*
Yes	117	19.15
No	487	79.71
No comments	7	1.15
Total	**611**	**100.00**

Source: Personal survey.

It is seen that 79.71 per cent of respondents did not approach any one to redress their grievances and preferred to accept it as *'fait accompli'*. In other words, these respondents find that there is no point in making a complaint against the police. It is only an intrepid 19.15 per cent of respondents, who addressed to their grievances to departmental superiors, political leaders and others. It is not clear whether their efforts yielded satisfactory results.

Table 5.28: If yes, whom did you approach?

	Number	*Percentage*
Departmental superior	34	29.06
Political leader	77	65.81
Any other	6	5.13

Source: Personal survey.

As Table 5.27 reveals 19.15 per cent of respondents took courage in both hands and approached departmental superiors, political leaders and others to demand satisfactory service from the police. Of the 19.15 per cent respondents 29 per cent of respondents approached departmental superiors, 65.81 per cent political leaders and 5.13 per cent, other agencies to redress their grievances. It may be remembered that they were making use of the existing machinery for the redressal of grievances which is not known for neither deterrence nor retribution. As a result, the process of making a complaint would not have delivered the desired results. It is therefore necessary that an adequately effective machinery for redressal of public grievances against the police is essential in a reformed and re-structured police force. The machinery should be simple, easily accessible, transparent and capable of disposing the complaints fast. The result of the disposal must have a sobering effect on the delinquent police personnel. It is the lack of such grievance redressal machinery for the public that generates mutual suspicion and distrust and conflict between the community and the police. Therefore, it is evident that a functioning grievance redressal mechanism closely monitored by responsible levels of leadership is an essential safeguard ensuring satisfactory police service to the community.

Table 5.29: Where do you find deficiency in police functioning?

	Number	*Percentage*
Registration and investigation of crime	301	49.26
Handling of law and order situation	143	23.40
In handling communal or caste situation	11	1.80
In keeping proper statistics and records	29	4.75
In prosecution of cases	180	29.46
Maintaining good public relations or image	291	47.63
Management of traffic	21	3.44
In handling organized crime/mafia	63	10.31
In dealing with weaker sections and women	66	10.80
Any other	00	00.00

Source: Personal survey.

There has been an attempt to identify the areas, where police service found deficient. The respondents were given nine answers to choose from and one to give their own reasons making a total of Ten (10) options. It is seen that 49.26 per cent of respondents have found the police deficient with regard to registration and investigation of crime. 29.46 per cent of respondents have found prosecution of cases to be deficient. 47.63 per cent of respondents have found the police deficient in maintaining good public relation or image. In dealing with weaker section and women 10.80 per cent of respondents found the police to be deficient. 10.31 per cent of respondents have found that the police did not effectively handle organized crime/mafia.

Leaving police and the management of crime aside for a while, when we look at Police handling of law and order situation 23.40 per cent of respondents have said that police performance is deficient. 4.75 per cent of the respondents have said that police deficiency is apparent in keeping proper statistics and records. 3.44 per cent of respondents found the police deficient in the management of Traffic and 1.80 per cent found the police deficient in handling communal or caste situations.

The composite picture that emerges from these responses is that the police handling of both crime and law and order and police service to the weaker sections, women and children, in the management of traffic, in dealing with caste and communal situations are all deficient. It is seen that, the development process depends upon satisfactory conditions of order prevailing in the community. Crime and the social cost involved have not been precisely related yet. However, it is evident that crime and the consequences of crime have far-reaching implications for social security and social defence. It has been indicated earlier that police service fall almost nearly into two equal halves—one centered on the management of crime and the other on the management of order. All other areas are incidental or consequential to these broad areas. We find that both these areas are, in the eyes of the respondents deficient and falling short of delivering satisfactory service. Therefore, police reform has to aim at adequately designing, equipping and training the police to deal with disorder and crime. In fact, the police are able to provide conditions where crime and disorder are adequately controlled. It would boost both the development process and social distribution. Therefore, it is evident that police reforms have to be focused sharply on police management of crime and order.

Table 5.30: Where do these deficiencies appear more often?

Purpose	*Number*	*Percentage*
Police stations	389	94.88
Field officers	144	35.12
Lower level supervisory officers	102	24.88
Supervisory officers in IPS	2	0.49
All ranks	14	3.41

Source: Personal survey.

As shown in the above Table, the respondents have identified the areas which are susceptible to deficiency. 94.88 per cent of respondents have found deficiencies in the police station, 35.12 per cent in the field officers and 24.88 per cent in the lower level supervisory officers. 3.41 per cent of respondents found deficiencies in all ranks and a small percentage 0.49 per cent in the supervisory officers in IPS. Though the percentage as high as 3.41 per cent find deficiencies in all ranks it would not be prudent to ignore the convincing data which isolates and identifies areas of deficiency. Whatever be the negligence of superior levels, the fact of the matter is that, the public who have their interface with the police at the lower levels are mostly dissatisfied. An overview of these findings would suggest that police reform attempts would target the police stations, the field offices and lower level supervisory offices as the most vulnerable area. In his perspective study on police reforms and what the police can do by themselves P.J. Alexander has asked "Can the police do something for police reforms themselves".[17] He has gone on to answer that police reform has to start at the police level. Therefore one of the areas where police reforms should start with is the police stations, field offices and lower level supervisory offices.

Table 5.31: How would you rate the police in Kerala in comparison with the police force of other States?

	Number	Percentage
Better than other States	392	52.27
As good as other States	269	35.87
Lower than other States	89	11.87
Total	750	100.00

Source: Personal survey.

Table 5.32: If better, identify the areas where they excel?

	Number	Percentage
Detection of crimes	372	94.90
Being people friendly	9	2.30
Managing traffic	11	2.81
In not being corrupt	3	0.77
In resisting political pressures	6	1.53
Handling of law and order situations	73	18.62
In eschewing third degree methods	8	2.04
In the application of science & technology	4	1.02
Being helpful to weak and underprivileged	4	1.02
In developing good rapport with the community	1	0.26
Any other	1	0.26

Source: Personal survey.

The responses as shown in Table 5.31, 5.32 and 5.33 were elicited to ascertain whether the respondents perse were anti-police or hostile to the police. It is seen that 52.27 per cent of respondents have rated the police in the State to be better than the police of other states and 35.87 per cent of respondents to be as good as the police in other states. It is only 11.87 per cent of respondents who have said that the police in the State is below the police of other states in India.

Table 5.33: If lower than the police of other states, what are the reasons?

	Number	*Percentage*
High handed and arbitrary	49	55.06
Rude and ill-mannered	46	51.69
Poor detection of crime	23	25.84
In not being accessible	45	50.56
Corruption	50	56.18
Nexus with crime protection rackets (mafia)	41	46.07
Subservience to political leaders	63	70.79
Using illegal techniques and third degree methods	22	24.72
Poor handling of law and order situations	9	10.11
Lack of exposure to latest developments	8	8.99
In failing to use modern techniques in crowd management	4	4.49
In discriminating against poor and underprivileged	30	33.71
Unsatisfactory management of traffic	2	2.25

Source: Personal survey.

The reasons for the high rating of the Kerala police by the respondents are many. According to 94.90 per cent of respondents Kerala police is good at the detection of crimes. 18.62 per cent of respondents have found the police in the State good at handling of law and order situations. The respondents were also complementing the police, though in smaller percentages that the police here are better because they eschew third degree methods, they apply the benefits of science and technology in investigation, they attempt to develop good rapport with the community and for being helpful to the weak and the underprivileged. A very small per cent of respondents who have pointed this on the credit side can be taken as those with a wishing list, those optimists who see change for the better and hope for the best police functioning. But the crux lies in the management of crime and order.

The respondents who have rated the police in the state to be lower than the police in other states have identified the reasons also. 50 or 56.18 per cent of the respondents have identified corruption as the reason for rating the police in the State lower than the police in other states. 49 or 55.06 per cent have identified high handed and arbitrary behaviour of the police, 46 or 51.69 per cent have found the rude and ill-mannered behaviour, 63 or 70.79 per cent have found subservience to political leaders, 45 or 50.56 per cent in not being accessible, 41 or 46.07 per cent, nexus with crime protection rackets (mafia) 30 or 33.71 per cent, in discriminating against poor and underprivileged, 23 or 25.84 per cent, poor detection of crime 22 or 24.72 per cent, using illegal techniques and third degree methods 9 or 10.11per cent, poor handling of law and order situations, 8 or 8.99 per cent, lack of exposure to latest developments, 4 or 4.49 per cent, in failing to use modern techniques in crowd management and 2 or 2.25 per cent, unsatisfactory management of traffic as the reasons for lower rating they have given to the Kerala Police. These responses confirm our earlier findings that the police behaviour while dealing with the clientele is a very important area in determining the chords of relationship between the police and the community. It has also been found earlier that first and foremost, the police have to deliver the goods or fulfil their mandate before they aspire to be accepted by the community.

Table 5.34: The police being an index to measure the quality of life in society would you suggest that the Kerala police need to be reformed?

	Number	*Percentage*
Yes	743	99.07
No	1	0.13
Do not know	6	0.80
Total	**750**	**100.00**

Source: Personal survey.

An overwhelming per cent, 99.07, have unmistakably pointed out that the Kerala Police needs to be reformed. In fact, this is a very convincing quantity of evidence that can hardly be ignored.

Table 5.35: If yes, indicate areas for reform?

Areas for reform	*Number*	*Percentage*
Acts and rules governing the police	215	28.94
Training and training methodology	611	82.23
Organisation and structure of the police	208	27.99
Functional style of the police	655	89.50
Implementing the recommendations of National and Kerala Police Commissions	429	57.74
Any other	4	0.54

Source: Personal survey.

The respondents have identified the areas for reform in Table 5.35. An overwhelming majority of respondents 89.50 per cent have identified reform in the functional style of the police. 82.23 per cent have identified that training and training methodology are to be reformed. 57.74 per cent of respondents suggested the implementation of the recommendations of the National and Kerala Police Commissions and 28.94 per cent of respondents indicated that the Acts and rules governing the police need to be reformed. 27.99 per cent of respondents have pointed out that the organization and structure of the police shall also be reformed.

Question number X was intended to measure the rating of the police by all the respondents in their relation with the different sections of the society (Table 5.36). These included seven sections—the people who come into contact with the police, students, labourers and other organized sections, important people in the society, the public at large, women and weaker sections, political workers and leaders and any other. Under all categories police relation has been rated as unsatisfactory on all counts. 47 or 59.60 per cent of respondents have rated the police in their relation with the people they come into contact with as unsatisfactory and 282 or 37.60 per cent as satisfactory 21 or and 2.80 per cent of the respondents have reserved their comments on this question. To the question, to rate the police in their relationship with students, labourers and other organized sections, 59.33 per cent of respondents have stated unsatisfactory, 37.60 per cent satisfactory and 3.07 per cent no comments. But 47.73 per cent of the respondents have rated the

Table 5.36: How would you rate the police in their relationship with the people they come into contact students, labourers and other organized sections, important people in society, the public at large, women and weaker sections, political workers and leaders

Sl. No.		*Satisfactory*	*Unsatisfactory*	*No comments*	*Total*
1.	The people they come into contact	282 (37.60%)	447 (59.60%)	21 (2.80%)	750 (100%)
2.	Students, labourers and other organized sections	282 (37.60%)	445 (59.33%)	23 (3.07%)	750 (100%)
3.	Important people in society	358 (47.73%)	315 (42.00%)	77 (10.27%)	750 (100%)
4.	The public at large	250 (33.33%)	473 (63.07%)	27 (3.60%)	750 (100%)
5.	Women and weaker sections	237 (31.60%)	465 (62.00%)	48 (6.40%)	750 (100%)
6.	Political workers and leaders	332 (44.27%)	263 (35.07%)	155 (20.67%)	750 (100%)
7.	Any other	000	000	000	000

Source: Personal survey.

police in their relation with important people in the society satisfactory, 42.00 per cent unsatisfactory and 10.27 per cent had no comments. 63.07 per cent of respondents had found the police unsatisfactory in their relation to the public at large, 33.33 per cent satisfactory and 3.60 per cent had no comments to this question. With regard to the relationship of the police with women and weaker sections, 62.00 per cent had rated unsatisfactory, 31.60 per cent satisfactory and 6.40 per cent had no comments. 44.27 per cent of respondents had rated the relationship of the police with political workers and leaders satisfactory, 35.07 per cent unsatisfactory and 20.67 per cent of respondents had no comments on this question.

Table 5.37: Are you aware of your duty as a citizen to help and co-operate with the police?

	Number	*Percentage*
Yes	744	99.20
No	6	0.80
Total	**750**	**100.00**

Source: Personal survey.

An important question tendered to the respondents was whether they were aware of their duty as citizens to co-operate with the police. 99.20 per cent of the respondents have confirmed that they were aware of their duty as citizens and that the duty entailed helping and co-operating with the police. This is a very revealing and suggestive response and it augurs well for the police in the State that the public are aware of their duties and are desirous of cooperating with the police and helping them. The important question that has to be answered here is if, as the respondents indicate, the public are willing to co-operate and help the police and consider it their duty as citizens what stands in the way of a harmonious relationship between the police and the public. The data from the respondents in the Tables above also provide the answer to this question viz. aberrations in police behaviour. Therefore, just as a bridge needs two stable banks, the police and the community have to interact and evolve modalities which would help the police to accept the public's offer of help and assistance as part and parcel of their duty as citizens and the police should prepare themselves to be accepted by the public. It would be no exaggeration to say that this area is very important from the point of view of police reforms.

Table 5.38: If yes; mention how such co-operation and help can be made effective or useful?

	Number	*Percentage*
By organizing police-community relation exercises	281	37.77
By decentralization of some powers and functions of the police to Panchayat Raj Institutions	438	58.87
By making police stations accessible to people and in encouraging them to demand satisfactory services from the police	722	97.04
By separating crime investigation and law and order management	421	56.59
Any other	00.00	00.00

Source: Personal survey.

The various options given to the respondents to make police-public cooperation effective and useful have been welcomed enthusiastically by the respondents. It is again very revealing to find that 97.04 per cent of respondents felt that one important step in this direction would be to make the police stations accessible to the people. 58.87 per cent of the respondents have welcomed the idea of decentralizing some powers and functions of the police to Panchayat Raj Institutions. Separating crime investigation and law and order management has received the support of 56.59 per cent of respondents. Police community relation exercises have surprisingly received welcome response only from 37.77 per cent of respondents which clearly indicates the distance to be traversed by the police to make their credibility palpable enough to secure the support of the people. It is no doubt, not an easy task but, certainly attainable if pursued with determination.

Question No. XII asked the respondents to make suggestions on making supervision of police work (policing the police), reducing corruption in the police, making police people-friendly, introducing police reform measures and modernizing the police organization and functions. A number of useful suggestions have come from the respondents on the question. These responses are summarized thus.

1. By and large the respondents felt that supervision has suffered on account of unionization of the police and the performing ranks working in tandem. A new sense of camaraderie has evolved which forces higher ranks to turn a Nelson's eye on most delinquencies. Therefore, the most important of the suggestions is having a separate inspection team, which is neither too friendly nor familiar with the staff manning the field offices, would be a useful idea. Another important suggestion was to accelerate the process of computerization and introduce MIS techniques for securing necessary information from the organization on a continuing basis.

2. On the question of reducing corruption in the police most of the suggestions encouraged greater transparency and an effective machinery for quick redressal of public grievances. A number of respondents have suggested adopting the e-SEVA-measures of Andhra Pradesh, *mutatis mutandis*.

3. To make the police people-friendly, the respondents have stressed intense training programme aimed at greater concern for the Human Rights of the public, victims, accused and witnesses and to abjures personal violence, use of intemperate language, misuse/over-stepping of power and areas of discretion.

4. The respondents were almost unanimous in indicating that the police in the state needs to be reformed and police reform measures should produce a "Kerala Model" which could be a beacon for other states. They have distinguished subtly between modernizing the police and reforming the police and while welcoming more facilities, equipments and scientific aid to the police to discharge their duties, stressed that police

reforms are the crux and that modernization efforts are no substitute to police reform. In all, the responses have been well considered and mature.

In Question No. XIII the respondents were asked to outline their vision of a police system in a highly literate and politically sensitive state like Kerala in any order of preference. The ratings of the respondents are shown in Table 5.39.

Table 5.39: Vision of a police system

	Rank	*Mean Score*
Accountable to law	1	7.82
People friendly and accessible	4	5.40
As eschewing violence and third degree	5	5.31
Committed to Human Rights and Fundamental Rights of the people	2	6.61
Using science, technology, I.T. and communication skills	7	2.99
Officer-oriented than manpower-oriented	9	2.02
Politically neutral and independent	3	5.95
Decentralized in some powers	6	4.59
Women well represented	8	2.62
Any other	0	0

An analysis of the rating of the respondents shows that they have put accountability to law which secured 7.82 mean score as the first important aspect of their vision of police system suited to a highly literate and politically sensitive state like Kerala. The aspect which secured the second position with 6.61 mean score was commitment to Human Rights and Fundamental Rights and close at the heels was a police, politically neutral and independent and remaining people friendly, accessible, eschewing violence and third degree methods. Decentralisation of some police functions was also a priority with the respondents. Using science, technology, IT and communication skills, women well represented and making the police officer oriented than manpower oriented were rated seventh, eighth and ninth respectively in the ranking by the respondents.

REFERENCES

1. Government of Kerala, *Final Report of the Kerala Police Re-organization Commission*, Thiruvananthapuram, 1986, p. 109.

2. Data Provided by the Census Directorate.

3. Data Provided by the State Election Commission, Trivandrum, Kerala.

4. *Malayala Manorama Year Book,* 2003.

5. *Kerala Police Act*, Section 23.

6. *Cr.P.C*, 1973, Schedule 1.

7. Data Provided by the Eelection Commission, Trivandrum, Kerala.

8. Data Provided by the State Election Commission, Trivandrum, Kerala.

9. P.J. Alexander, *Legal Framework of Police Process: Tortion and Distortion*, Bangalore, Ecumenical Christian Centre, 2003.

10. N. Vittal, "Strategy for Better Governance", *The Hindu*, March 31, 2002.

11. Government of India, *Report of the Vohra Committee*, New Delhi, 1993

12. Harish Khare, "The New Netha-Babu Nexus", *The Hindu*, 2 April 2002.

13. See: *The Hindu*, September 28, 2002

14. Government of Kerala, *Annual Administration Report of the Kerala Police*, 1998, p. 120.

15. The pay scale of a police constable is Rs. 3050-5230 and the S.I. is Rs. 5500-9025.

16. Community Policing has been accepted as a style of grassroot policing in most countries. Curiously enough this was one of the subjects in the terms of reference of Kerala police Re-organisation Committee of 1959.

17. P.J. Alexander, (ed) *Policing India in the New Millennium*, New Delhi, Allied Publishers, p. 1053.

Police Reforms–Need and Directions

Police Perspective

The police is an important government department engaged in maintaining order in society and in controlling crime and infractions of law. It is generally conceded that they perform a variety of functions and touch upon the life of the individual in society in a number of ways. The study, therefore, aimed at eliciting the views of the people as clientele or consumers of police service, on the need and directions of reforms in the police. It is a limitation of studies on police reforms that the police view point on reforming their own department and on empowering themselves to initiate the process of change and reform are not usually elicited. Therefore, it was considered necessary to ascertain police responses on the need and direction of police reform. In a recent study on the police in India, this aspect has been highlighted and it was suggested that the police themselves may initiate such changes as are possible within their power.[1] One of the papers in the above volume specifically deals with this question and the author has identified adoption of fair, quick and responsible methods of redressal of complaints against the police, transparency in the dealings of superior officers and a drastic revision of the system of training, to include Human Rights as an important module in the training programme,[2] as the areas where police themselves can initiate reform. In this background, it was decided to elicit the views from three (3) different segments of the police personnel viz, Field Formations (S.Is, A.S.Is, H.Cs and

P.Cs), Middle Management (S.Ps, Dy. S.Ps and C.Is) and Senior Management (IPS officers), on the need and directions of police reforms.

The police in Kerala as on 31 December 2002, has 44268 officers[3] in the Field Formations. From them a sample of three hundred (300) was selected, at the rate of fifty (50) from each district from which data from the public was collected. Out of the 827[4] Middle Management level officers serving in the State a sample of hundred and fifty (150) was selected at the rate of twenty-five (25) from each of the above districts. As on 31 December 2002, there are a total of ninety-six (96)[5] I.P.S. officers borne on the Kerala Cadre who could be called the police senior management. Of these twenty (20)[6] are currently on deputation outside the department to different non-police departments under the Central Government, the State Government and to other instrumentalities of the State. Therefore there were only seventy-six (76) I.P.S officers in the State Police Department to approach for eliciting their responses. The researcher mailed the Questionnaire to all I.P.S officers and personally interviewed some of them who are currently working in the police department, and collected fifty (50) samples. The researcher also personally interviewed the samples selected from the field formations and the middle management. Since the questionnaires employed were different for the three different samples, the responses to the three are arranged separately in Tables in 6.1 to 6.15, 6.16 to 6.27 and each of them are discussed below.

FIELD FORMATIONS

Table 6.1: Personal Profile

Age distribution of the respondents

Age	*Number*	*Per cent*
Below 35 years	55	18.33
35-39 years	56	18.67
40-44 years	104	34.67
45-49 years	34	11.33
50 years & above	51	17.00
Total	**300**	**100.00**

Source: Personal survey.

The age distribution of the three hundred respondents interviewed from the category of field formations can be seen from Table 6.1. Of the respondents 18.33 per cent were in the age group of below 35 years, 18.67 per cent in the age group of 35 to 39 years, 34.67 per cent in the age group of 40 to 44 years, 11.33 per cent in the age group of 45 to 49 years and 17.00 per cent above 50 years of age. The age of entry in respect of those who enjoy the benefits of reservation being 33 years, the respondents come from a very representative age group. The respondents came from nine (9) districts in the State.

Table 6.2: Gender distribution

Sex	*Number*	*Per cent*
Male	276	92.00
Female	24	8.00
Total	**300**	**100.00**

Source: Personal survey.

Table 6.2 shows that of the respondents, 92 per cent were males and 8 females. The total strength of Field Formations being 44268 and the strength of women police being 1447,[8] this distribution would appear to be representative.

Table 6.3: Marital status

Marital status	*Number*	*Per cent*
Unmarried	11	3.67
Married	289	96.33
Total	**300**	**100.00**

Source: Personal survey.

An interesting feature of the respondents about their marital status can be seen from the data in Table 6.3. 96.33 per cent of the respondents were married and enjoy the benefits of stable marriage and 3.67 per cent of respondents were unmarried. It is a reflection of the discipline under which the police personnel live, that discord in marriage leading to dissolution or break down appears to be almost non-existent.

Table 6.4: Present post

Present Post	Number	Per cent
PC	158	52.67
HC	81	27.00
ASI	17	5.66
SI	44	14.68
Total	**300**	**100**

Source: Personal survey.

Table 6.4 reveal that of the 300 respondents 52.66 per cent were holding the lowest post, that of the Police Constable, 27 per cent were holding the next higher post of Head Constables, 5.66 per cent were holding the next promotion post of Additional Sub-Inspector and 14.68 were holding the post of Sub-Inspectors, which is filled up by direct recruitment as well as promotion from the ranks in the ratio of 50 : 50.

Table 6.5: Number of promotions

No. of Promotions	Number	Per cent
0	189	63.00
1	82	27.33
2	17	5.67
3	12	4.00
Total	**300**	**100**

Source: Personal survey.

Table 6.5 show that of the respondents, 63 per cent remain at the entry stage and did not receive any promotion yet. Obviously, they are those who directly entered the department from the open market like Constable and Sub-Inspectors. 27.33 per cent of respondents have received one step promotion, 5.67 per cent have received two promotions and 4.00 per cent of respondents have received three, clearly indicating that they belonged to the Constabulary, and have received promotion to the post of Sub-Inspectors.

Table 6.6: Educational status

Education	*Number*	*Per cent*
Above SSLC	81	27.00
Upto 12	58	19.33
Graduation	147	49.00
Postgraduate	13	4.33
Professional	1	0.33
Total	**300**	**100.00**

Source: Personal survey.

The educational standard of the respondents are impressive and appropriately high for a State like Kerala with 90.92 per cent of literacy.[9] Table 6.6 show those who have studied above S.S.L.C. were 27 per cent of the respondents, 19.33 per cent of respondents have studied upto standard 12, 49 per cent were graduates and 4.33 per cent were postgraduates. One respondent had professional education—a degree in Law. In respect of computer literacy the picture is not as bright. 25.67 per cent of respondents were computer literates and the remaining 74.33 per cent were computer illiterates. This is an aspect that deserves to be taken serious notice of since computerization of crime records was introduced as early as 1975-76 in Kerala[10] and computer is extensively used in the storage and retrieval of data and information relevant for investigation of cases. It is therefore surprising that the police department has nearly 75 per cent of people who are computer illiterates. It is obvious that there is a serious flaw in the IT policy regarding the training in the police department. If at the point of entry or during exposure to in-service training programmes or as an in-service programme itself, the personnel were exposed to appropriately designed computer awareness programme, the picture would have been different. It may be pointed out here that in Andhra Pradesh, the benefits of IT has been taken to the police station level and the networking has enabled the public to register online complaints.[11]

Table 6.7: Achievements in sports and games

Achievements in Sports and Games	*Number*	*Per cent*
Yes	14	4.67
No	286	95.33
Total	**300**	**100.00**

Source: Personal survey.

The achievements of the respondents in sports and games as Table 6.7 shows appear not at all impressive except in the case of 4.67 per cent who have notched some success. The large majority 95.33 per cent has hardly any achievements in sports and games. However, this yields some broad conclusions on the recruitment policy of the police department. One reason could be that the emphasis has shifted from sheer brawn to other attributes and it is not crude physical strength that is demanded from the lower levels. The educational status of the respondents shows that at the formative stages, the emphasis of the personnel would have been on clearing the academic examinations and not to distinguish in sports and games. It may be recalled that in Kerala, recruitment to the ranks of constables and sub-inspectors is done by the Kerala Public Service Commission which lays down general norms and no special weightage is given to those who excel in sports and games. Another reason could be that the police department does not find time to give its personnel enough leisure and opportunities to train themselves in sports and games.[12] A still more relevant reason could be that the work of the police personnel takes up most of their waking hours and as the Police Act says 'all police personnel are expected to be available for duty on Tap' all the twenty-four (24) hours of the day.[13] Both the clamour and the promise for eight (8) hour working for policemen have been found impracticable.

The respondents were specifically asked whether they were satisfied with the present image of the Kerala Police and if they found the image to be distorted the primary reasons for the same. The responses are arranged in Table 6.8.

Table 6.8: Are you satisfied with the present image of the Kerala police?

	Number	*Per cent*
Yes	133	44.33
No	161	53.67
No comments	6	2.00
Total	**300**	**100.00**

Source: Personal survey.

In Table 6.8, 53.64 per cent of the respondents have stated that they were not satisfied with the present image of the Kerala Police. 2 per cent of the respondents have opted to remain silent. These two categories make up nearly 56 per cent of the respondents. While the response of 44.33 per cent, that they were satisfied with the image of the police cannot be brushed aside, the fact remains that the majority were not happy with the image. The reasons for not being happy with the image of the Kerala Police have been identified by the respondents from the suggestions given in the questionnaire. The respondents were given the freedom to select one or more reasons and the responses are arranged in Table 6.9 below.

Table 6.9: If not satisfied, briefly indicate the reasons?

Reasons	*Number*	*Per cent*
Police-public discord	37	22.98
Hostile relation with politicians and political parties	116	72.05
Poor pay and working conditions	78	48.45
Harsh disciplinary control	66	40.99
Image of the Police as insensitive and oppressive	23	14.29

Source: Personal survey.

In Table 6.9, 72.05 per cent of the respondents have identified hostile relation with politicians and political parties as the reason for the dissatisfaction with the present image of the Kerala Police. Poor pay and working conditions were pointed out by 48.45 per cent of the respondents and 40.99 per cent of respondents have identified harsh disciplinary control as the reasons. 22.98 per cent of respondents have identified police-public discord and 14.29 per cent of respondents put the image of the police as insensitive and oppressive as reasons for the police image being unsatisfactory.

A question was asked to the respondents to identify the major handicaps, if any, they face in their profession. The respondents were given the freedom to give their own answers. These responses may be seen in Table 6.10.

Table 6.10: What according to you are the major handicaps, if any, in your profession?

Handicaps	*Number*	*Per cent*
No handicaps	23	7.67
No timely promotion	70	23.33
Heavy work and continuous duty	56	18.67
Poor working conditions	34	11.33
Poor pay and allowances	33	11.00
Political interference	17	5.67
Lack of modern tools for scientific investigation	15	5.00
Lack of exposure to modern developments in policing	14	4.33
No meaningful powers to the lower level officers	14	4.33
Low level of participation from the public	12	3.67
Inhuman treatment by senior officers	12	3.67
Total	**300**	**100.00**

Source: Personal survey.

In Table 6.10 shows that the respondents have identified the major handicaps which they face in their profession, though 7.67 per cent of the respondents have pointed out that there were no such handicaps. 23.33 per cent of the respondents have pointed out the absence of a sound promotion policy in the department as the major handicap. Heavy workload and continuous duty were identified as the major handicap by 18.67 per cent of respondents, poor working conditions by 11.33 per cent, political interference by 5.67 per cent, lack of modern tools of scientific investigation by 5.00 per cent and lack of exposure to modern developments in policing by 4.33 per cent of respondents. Respondents coming to 4.33 per cent have pointed out that no meaningful powers were given to the lower level officers, 3.67 per cent have identified low level of participation from the public and an equal per cent (3.67) have pointed out the inhuman treatment of senior officers as the major handicaps which they face in the profession.

A sequel to this question was whether the respondents would like the police to be reformed. The responses to that question are shown in Table 6.11.

Table 6.11: Would you like the police to be reformed?

	Number	*Per cent*
Yes	278	92.67
No	16	5.33
No comments	6	2.00
Total	**300**	**100.00**

Source: Personal survey.

From Table 6.11 it is of interesting to note that 92.67 per cent of respondents have stated that they want the police to be reformed. Those who were satisfied with the *status quo* come to 5.33 per cent only. 2 per cent of the respondents had no comments on the question. Thus, it is very evident that the large majority of personnel in the Field Formations yearn for police reform.

A question was asked to the respondents who wanted the police to be reformed, to prioritise the areas of reform. The respondents were given freedom to give one or more answers of their own choice. The areas of reform prioritized by the respondents are shown in Table 6.12.

In Table 6.12, 38.38 per cent of respondents have suggested revision of Police Acts and Rules as the first area which demands reform, 31.68 per cent have identified fixed duty time, 28.17 per cent have pointed out service conditions, 26.05 per cent have identified increasing the strength of police force and 25.70 per cent of respondents have stated training as the priority areas of reform. Better infrastructural facilities, police-public rapport creating exercises, delegation of powers to lower level officers, adoption of scientific methods of investigation and functional style of the police were identified by 25.35 per cent, 25.00 per cent, 16.56 per cent, 15.85 per cent and 15.50 per cent of respondents respectively as priority areas of reform. It can be seen that the respondents have touched practically every important aspect of the functioning of the police department and it is evident that what they hope for is a comprehensive police reform process rather than cosmetic changes. It may be kept in view here that the Field Formations make up 97.5 per cent of the police force in Kerala or in raw figures 44268. This figure makes the demand for total reform a priority.

Table 6.12: If yes, which are the priority areas?

Areas of Reform	*Number*	*Per cent*
Police Acts and Rules	109	38.38
Fixed duty time	90	31.68
Service conditions	80	28.17
Increasing the strength of police force	74	26.05
Training	73	25.70
Better infrastructural facilities	72	25.35
Police public rapport creating exercises	71	25.00
Delegation of powers to the lower level officers	50	16.56
Adoption of scientific methods of investigation	45	15.85
Functional style of the police	44	15.50

Source: Personal survey.

The next step was to assess the familiarity of the respondents with the recommendations of the National Police Commission of 1977 and the Kerala Police Re-organization Committee, 1959 and the Kerala Police Re-organization Commission, 1982-1986 (See Table 6.13).

The responses as can be seen from theTable 6.13 show that 86.33 per cent of respondents are familiar with the recommendations of the Commissions and the Committee, 5.33 per cent of respondents have stated that they were not familiar with those recommendations and 8.33 per cent of respondents have reserved their comments to the question.

Table 6.13: Are you familiar with the recommendations of the National Police Commission of 1977 and the Kerala Police Re-organization Committee/Commission of 1959 and 1982-86?

	Number	*Per cent*
Yes	259	86.33
No	16	5.33
No comments	25	8.33
Total	**300**	**100.00**

Source: Personal survey.

Table 6.14: If yes, are those recommendations still relevant?

	Number	*Per cent*
Yes	36	13.90
No	211	81.47
No comments	12	4.63
Total	**259**	**100.00**

Source: Personal survey.

As shown in Table 6.14, 81.47 per cent of respondents have pointed out that the recommendations of the National Police Commission and of the Kerala Police Re-organization Committee/ Commission were not relevant, 13.90 per cent as still relevant and 4.63 per cent had no comments on the question.

Table 6.15: Do you think that there is a case for a new State Police Commission

	Number	*Per cent*
Yes	235	78.33
No	33	11.00
No comments	32	10.67
Total	**300**	**100.00**

Source: Personal survey.

As can be seen from the responses shown in Table 6.15, 78.33 per cent of respondents have stated that there is a case for a new State Police Commission. 11 per cent of the respondents have pointed out that a new State Police Commission was not needed and 10.67 per cent had no comments to the question.

MIDDLE MANAGEMENT

Middle Management in the police department, as is the case with large organizations anywhere, is the backbone of the organization. They, in fact, function as the conduit for transmitting and translating visions, ideas and policies generated by the top management level to the lower levels which are, in fact, the base of the organizational pyramid. The middle management also functions as the link between the base and the superstructure. Their role is invaluable for feedback from lower levels which is a necessary input for structuring and re-shaping of approaches and policy initiatives. The middle management are those who have done some spell in the organization and have been promoted to the higher rank and thus, carry with them substantial work experience and insights into the strengtns and weaknesses and the behaviour of the organization. Thus, the middle management, is a stabilizing factor in the structure of the police department. Therefore, the three (3) supervisory levels, Circle Inspectors (C.Is), Deputy Superintendents of Police (Dy. S.Ps) and Superintendents of Police (S.Ps) generally identified as the middle management was taken up for their study. It may be recalled that the Police Station is the most important field office in the police department and practically every level above the police station, is for supervision of the work done at the police station level and for appropriate intervention with a view to correcting or re-directing what has been done. The Circle Inspector of Police, thus looks after a small cluster of Police Stations roughly equivalent to a Taluk in area, a Deputy Superintendent of Police, a few circles roughly equivalent to a sub-division or half a district and a Superintendent of Police, a district or an organization which is placed in a district, functionally, if not territorially. It may be clarified here that these three ranks in the police department have territorial and non-territorial jurisdiction and sometimes in an organization they are so designated to signify the level in the hierarchy. Thus, in an armed police battalion or an armed reserve unit a Circle Inspector is known as an Armed Police Inspector, a Deputy Superintendent of Police as Assistant Commandant and a Superintendent of Police as Commandant. In city police formations the last two designations are generally known as Assistant Commissioner and Commissioner.[14]

It is estimated that the Middle Management has a strength of 827 officers. For the purpose of this study samples were collected from 150 officers belonged to this category at the rate of 25 samples from each district from which data was collected from the public. The method of simple random sampling was applied for data collection. The respondents from the middle management comprises of eleven (11) S.Ps/Commandants, Seventy-five (75) Dy. S.Ps/ Assistant Commandants and Sixty-four (64) Circle Inspectors/ Armed Police Inspectors. Though officers borne on the IPS cadre are also known as Superintendents of Police, when they hold charge of districts or an equivalent post on the senior scale of the I.P.S., they have been omitted from this sample in view of the fact that they do belong to the top management as members of the IPS. The responses are arranged in tabular form in Tables 6.16 to 6.27.

Table 6.16: Personal Profile Age distribution of the respondents

Age	*Number*	*Per cent*
35-39 years	22	14.67
40-44 years	20	13.33
45-49 years	30	20.00
50 years and above	78	52.00
Total	**150**	**100.00**

Source: Personal Survey.

The Table 6.16 gives the personal profile of the respondents. There were 14.67 per cent of respondents in the age group of 35 to 39 years, 13.33 per cent in the age group of 40 to 44 years, 20.00 per cent of respondents in the age group of 45 to 49 years and 52 per cent of respondents above 50 years of age. The samples are all males, clearly indicating that police women are not yet occupying positions in the Middle Management of the police department in Kerala.

Table 6.17: Educational status

Education	*Number*	*Per cent*
Degree	72	48.00
P.G.	76	50.67
M.Tech.	2	1.33
Total	**150**	**100.00**

Source: Personal survey.

The Table 6.17 shows that 48.00 per cent of the respondents were graduates and 50.67 per cent post-graduates in one discipline or other. 1.33 per cent of respondents were professional degree holders. It was seen that the large majority did not have any special education, though there were a few with qualifications like a degree in law, post-graduate diploma and an M.Phil.

Table 6.18: Present rank

Present Rank	*Number*	*Per cent*
SP/Commandant	11	7.33
DYSP/Assistant Commandant	75	50.00
Circle Inspector/Armed Police Inspector	64	42.67
Total	**150**	**100.00**

Source: Personal survey.

The Table 6.18 reveals that 7.33 per cent of the respondents were holding the rank of S.Ps/Commandants, 50.00 per cent Dy. S.Ps/Assistant Commandants and 42.67 per cent Circle Inspectors/Armed Police Inspectors.

Table 6.19: Rank at entry

Rank at Entry	*Number*	*Per cent*
S.I.	142	94.67
P.C.	5	3.33
Dy.S.P.	3	2.00
Total	**150**	**100.00**

Source: Personal survey.

As shown in Table 6.19 the rank of entry in respect of 94.67 per cent of respondents were that of the Sub-Inspector, while there were 3.33 per cent of respondents who entered the service in the rank of Police Constable and 2.00 per cent of respondents in the rank of Deputy Superintendent of Police.

At this stage, it is necessary to clarify that, the personnel management policy of the police department in Kerala is a mix of open market recruitment and in-house promotions. Normally, direct enlistment is resorted to only at the ranks of Constables, Sub-Inspectors and Assistant Superintendents of Police (IPS), although occasionally, to give representation to members of Scheduled Caste (S.C.) and Scheduled Tribes (S.T.), recruitment is made to the rank of Deputy Superintendent of Police (Dy. S.Ps). Therefore, it can be seen that an overwhelming majority, of about 95 per cent of respondents, have joined the service as Sub-Inspectors and earned their promotions in due course, by diligent discharge of duties and blameless official conduct. The long service they have put in the department, their familiarity with the rungs of the middle management, the duties they discharge and the powers they exercise give considerable credibility to their responses.

Table 6.20: Number of promotions

No. of Promotions	*Number*	*Per cent*
0	2	1.33
1	60	40.00
2	75	50.00
3	10	6.67
4	3	2.00
Total	**150**	**100.00**

Source: Personal survey.

In Table 6.20, of the respondents 1.33 per cent remain at the entry stage and did not receive any promotion, 40.00 per cent of the respondents have received one step promotion and 50.00 of two step promotions. 6.67 per cent of respondents have received three promotions and a small per cent viz, 2.00 have received four promotions. This is a rosy picture of vertical promotion prospects in the middle management level of the police in Kerala.

Table 6.21: Employment prior to joining the police

	Number	*Per cent*
Employed	64	42.67
Unemployed	86	57.33
Total	**150**	**100.00**

Source: Personal survey.

A question was asked to the respondents whether they were employed before joining the police and if so, what was the nature of that employment and how many years of service they have put in Table 6.21. 42.67 per cent of the respondents were employed and 57.33 per cent were unemployed.

Table 6.22: If employed, name of the post

	Number	*Per cent*
LD auditor	5	7.81
Teacher	10	15.63
LDC	13	20.31
Police Constable	17	26.56
Accountant	6	9.38
Indian Railways	1	1.56
Legal Assistant	1	1.56
Private sector	11	17.19
Total	**64**	**100.00**

Source: Personal survey.

From the data in the Table 6.22, it is very clear that the respondents were having work experience in different departments both in the public as well as in the private sector. 7.81 per cent of respondents were lower division auditors, 15.63 per cent Teachers and 20.31 per cent lower division clerks, before joining in the police service. 26.56 per cent of respondents were police constables, 9.38 per cent accountants, 1.56 per cent were working in the Indian Railways, 1.56 per cent were Legal Assistants and 17.19 per cent of respondents were employed in the private sector. The respondents have put in 6 months to 7 years of service before they were drawn into the police service.

To enable the members of the middle management to comment freely on the need and directions of police reform, the respondents were asked to differentiate between 'modernization' and 'police reform'. Their responses are tabulated and given in the Table 6.23.

Table 6.23: As a member of the middle management of the Kerala police, please differentiate between modernization and police reform

	Number	*Per cent*
Modernization is the application of modern tools for policing, whereas reform aims at a complete change	99	66.00
Modernization must be preceded by reform	30	20.00
Modernization without reform is only a futile attempt	15	10.00
Modernization aims at operational change only. But reform aims at a total change including training, behaviour etc.	6	4.00
Total	**150**	**100.00**

Source: Personal survey.

During the period of this study there was a controversy in the State as to whether modernization is what the police require or reform. In fact, a careful scanning of comments in the press by the Chief Minister, who is handling the police portfolio also, did not even mention once, even in the height of the controversy concerning efforts to de-politicise the control over the police, that there is a case for reforming the Kerala Police. He was also repeating the efforts made to modernize the police which in effect, meant giving them more vehicles, access to sophisticated communication gadgetry and such other technical services and facilities. In fact, many perceptive commentators on the police had during this time very clearly differentiated between police reform and modernization.[15] Therefore, it was necessary to ascertain whether the middle management was aware of the difference between modernization and police reform. As can be seen from Table 6.23, the middle management in the Kerala Police had very clearly distinguished between the two. 66.00 per cent of the respondents spelled out that modernization was nothing but the application of modern tools for efficient policing whereas reform aims at a complete change. 20.00 per cent of the respondents have stated that modernization must be preceded by reforms. 10.00 of the respondents were of the view that modernization without reform was only a futile attempt. 4.00 of the respondents have clearly differentiated modernization from reform by stating that the first aims at operational change only and the latter at a total change. This perception of the middle management is very significant and it has to be commented that it augurs well for the future of the police department. This is particularly so because, all reform measures and initiatives for change have to be carried out through the middle management, as they are the most important cogs in the communication mechanism of the police organization.

A significant corollary to the above findings can be seen from the responses of the middle management on their familiarity with the recommendations of the National Police Commission of 1977, the Kerala Police Re-organization Committee of 1959, and Kerala Police Commission of 1982-1986. The respondents were given the freedom to suggest those recommendations which they consider relevant today. Their responses are given in Table 6.24.

Table 6.24: What recommendations of the National Police Commission, 1977 and the Kerala Police Re-organization Committee/Commission of 1959 and 1982-1986 appear to be relevant today?

	Number	*Per cent*
Not familiar with the recommendations	30	20.00
Setting up of the State Security Commission	60	40.00
Functional Independence	45	30.00
Professionalism	21	14.00
New Police Act	18	12.00
Fixed Tenure for the Head of the Department	15	10.00
Frequent exposure to training	6	4.00

Source: Personal survey.

It was very interesting to find from Table 6.24 that an overwhelming majority, 80.00 per cent of the respondents, were familiar with the recommendations and more importantly some of the very sensitive and crucial recommendations of the National Police Commission and the Kerala Police Re-organization Committee/Commission. However, 20.00 per cent of the respondents have stated that they were not familiar with those recommendations. 40.00 per cent of the respondents have stated that the recommendation to establish a State Security Commission was relevant and 30.00 per cent of the respondents were found favouring Functional Independence for the police recommended by the National Police Commission, 14.00 per cent of respondents found the recommendation regarding professionalism and 12.00 per cent found the recommendation for substituting the present Police Act with a new Police Act relevant. The recommendation for a Fixed Tenure for the Head of the Department and frequent exposure to training were found relevant by 10.00 per cent and 4.00 per cent of the respondents respectively. These responses very clearly indicate that the police personnel at the Middle Management level were aware that there has not been any worthwhile effort at reforming the Kerala Police so far and that most of them view the various recommendations, even those which mark a complete departure from the past, with favour. These responses make it necessary to observe that ground within the police structure is ready to receive the seeds of police reform. They were also clear in their minds that despite several opportunities, the State has failed to evince the required earnestness to introduce reforms.

Table 6.25: Are you happy with the present image of the Kerala police?

	Number	*Per cent*
Yes	33	22.00
No	90	60.00
No Comments	27	18.00
Total	**150**	**100.00**

Source: Personal survey.

The respondents were asked to express themselves regarding the image of the Kerala Police. As can be seen from Table 6.25, 60.00 per cent of the respondents were not happy with the present image of the police in the State. 22.00 per cent of the respondents have stated that they were happy with the present image of the Kerala Police and 18.00 per cent of respondents had no comment to the question. It may be recalled here that, as Table 6.8 shows, 53.67 per cent of the respondents from the field formations were also not satisfied with the present image of the Kerala police. These responses when added with responses of the public about their impression of their contact with the police as shown in Table 5. 19, in which 59.41 per cent have rated the impression unsatisfactory substantiate that the police sub-system is deficient and that there is a pressing need for reform.

Table 6.26: If not, please indicate a few steps to correct the present distortions?

	Number	*Per cent*
Take steps to obviate political interference at lower levels	72	80.00
Norms to be adopted and strictly followed to avoid frequent transfers and postings	54	60.00
Provide better infrastructural facilities	45	50.00
Re-structure the training modules to include training in the use of computers	36	40.00
Computers of all police stations	27	30.00
Take strict disciplinary action against corrupt officers	18	20.00

Source: Personal survey.

The respondents who were not happy with the present image of the Kerala Police, as shown in Table 6.25, (60 per cent of the total respondents) were asked to indicate a few steps to correct the present distortions in the image of the police. They were given the freedom to make one or more suggestions of their own choice. Their suggestions are given in Table 6.26. 80.00 per cent of the respondents have suggested that steps should be taken for obviating political interference at lower levels. 60.00 per cent of respondents have recommended adoption of norms for promotions and transfers, 50.00 per cent of respondents have suggested better infrastructural facilities, 40 per cent of respondents have indicated re-structuring the training methodology, 30.00 per cent of respondents have suggested computerization of all police stations and 20.00 per cent of respondents have recommended strict disciplinary action against the corrupt officers as steps to correct the present distortions. It can be seen that these are all very important suggestions.

Table 6.27: Indicate in a rough order of preference areas of reform in the Kerala Police

Areas of Reform	*Rank*	*Mean score*
Re-write the Kerala Police Act. Please indicate whether you would like it to be remodelled on the draft 'Police Act" given by the N.P.C. 1977.	1	12.15
Re-write the Criminal law I.P.C, Cr. P.C, I.E. Act and Special and Local Legislations like the Arms Act, M.V. Act etc.	2	10.73
Introduce stringent laws to manage violations of Law and Order	12	5.05
Provisions to ensure quick prosecution and adjudication of cases in courts	3	10.65
Delegation of some powers and duties to the constabulary	14	2.53
Drastic revision of training modules at the induction level	5	8.35
Introduction of Human Rights jurisprudence in police functioning at all levels	7	6.87
Provisions to insulate police officers against political interference for partisan purposes and to ensure police neutrality	6	7.23
Introduce steps to obviate corruption by SMART or e-governance	8	6.29
Improve individual police behaviour during interface with Members of the public	11	5.63
Frequent exposure to training to keep pace with the change and development both in the work environment and in state and society	9	5.78
Introduce scientific methods of investigation	4	8.89
In the place of non-cognizable offence introduce some mechanism for community response	13	3.34
Introduce computerization of police records and computer literacy for the police	10	5.65

Source: Personal survey.

The respondents were also asked to indicate in a rough order of preference areas of reform in the Kerala Police. They were given the freedom to express their preferences going beyond the choices given as illustration in the questionnaire. The views of the respondents are arranged in the Table 6.27.

The areas of police reform prioritized by the respondents yield valuable insights. Introducing a new Police Act as given in the VIII report of the National Police Commission has taken precedence over all other options. Re-writing the criminal laws and special and local legislations and provisions to ensure quick prosecution and adjudication of cases before the courts have secured second and third positions among the reform areas. Introduction of scientific methods in investigation and drastic revision of training modules at the induction level follow as priority areas. Insulating police officers and their work against political interference and Introduction of Human Rights Jurisprudence in police functioning have been indicated as next in priority in the areas of reform. Steps to introduce SMART or e-governance to obviate corruption, frequent exposure to training to keep pace with changes in the socio-political milieu, computerization of police records and computer literacy for the police and improving individual police behaviour during interface with members of the public have also been identified by the respondents as reform areas. Introduction of stringent laws to respond to violations of law and order, the irrelevance of categorizing offences as given in the present Indian Penal Code, as cognizable and non-cognizable and delegation of some powers and duties to the constabulary secured the next three positions in the order of priority marked by the respondents.

It would thus appear that the Middle Management in the Kerala Police has more or less a very clear idea about areas of the police corpus that require to be reformed. It may be seen that they have also identified factors contributing to distortions in the image of the police and have also recalled earlier reform efforts. It can therefore, be safely concluded that the middle management have familiarized themselves with the various recommendations for police reforms in the past, they have quiet clearly identified and prioritized the areas for police reform and have expressed themselves clearly that what the Police in Kerala need today is police reform rather than police modernization. True to the assumptions of the researcher, the middle management has expressed themselves specifically on each of the questions administered to them.

SENIOR MANAGEMENT

The Police Senior Management denotes members of the Indian Police Service (IPS). The IPS is one of the two All-India services constituted under the Constitution of India at its very inception. The All-India Services constitute "An extra-ordinary feature of the Indian federal system. They are common to the Union and the States. Recruited by the Government of India and controlled jointly by Central and State Governments, they supply officers for high administrative and secretariat appointments required both by the Centre and the States".[16] They are governed by the All-India Services Act and Rules which provide for greater administrative independence and insure against personal career hazards to its members.[17] The strength has in its fold thirty-three (33%) per cent of promotees from the State Service. The rest of the strength is met by direct recruitment by the Union Public Service Commission. They occupy all the cadre posts of the IPS in every state. For the purpose of evolving a national character, direct recruits belonging to various states are allotted to various state cadres other than their own home states on a roughly 1 : 1 basis. This means that at any given time fifty per cent (50%) of the strength of the IPS/IAS cadre will be occupied by those who do not belong to the state. This arrangement, it is believed, would provide besides national character, the elements to strengthen national integration and broad basing of the cadres of the different states. It also provides an opportunity for the members of the All-India Services to function without the constraints of narrow loyalties—caste, region, religion and importantly 'Sons of the Soil' parochialism. It was therefore, very important for this study to find out the views of the IPS of the cadre on police reform.

Since the strength of the IPS in Kerala is Seventy-six (76) excluding those on deputation, it was decided to include all of them in the universe. Copies of the questionnaire were mailed to them with the assistance of the Police Headquarters. The researcher also met with a few of them while out on the districts interviewing the members of the public and the police subordinate levels and middle management. The access, the researcher had with members of the service on account of his membership of the Indian Institute of Public Administration and the Indian Institute of Police Studies also helped to interact freely with them. In all fifty samples were received from the senior management. The responses from the members of the Kerala Cadre of the IPS are arranged in Table 6.28.

Table 6.28: Personal profile Age distribution of the respondents

Age	*Number*	*Per cent*
Below 35 years	6	12.00
35-39 years	8	16.00
40-44 years	1	2.00
45-49 years	20	40.00
50 years & above	15	30.00
Total	**50**	**100.00**

Source: Personal survey.

As can be seen from the Table 6.28, 12 per cent the respondents were below 35 years of age, 16 per cent of the respondent between 35 to 39 years of age, 2 per cent between 40 to 44, 40 per cent between 45 to 49; and 15 per cent above 50 years of age. There were among them two respondents (2) females and forty-eight (48) males.

Table 6.29: Year of entry in to the IPS

Year of entry into the IPS	*Number*	*Per cent*
1970-1979	8	16.00
1980-1989	23	46.00
1990+	19	38.00
Total	**50**	**100.00**

Source: Personal survey.

The year of entry into the service arranged on the basis of decadal cadre strength as Table 6.29 shows that 16.00 per cent of the respondents have entered into the service between 1970 and 1979, 46 per cent between 1980 and 1989 and 38 per cent from 1990 on wards.

Table 6.30: Academic qualifications

	Number	*Per cent*
Degree	7	14.00
MA/M.Sc.	37	74.00
B. Tech	5	10.00
M. Tech	1	2.00
Total	**50**	**100.00**

Source: Personal survey.

The academic qualifications of the respondents are very impressive, it is evident from Table 6.30, 14 per cent of the respondents were graduates and 74 per cent post-graduates. 10 per cent of the respondents had a B.Tech degree and 2 per cent had an M. Tech degree. It is obvious that those with higher qualifications are from those who have entered the service from the open market and others by promotion.

Table 6.31: Employment before joining the IPS

	Number	*Per cent*
Employed	26	52.00
Unemployed	24	48.00
Total	**50**	**100.00**

Source: Personal survey.

Table 6.31 shows that 52 per cent of the respondents were employed before they joined the IPS, but for 48 per cent, I.P.S. was their first appointment.

Table 6.32 reveals that the respondents who were employed before joining the IPS came from a variety of professional background. 34.69 per cent of respondents came from the academic sector, 19.31 per cent were Bank Officers, 15.41 per cent were from the lower and middle rungs of the Police Department, an equal per cent (15.41) were Engineers, 7.79 per cent were Production Managers and 7.79 per cent of respondents were Scientists.

Table 6.32: Nature of employment

	Number	Per cent
Lecturer	9	34.69
Bank Officer	5	19.31
Police Department	4	15.41
Engineer	4	15.41
Production Manager	2	7.79
Project Scientist	2	7.79
Total	**26**	**100.00**

Source: Personal survey.

Table 6.33: Length of service

Length of Service	Number	Per cent
1-3 years	5	10.00
3-5 years	7	14.00
5-10 years	6	12.00
10-15 years	12	24
15-20 years	10	20
20-25 years	4	8
25-30 years	5	10
35 years and above	1	2
Total	**50**	**100.00**

Source: Personal survey.

In terms of length of service in the cadre, as shown in Table 6.33, the respondents had one (1) to more than thirty-five (35) years, which is happily a vertical cross section of the cadre because the maximum length of service of an IPS officer, is by virtue of the recruitment and superannuation rules, would not be more than thirty-six (36) years, on the average.

It was considered necessary to confront the respondents with the strained police media relationship and the adverse reports appearing against them in the press and they were asked to identify the basic reasons. The responses are shown in Table 6.34.

Table 6.34: The media in recent times in the State have been focusing attention on police lapses and criticize the police rather than complementing them. It is obvious that the police-media relationship is not all that happy. Could you identify the most basic reasons?

Reasons	*Number*	*Per cent*
Media wants to sensationalize news	24	48.00
To increase circulation	19	38.00
Prejudice of the management and employees of the visual media	18	36.00
Lack of accountability of the media men	15	30.00
Lack of transparency in police work	14	28.00
Immaturity and lack of training of the media personnel	11	22.00
Communication gap between the police and the media	9	18.00
Corrupt police officers are behind some cases	6	12.00
Competition among the media personnel	5	10.00
Politically oriented news making	4	8.00

Source: Personal survey.

It was seen that the respondents have been very objective with regard to their reactions to the question, it is clear from the Table 6.34. 48per cent of the respondents have identified the craze for sensational news making and 38 per cent have identified the purely business interest of increasing circulation as the reasons. Prejudices of the management and employees of the visual media were identified as the basic reason by 36 per cent of the respondents and 30 per cent of the respondents identified lack of accountability of the media personnel as another reason. Lack of transparency in police work, immaturity and lack of training among the media personnel, communication gap between the police and the media and involvement of some police officers themselves were stated as the reasons by 28 per cent, 22 per cent, 18 per cent and 12 per cent of respondents respectively. 10 per cent of the respondents have identified competition among the media and 8 per cent the sharply differing political loyalties of the media as the reason behind the strained police media relationship. On the whole the responses very clearly indicate that the respondents are aware of the poor image the police has in the media. The fact that the respondents did not shy away from responding to this question was very encouraging and was indicative of their willingness to discuss areas and issues with which they were not in the best of terms. The respondents were asked on their views regarding the policy of the United Democratic Front (UDF) government under the Chief Minister A.K. Antony, who also holds the Police portfolio, to de-politicise the control over the police so as to ensure police political neutrality. They were specifically asked whether such a policy would survive change of Governments, change of police ministers or political vicissitudes without necessary changes in the statutes. The responses are arranged in Tabular form in Table 6.35.

Table 6.35: The police policy of the present Government was under attack from various quarters including some of the constituents of the U.D.F. However, the public by and large have come to believe that a non-interfering political executive (in the details of routine police response) and a strong professional leadership would ensure political neutrality of the police. Do you think this arrangement would continue without necessary change in the statutes?

	Number	*Per cent*
Yes	32	64.00
No	14	28.00
No comments	4	8.00
Total	**50**	**100.00**

Source: Personal survey.

As per Table 6.35, 64 per cent of the respondents have stated that the present arrangement could continue without changes in the statutes. 28 per cent of the respondents were of the view that changes in the statutes are necessary and 8 per cent of the respondents had no comments to the question.

Table 6.36: Would you support the recommendation of the National Police Commission, 1977, for functional independence of the Head of the Department?

	Number	*Per cent*
Yes	46	92.00
No Comments	4	8.00
Total	**50**	**100.00**

Source: Personal survey.

The respondents were asked whether they were in support of the recommendation of the National Police Commission of 1977 on functional independence to the Head of the Department. The responses were very revealing, it is evident from Table 6.36. An overwhelming majority of 92 per cent of respondents have stated that they were in support of that recommendation, though a few respondents (8 per cent) had no comments on the question.

Table 6.37: Which other recommendations of the National Police Commission would you highlight to ensure police neutrality?

	Number	*Per cent*
Setting up of State Security Commission	36	72.00
Fixed tenure for the Head of the Department	34	68.00
No comments	14	28.00

Source: Personal survey.

The respondents were asked to identify the other recommendations of the National Police Commission, which would ensure police neutrality. Their responses are shown in Table 6.37. 68 per cent of the respondents have highlighted the recommendation for Tenure Appointment of the Head of the Department to ensure police neutrality and 28.00 per cent of respondents had no specific opinion on the issue.

The allegations and criticism of the police pertain overwhelmingly to the manner in which they handle law and order situations and their failure in quickly detecting important and sensational crimes. The respondents were asked whether they would agree to a bifurcation of the functions of management of order and investigation of crime. It may be recalled that the very first police reform effort in Kerala, the 'Kerala Police Re-organization Committee, 1959' and the subsequent 'Kerala Police Re-organization Commission,' 1982-1986, had recommended such a bifurcation. Hence it was thought appropriate to elicit the views of the respondents whether there was a case for such a bifurcation. The responses can be seen from Tables 6.38 and 6.39.

Table 6.38: Is there a case for bifurcating the management of order and investigation of crime?

	Number	*Per cent*
Yes	46	92.00
No	4	8.00
Total	**50**	**100.00**

Source: Personal survey.

Table 6.39: If yes, would it create personnel management problems?

	Number	*Per cent*
No	42	91.30
Yes	4	8.70
Total	**50**	**100.00**

Source: Personal survey.

From Tables 6.38 and 6.39 can be seen that 92 per cent of the respondents have suggested bifurcating the functions of management of order and investigation of crime. Of these 91 per cent have stated that such a bifurcation would not create personnel management problems for the police. It may be remembered that maintenance of order and prevention and detection of crime are the basic functions of the police and introduction of professional expertise and sophistication so as to be ready to confront the emerging trends in the violations of law is not only basic but imperative for police success in their basic functions. This suggestion also involves a whole range of re-thinking with regard to police recruitment, training, placements, overseeing and evaluation. The readiness with which the senior management of the Kerala police agreed to this proposal indicates a willingness on their part to reconstruct and re-deploy their personnel and resources towards ensuring a much better satisfaction level to their clientele.

Table 6.40: There is a general feeling that Police Reform efforts often come to nothing. The reports of the National Police Commission and Kerala Police Re-organization Committee, 1959 and Kerala Police Re-organization Commission 1982-1986, are instances. Would you comment as to why such situations persist?

	Number	*Per cent*
Lack of political will	26	52.00
Politicians as well as police leadership are happy with the status quo	12	24.00
Resistance to reform from vested interests	8	16.00
No comments	4	8.00
Total	**50**	**100.00**

Source: Personal survey.

The respondents were asked to comment on the general impression that police reform efforts often come to nothing, on the strength of the proven failure of the National Police Commission and the various committees/commissions appointed in the State of Kerala. It may be added here that the experience in other states with regard to police reforms also are not dissimilar. The responses are very revealing, it is evident from data shown in Table 6.40. 52 per cent of the respondents categorically said that it was the lack of political will that was frustrating police reforms. 24 per cent of the respondents have indicated that politicians as well as Police leadership are to be blamed for the failure to reform the police. Resistance to reform from vested interests was identified as the reason for the sorry state of affairs by 16 per cent of the respondents and 8 per cent of the respondents offered no comments to the question, indicating the utter futility and sense of desperation with regard to the prospect of police reforms. When all these responses are put together the obvious conclusion that can be drawn is that the Police Senior Management in the State has the feeling that police reform efforts are not likely to be seriously floated, pursued or executed. Since these are prima-facie beyond their purview and rests on *sober* political will aimed at committed, sustained good governance, it is, obvious that the senior management is more frustrated than other segments of the police sub-system.

The respondents were asked to identify in a rough order of preference the areas that should be prioritized for reform. As shown in Table 6.41, amenaing the Police Act to incorporate the recommendations of the N.P.C to provide a tenure appointment for the Head of the Department and setting up of State Security Commission have received the top priority from the respondents. Insulating the Police against political vendetta through appropriate statutory safeguards and enactment of necessary statutes to ensure political neutrality and professional independence, transparency and accountability of the police have received the next two slots in terms of urgency. Amending the Criminal law trilogy and making the police accountable to the Judiciary only, in respect of investigation of cases, have secured the fourth and fifth positions respectively. Separation of the two basic police functions of investigation and prosecution sixth in priority and introduction of new legislations for managing order, the seventh. The need to introduce appropriate training systems and exposure to modernization programme for all levels restructuring of police hierarchy by providing some meaningful role to the constabulary and strengthening internal control mechanisms have received the eighth and ninth positions respectively. In the order of priority marked by the respondents, introducing through e-governance SMART police governance to increase public confidence and community rapport have secured the tenth position and increasing the per cent of women and minorities in the police force the eleventh position. Differentiating police management of order and handling the terrorist's hostage taking, security threats to V.I.Ps/V.V.I.Ps, attempts at suicide attacks are marked as twelfth by the respondents. Introducing Human Rights and Police Response as an important theme in Police training and the linking of prison reforms with police reforms were given the thirteenth and fourteenth positions in the order of priority by the respondents.

Table 6.41 As a member of the Police Senior Management you must have identified areas where police reforms are urgent. Could you in a rough order of preference indicate these areas? A few illustrative, but not exhaustive, suggestions are given below. Please feel free to add areas of your choice.

Areas of Reform	*Rank*	*Mean score*
1	2	3
Police Act to incorporate the recommendations of the NPC, like a tenure appointment for the Head of the Department, State Security Commission etc.	1	11.76
Amendment to the Criminal Law trilogy; I.P.C, Cr.P.C., I.E. Act	4	11.08
Enactment of New Statutes to ensure political neutrality and professional independence, transparency and accountability (Recall the present arrangement of supervision of some cases investigated by the C.B.I. by Central Vigilance Commission)	3	11.30
Insulate the Police against political vendetta through appropriate statutory safeguards.	2	11.36
Make the Police accountable to the Judiciary only in respect of investigation of cases.	5	9.35
Introduce new legislations for managing order, keeping in view the pressures to which a soft State governed by a number of coalescing political parties, are likely to come under.	7	6.96
By law differentiate police management of order and handling of terrorists, hostage taking, security threats to V.I.Ps/V.V.I.Ps, attempts to suicide attacks etc.	12	4.71
Increase the per cent of women and minorities in the police force	11	5.08
Introduce through e-governance SMART Police governance to increase public confidence and community support.	10	5.68

(Contd...)

1	2	3
Provide some role for the police without compromising the separation of investigation and prosecution, to ensure effective prosecution and quick disposal by the courts	6	7.28
Link prison reform with police reform	14	4.34
Re-structure police hierarchy by providing some meaningful role to the constabulary and strengthen internal control mechanisms.	9	6.00
Introduce appropriate training and exposure to modernization programme for all levels	8	6.76
Introduce Human Rights issues and police responses as an important theme in police training.	13	4.35

Source: Personal survey.

It has to be observed that the respondents giving a lower or higher priority index to the options given to them under this question does not necessarily reflect a view that some of the areas can be relegated for the benefit of others or others can be push forward. In fact, the responses very clearly indicate that the question of 'police reform' is inclusive of the various options given in the questionnaire, as illustration and the responses are not for piecemeal reform of police and their areas of functioning. It is all a question of where to start and when to start. This can be seen from the fact that when the Police Act and the basic Criminal Acts, the I.P.C, Cr.P.C., I.E. Act, are amended or recast, Human Rights issues will have to be seriously considered and steps to accelerate disposal both by the investigating agency and the adjudicating agency provided. Similarly, such changes in the law will also have to look after accountability of the investigating agency to the judiciary and separation of the two segments looking after management of crime, political neutrality of the police, transparency in the exercise of authority and also styles and approaches to the handling of law and order. Increasing the per cent of minorities in the force or providing for gender justice also depend upon the enactment of new legislations. Providing for some meaningful role to the constabulary and strengthening internal control mechanisms are also stand rivetted on the provisions of the new legislations to be enacted. Similarly, linking prison reforms with police reforms touch upon the core concept of the very purpose of punishment-retribution or reformation and re-integration of the delinquent to society. It also indicates that the Criminal Justice System as a whole would be in need of review and reform consequent on police reform.

Table 6.42: Since the recommendations of the National Police Commission are about two decades old, would you support constituting a new Police Commission to study and report on Police Reforms in Kerala/ India?

	Number	*Per cent*
Yes	29	58.00
No	21	42.00
Total	50	100.00

Source: Personal survey.

It was considered appropriate to elicit responses from the senior management of the Kerala police about setting up a new Police Commission, since the recommendations of the National Police Commission, which submitted its VIII and Final Report in May 1981, are old, by more than two decades. As shown in Table 6.42, 58.00 per cent of the respondents have advocated the setting up of a new Police Commission, though 48.00 per cent, perhaps on the lessons of past experience, did not support the setting up of a new Police Commission to suffer the dismal fate of its predecessors.

The respondents who belong to three different strata of the police hierarchy have thus, conclusively canvassed the case for police reform. It may be recalled that the police views on police reforms have not been ascertained during any earlier police reform efforts. In fact, most of the responses have been one sided, from the public as to what changes they desired for the police. It was perhaps assumed that the police viewpoint can be taken for granted. Several studies have indicated that the difficulty with regard to implementing various legislations or various administrative directions, affecting the basic freedoms of the people have been enacted or issued without consulting the police, who are always condemned as the perpetrators of such lawless acts.[18] Therefore, these responses open our eyes to the views of the police department which is seldom expressed on account of the tight control of disciplinary mechanism and the various constraints on the police personnel airing their views in public. It may be recalled that in the questionnaires the respondents had been assured that the data will be used only for research purposes. They were also given the further option to remain anonymous in case they so preferred. It may not be idle to speculate that these caveats helped the candid and frank expression of views by the respondents from the different levels. The composite view of the respondents unmistakably indicates to a pressing need for police reform.

REFERENCES

1. P.J. Alexander (ed), *Policing India In The New Millennium*, New Delhi, Allied Publishers, p. 1058.

2. N.R. Madhava Menon, "Police Reform: Imperative for Efficiency in Criminal Justice in P.J. Alexander (ed.) *Policing India In The New Millennium*, New Delhi, Allied Publishers, 2002, p. 259.

3. Data provided by the State Crime Record Bureau, Pattom, Trivandrum.
4. *Ibid.*
5. Data provided by the Police Headquarters, Trivandrum.
6. *Ibid.*
7. *Ibid.*
8. Data provided by the State Crime Records Bureau, Pattom, Trivandrum.
9. Literacy rate as a whole 90.92%, Male 94.2, Female 87.86. District with highest literacy—Kottayam 95.9%, district with lowest literacy—Palakkad 84.3%. *Manorama Year Book*, 2003.
10. The Computer Programme for the Kerala Police started with preparing a data bank with punching machines of IBM and a T.D.C. 316 Computer [mainframe] as part of the modernization programme in 1975-76.
11. In Kerala, the police website is shown as under construction and the available data are not updated.
12. We do not hear of any Kerala Police Football or Volleyball team now as it used to be heard of a few years earlier.
13. Section 17 of *Kerala Police Act*, 1960, (Act V of 1961).
14. The Commissionerate system has not been introduced in Kerala yet, though the head of the district police organization in Calicut, Ernakulam and Trivandrum is known as commissioner of Police and the rank next below as Deputy Commissioner/Assistant Commissioner. They perform only the functions which Superintendents and Deputy superintendents perform. There was an announcement recently that the Commissioner of Police, Kochi is being vested with all the powers of a City Police Commissioner, parallelled to that of Mumbai, Chennai, Kolkatha, Nagpur, Pune, etc.
15. Comments in the Press by P.J. Alexander, *The Hindu*, 17 January, 2003.
16. R.N. Thakur, *The All India Services*, Patna, Bharathy Bhavan, 1969, p. 1.
17. See: *All India Services Manual*, New Delhi, Manager of Publications, 2002.
18. See: P.J. Alexander, Why We are not Consulted?—A Policeman's Dilemma, Trivandrum, (Mimeo), Institute of Management in Government, Kerala, 1986.

Conclusions and Suggestions

Every organization is a living and dynamic entity. Each activity is born, has its periods of experimental development, of vigorous and stable activity and in some cases of decline. One effort at arresting such decay and degeneration is to inject into the corpus of the organization, elements of re-construction, reform and reorganization. This process has to be dove-tailed into the organization whenever it is faced with challenges affecting its mission-objective or goals as well as dynamics of functioning. In other words, the process cannot be delayed till such time the organization faces a crisis or suffer atrophy. This axiom is applicable with considerable force to organizations like the police which is compelled to pass through sharp vicissitudes of transition and change. In fact, as and when new convulsions grip the society, new challenges are faced by the State, new demands are made of it and it is exposed to new threats, the police organization needs to be reformed. A close look at the police organization in Kerala would strongly indicate that no serious effort has ever been launched to reform the police, in spite of various serious challenges faced by the sub-system.

The Kerala police as we have today, it has been found, came through three different streams, the Travancore police system, the Cochin police system and the system that existed in the Madras Presidency as applicable to the Malabar district. It has been found that these three sources were not uniform either in their shape or in their content. In Travancore the police had derived their strength straight from the Monarch and exercised a good deal of influence in the State administration. In Cochin, although the initial growth was from the Kingship, as a small State with a much more cohesive administration, it had its distinct limitations and advantages. The most prominent feature that can be identified from the story of the growth and development of these two systems is that both had benefited from reforming interventions of the British administration through the Political Agent or Resident, who not only exercised a role of overseeing the State administration but also a benign modernizing influence which ultimately aimed at a uniformity common both for British India and the Princely States. This was reflected both in the laws which were introduced into these States on the pattern which existed in British India and also organization of the force, the command structure, ranks and designations of officers and at a later stage induction of officers from the Indian Police to head the police organizations. During the struggle for national freedom, the police in the Princely states of Cochin and Travancore were accused of being anti-people and anti-freedom struggle, but the stigma of being harsh, authoritarian and ruthless in the exercise of their powers was particularly that of the police in Travancore. The policy of the then Dewan regarding integration with the Indian Union and State Congress and popular uprisings like the Vayalar Punnappra struggles further hardened the image of the Travancore police in the minds of the people at large. When on attaining independence and the merger of the States, when Travancore-Cochin was formed, it was widely believed that the new political leadership, which had more or less directly experienced the response of the police both to specific events and the general array of the agenda for independence, would think of reforming the Criminal Justice System or at least the police sub-system. However, there was not even the slightest effort at pruning the police department or exorcising the police sub-system of the evil remnants of the past. It would appear that during the integration of the two States, the primary effort was to provide for the officers of the two State services and to make a few of them eligible for membership of the IPS, rather than weeding out the corrupt, the incorrigible and those who have unleashed brutal terror on the people who were agitating for political freedom. From 1 July 1949 to

30 October 1956, long seven years, the police of Travancore and of Cochin were struggling to integrate themselves rather than transforming themselves into a new police force in the wake of the new political dispensation that had dawned in this country. Unfortunately, the continuance of the Inspector General of police of Travancore who became the Inspector General of Police of Travancore-Cochin and the Inspector General of Police later when the State of Kerala was formed on 1 November 1956, a person who had risen from the rank of Sub-Inspector through the patronage of the palace, did not help the police in Travancore-Cochin either to aspire or to experiment for a police culture different from what existed in Travancore, which we have seen, had the worse image among the police forces of the three constituent parts of the State of Kerala. In fact, such a continuance of leadership led to the survival of many bad habits and practices in the force. The police continued to be an organization feared by the people.

The formation of the Kerala State and the assumption of the reigns of governance by a ministry spearheaded by the Communist Party of India (C.P.I.) was an unbelievable development and the State was not prepared for such a violent departure from the past. Not only were there unfamiliar political faces from the Malabar region but also unusual responses to policing at the grassroots. The formation of the Kerala State saw a few members of the I.A.S., I.P., and I.P.S officers coming from Madras State into the Kerala cadre. One of them, a member of the I.P. succeeded the I.G. of Travancore, Travancore-Cochin and later of Kerala as head of the Kerala Police department. However, as they were numerically too small, they were unable to introduce substantial changes in the style of police functioning in the State. A political development that stood in the way of any positive contribution likely to be introduced by the new Ministry led by the Communist Party was the eruption of the violent political agitation known as the 'Liberation Struggle'. Faced with unprecedented challenges to the maintenance of law and order, the C.P.I.-led ministry fell back on traditional police response and resources and the police leadership which rose from the rank rather than relying on the leadership of a member of the I.P. from the Madras Presidency, who was then the Head of the Department. The new Ministry had sown the seeds of hope for police reform, in fact for crafting a new police system, when they appointed the Kerala Police Re-organization Committee on 15 January 1959. However, when the State was seized by a violent political convulsion, a mass upsurge, sadly even they reverted to police styles of functioning which smacked of anti-freedom struggle tactics spawned by the colonial administration. It was no doubt, a great set back to all hopes and optimism. In fact, it once more confirmed that, faced with a crisis even progressive political elements would rather rely on tried out and time tested police techniques and tactics rather than experiment with restraint and sobriety, sending a message down the line that the government was bend upon a departure from the past. It has been pointed out earlier that the Kerala Police Re-organization Committee, 1959 was asked to conclude their efforts and send up their Report on select items of the Terms of Reference, as soon as possible. This was a decision taken when the State was under the President's Rule after the dismissal of the State Government under Article 356 of the Constitution of India. Consequent on the formation of the State of Kerala, the IAS/IPS cadre received a large batch of officers, six each, and their services were available to the State from about 1959. Had the Communist Party-led Government continued in office, not disrupted by popular agitation, the Kerala Police Re-organization Committee of 1959 would have submitted a well-contained report on several important issues seen in the Terms of Reference and with the presence of officers received from the cadre of the Madras State at the helm and a large posse of young entrants both in the IAS and IPS cadre, the State could have launched a pioneering effort at modernizing the administration and reforming the police sub-system which had again got mired in allegations of mindless brutality and high handedness to the people who took part in the liberation struggle. It would appear that the forces of history were unkind to the State. Taking a cue from Kerala, a number of other States in the country appointed Police Commissions and brought about important changes in several areas. The circumstances under which the Kerala Police Re-organization Committee, 1959 was appointed, their work circumscribed and they were directed to submit a report on some of the subjects in the Terms of Reference, all contributed to confer on the Report of the Committee a prejudice and a bias which inhibited successive governments and even the police leadership from taking up for implementation even those recommendations which were neither controversial nor too progressive. This mind-set to took at reform proposals and departure from the beaten track seem to shadow the police leadership *ad infinitum*. When a new incumbent sent a message to the members of the Kerala Police on assuming charge as the Inspector General of Police, highlighting for the first time a progressive and balanced perception of police role and functions in a democracy, it did not meet with any warm welcome from all relevant quarters.

The next and most opportune phase for police reform for the State was the post-Emergency period when on an allegation of custodial death of a student of the Regional Engineering College, Kozhikode, the Chief Minister who was handling the police portfolio had to demit his office and the police department itself was subjected to the indignity of arrest and prosecution of three (3) IPS officers. This was the time the new Janata Government at the Center appointed the National Police Commission and a Study Team was appointed in the State to prepare background material and to collate data on the different items in the Terms of Reference. The study team submitted a paper which is seen to have focused attention on "the causes of delay in the investigation" and disposal of cases rather than on other sensitive issues like police excesses or police image or making the police function within a democratic framework accountable to law. Though some of the recommendations of the Study Team, are seen accepted by the National Police Commission, it has not been entirely on the basis of the recommendations of the study team but on the basis of evidence given by individual officers before the National Police Commission and through personal discussion with members of the National Police Commission.

It is seen that the Reports of the National Police Commission did not create any impact in the State either with the political executive or with the administrative apparatus. One of the reasons attributed to the lukeworm reception given to the Reports of the N.P.C. was, it is pointed out, the change of political executive at the center and the nationwide police agitation launched by the Paramilitary groups like Central/Reserve Police Force (C.R.P.F.), Central Industrial Security Force (C.I.S.F.) etc and the intervention of the

Army to disarm and to deal with the striking police men. The story that makes the rounds in the corridors of power at the State capital was that the apparent indifference of the political executive under a Congress Chief Minister, an Indira Gandhi loyalist, was one of the reasons for the State's indifference to the recommendations of the National Police Commission and that this strengthened the general disdain entertained by the administrative service towards police reform efforts. Despite political differences, in many states committees of police officers had been constituted to submit selectively, proposals that could be implemented without serious budgetary burden. Such responses are seen in many states when the Committee on Police Training, popularly known as the 'Gore Committee' in which the then I.G. of Kerala was also a member submitted their Report. Large training complexes and supervisory levels have come up in most of the states to implement the recommendations of the Gore Committee. It is seen that this wave of enthusiasm did not touch Kerala. No doubt, some essential but necessarily cosmetic changes were introduced in the training scheme, but even this was due to individual initiative and not on the basis of an institutional response to the recommendations of the Committee on Police training.

The next landmark in the course of police reform was the appointment of the Kerala Police Re-organization Commission, 1982-86. Very strong and convincing evidence to prove that this attempt was neither earnest nor goal-oriented can be seen from the Note by the Member-Secretary who has exposed that many items in the Terms of Reference were physically lifted from the Terms of Reference of the National Police Commission, when the Commission had already submitted its report and copies were freely available in the market.

Thus, we find that neither the pioneering effort of 1959, nor the subsequent effort of 1982-86 did yield an iota of reform in the police setup in the State. Further, what is revealed is the absolute lack of mission-oriented effort to reform the police. It is an enigma wrapped in a mystery as to why such an attitude of indifference has survived for decades in this State which has claim for distinction in several fronts including the 'Kerala Model' of development, total literacy movement, people's planning etc.

This situation of indifference towards police reform has to be viewed from the sweeping changes that have taken place in the State and society of Kerala. It may be recalled that the State has had the rare opportunity to have practically every political party guide its destinies. Since a coalition of political parties have been in power in turns, some of the progressive policies like Land Reforms, Housing for the Poor, Social Security (Pension) measures for various weaker sections, Public Distribution Systems for basic essentials, medicines etc., have survived political changes. Over the years or from the formation of the State in 1956, the population of the State has increased and stabilized, there has been rapid urbanization, the number of vehicles of all description has registered substantial growth without matching road development, which has resulted in almost daily fatal motor accidents. There has been unionization of practically every section of society and there have been almost continuous demonstrations on the streets for ventilating the grievances of each or the demands of the many inviting the ire of the High Court which was constrained to issue directions to regulate such assemblies and processions not to hinder the right of the public to use the roads and streets. Students of both schools and colleges have been getting organized on political lines and often their elections have led to violent clashes, which have also prompted the High Court to ban election on political lines in schools and to have a re-thinking on such elections in the colleges. There have been violent demonstrations and direct action by Tribals and other marginalized sections of the society leading to offences accompanied by violence and loss of life like the Muttanga firing. Striking government employees have been on a confrontation status with the government for long. Extremist movements like naxellites and assorted militant groups have had their presence in the State for long. Caste and communal tensions leading to clashes and loss of life have not been rare. In crime, the State has seen a phenomenal growth under all heads. The operation of inter-state gangs in the state has surfaced quite often. Loss of revenue through economic offences have been an alarming feature of crime in the state. Organised gangs have been freely indulging in white-collar crimes like fake mark-lists from the Universities and various quick-rich schemes in the state. There have been several instances of offences against women, both gender violence and other serious offences like rape and molestation. The State has been in the grip of a spate of suicides mostly as a result of the consumption fever and the craze to "keep up with the Jones'". The fast aging population of the State has increased the geriatric problems faced by the community and the elderly have been easy targets of violence in the State. Migratory labour from neighbouring states and also from far away states like Bihar and from some of the neighbouring countries have generated new trends of crime. Thus, on the whole, both on the front of law and order and crime, the State has been undergoing rapid changes unparalleled in any other state in the country. There have also been non-traditional crimes, crimes aided by technology and cyber crimes and other sophisticated crimes, in the State.

These changes gripping the State in the short span of about a few decades, is violently shaking the very foundations of the traditional society and its institutions. It has already been pointed out that the law and order scene is witnessing new techniques and methods. Thus, the problems the police have to deal with have become very complex and massive.

Corruption, which used to be discussed in hushed terms is no longer so in the State. In fact, it has come to be believed that corruption is a way of life and there is no escape from it. The poor conviction rate and the many acquittals have contributed to a sense of cynicism among the people.

Several social and political activists and N.G.Os have also been making their presence in the State championing causes and issues like pollution, environmental degradation, encroachment of public lands, violations of Human Rights, gender justice, child labour etc. In fact, in the last few years, Human Rights concerns have been playing a high visibility role. Several police officers themselves have been raided by anti-corruption agencies and the Director General of Police himself has said that the strength of the police in the State suffer a short fall of nearly ten thousand. Failure of important cases in the courts, long delays in the trial process, long pendency of cases, both the prosecution and the prison's administration have contributed to confound the situation further. It is generally believed that the Apex Court or the State High Courts have to be approached for relief. It has been pointed out by Rajeev Dhawan, a noted lawyer and columnist that the jubilance that the

Supreme Court's verdict has averted injustice has another side. "If we are delighted that corrective justice has been done, these cases are disturbing warning of the internal collapse of the State Judicial System—requiring urgent attention especially in respect of investigation, prosecution trials and judicial integrity. Transferred justice is the ultimate unnecessary corrective when primary in-State remedies fail. These remedies are failing and falling. Politics is corrupting the justice system. This is how failed states are born."

It is obvious from the very general observation above that the crime and law and order situation in Kerala call for serious intervention with the objective of reforming the police sub-system.

It was observed earlier in this study that the case of police reform must be seen from the viewpoints of two of its important functionaries—the dispensers and the recipients. On this basis, studies are made of the perspectives of the police and the public with regard to the need and direction of police reform. The findings have been discussed separately in preceding chapters. During the interaction of the researcher with various levels of the police hierarchy, particularly with the Senior Management, (IPS officers), several former police officers, academics, members of the public, those from the media, political workers and others, a number of view points have come up both regarding areas of police reform and concerning the nature of reform. These have been discussed and incorporated in the relevant Chapters. However, by way of conclusion of the study, some of the more important suggestions that have come up during such interactions are briefly summed up below.

Police reform measures have been distinguished from modernization. The police were for long not a Plan subject in the country. The needs of the police were met from regular budgetary sources. A departure from this occurred during the mid seventies, when specific provisions were made to meet police needs for modern equipment of communication, Forensic Science Laboratories, computerization and other facilities. Such assistance came from grants from the Central Government and also from the resources of the State Government. The police were later, made a Plan subject for necessary allocations, but the modernization programme also continues. The modernization programme in sum, is an attempt to replace equipment and facilities which have become useless due to wear and tear and also to make available the gains of Science and Technology to the police in their quest for keeping pace with the lawless and criminal elements. This difference of modernization as a process of re-equipping the force and police reform as an approach towards reforming the police by re-writing the basic laws, supplying legal enactments and statutes were required, realigning the focus of the police department towards emerging challenges to order and tranquility in society and enabling it to keep pace with the rapid changes taking place all round, is a distinction that has come out of this study. In other words, any effort to supply the police forces with modern transport and communication facilities, cyber science support, strengthening of the Forensic Science back up, giving the police sophisticated weaponry and accoutrements for crowd control and traffic management and generally making the police spit and polish to match with forces elsewhere, would not be police reform since they are only 'aids to performance and not guides to performance'.

The next question that has been highlighted during the study is the need for replacing the Police Act of 1861 which provides the objectives and organizational framework of the police force in the country. This enactment was on the recommendation of the Police Commission of 1860, appointed in the wake of the revolt of 1857. The Police Acts, existing in the different states including the Kerala Police Act, 1960 (Act V, 1961) were all framed after the Act of 1861. The Act of 1861 envisaged a structure and conceived an array of objectives for the Police forces of British India to enable them to discharge the limited obligations of an alien government to its colony. The Act was, thus, enacted to cater to a set of narrow objectives as is seen spelt out in its preamble. In the last about one and a half century, India has changed beyond recognition. The objectives of the State itself has become wider and all embracing. The Preamble, Part III and Part IV of the Constitution created a State in free India that went far beyond even the concept of a Welfare State. The Universal Declaration of Human Rights did make its impact on the Constitution. Yet, the Police Act was not recast. Among the three major Criminal Laws, revision was made only on the Criminal Procedure Code in 1973. Some of the important Special and Local legislations are also of pre-independence vintage. That there is a pressing need for revising these enactments have been highlighted by the National Police Commission, 1977 by the Kerala Police Re-organization Committee, 1959 and also the Kerala Police Re-organization Commission, 1982-86. The National Police Commission in its VIII and Final Report appended a draft Police Act. However, there has not been any follow-up action even on this suggestion of the N.P.C. One of the suggestions that received massive support from the Police samples was that the need for a 'New Police Act' can no longer be delayed. This has been more or less the view of other respondents also. With regard to the various provisions of the Indian Penal Code and the Indian Evidence Act, several recent studies have highlighted that, these acts have within them provisions that could be so used to make denial of even basic Human Rights well supported by law. The use of explosives and fire arms have become very common in crimes perpetrated in the context of caste and communal clashes as well as offences committed to disturb internal security. This situation has exposed that the Indian Arms Act and the legislations on explosives are worn out and archaic. The massive amount of fatal motor accidents have similarly exposed the fact that the Motor Vehicle Act is obsolete. The provision in the Indian Penal Code dealing with rash and negligent acts on the roads were framed long before even the steam engines were used on the Indian roads. This study has brought out very clearly that there is an urgent need to enact a new Police Act, amend the Indian Penal Code and the Indian Evidence Act to incorporate among other things Human Rights Jurisprudence emerging in this country and to re-draft the Special and Local legislations most of which are apparently obsolete.

It has been seen that the spread of education and literacy and with matching political education, the people are seeking various measures to secure the redressal of their grievances. These take the form of Public Interest Litigations (PILs), public agitations and various other measures that make up the broad agenda of political activity. In a democracy, the right to dissent lies at the core of its value system. The right of the people to express their dissent cannot be curbed through restrictive measures on freedom of assembly or the freedom of expression and association. Therefore, the police style of crowd control and management of order has to attune itself to the need for maintaining public order without curbing the right of the people to articulate their demands and grievances. The existing provisions of law and the response package in the Police Standing Orders have to be therefore re-written to accommodate these two cardinal aspects of public life. This study has indicated that there is need for new legislations for maintenance of public order without detriment to the values of democratic life.

The crime profile of the State is alarming and crime figures are spiralling to all time high levels. The measures for crime control with the police are embedded in the basic Criminal Law trilogy, which are pre-independence legislations and which did not envisage the development of such sophistication in the commission of crime. While, it is necessary that the Human Rights of the accused are not denied, the Human Rights of the victim and the social cost of crime and the consequent heavy loss to the exchequer also have to be taken into account in designing police response to confront the burgeoning crime trends. When in scams and frauds important luminaries of the political firmament and police brass are also involved, the case for a fresh look at the legal enactments cannot be overstated. Even developed western countries are struggling to hold a balance between Human Rights of the offenders and national security in the wake of strident public outcry against violations of basic rights. The law and regulations relating to the management of crime-prevention as well as detection—have to be recast. This is a conclusion that has surfaced at several stages during the study.

A disturbing aspect of crime management that has been thrown up by the study is the long pendency of cases at the stage of investigation, at the stage of prosecution and adjudication and the poor rate of successful prosecution. The cost of crime and the cost of crime control should under ideal conditions create a crime free society. However, this may be more in the nature of a pious wish in the existing circumstances. But, it is essential that crime is controlled and successfully prosecuted to ensure that the developmental agenda of the State is not defeated. Management of crime is as important as the management of order to ensure orderly development in society. Therefore, to meet special and sophisticated crime and manage resourceful crime syndicates and mafia with transnational linkages, it is necessary to have ad hoc legislations, competent prosecutors and Special Courts. This is one of the important conclusions of the present study. It follows that police reform should embrace reforms in other components of the Criminal Justice sub-system, particularly prosecution machinery, the lower judiciary and the prison administration.

The police organization, it has been brought out during this study, is a monolith and is deeply influenced by the top leadership both in the style and content of management. Therefore, it is essential that the selection of the Head of the Department is free from narrow political or partisan considerations. The selection process of the Director, C.B.I. has contributed to assuring the country that the incumbent could be not only competent but capable of holding his own professional independence and ensuring neutrality in his response. The N.P.C., has underscored the need for keeping the office of the Director General (Head of the Department) beyond the reach of manipulative politics. A security of tenure for a properly selected Head of the Department is only a logical next step. A corollary to this is some effective measures against arbitrary functioning by the police authorities. The N.P.C had, therefore, suggested setting up of the State Security Commissions. One of the findings of the present study is that policing the police has to be not only a convincing exercise but also one that is user-friendly and totally transparent.

The satisfaction of the clientele has to be the basic objective of any organization. The study has exposed that there is an underlying distrust and an ever-widening gap between the police and the public. While in areas of functioning like investigation of sensational crimes, response to threats to national security, protection of VIPs/ V.V.I.P.s, the police have to keep some distance with the public, there are areas calling for less specialization where the public and the Police can function in tandem. Experiments in the west and elsewhere in involving the public in controlling crime, managing traffic, maintaining order on the streets, monitoring the movements of strangers and suspects, have taken the shape of Neighbourhood Watch, Community Policing, Special Police Officers, Traffic Wardens and Friends of the Police etc. It is time that, in areas where public involvement and participation are possible and beneficial, the police should launch initiatives on their own and welcome community participation. This is particularly so in the context of this country where it is generally believed that the weaker and vulnerable sections do not receive fair treatment at the hands of the police at interpersonal level as well as on occasions of official interaction. The study has forcefully suggested that police officers have to be more accessible to the needy victims, particularly from the vulnerable sections of society. The responses from the public have indicated clearly that there is a willingness on their part, to help and cooperate with the police in their effort to manage order and crime

A change in the style of functioning of the police would be necessary to make them people-friendly. It has been made abundantly clear during this study that appropriate training and reorientation alone can change negative mindset and encourage necessary attitudinal change. Therefore, police training has to undergo drastic revision and police have to organize training and orientation programme for those who are likely to associate themselves in police-community programmes. In other words, training has to take into account the need to re-orient the police for attitudinal change and to be people-friendly and also training should aim at educating the clientele on their duties and obligations as well as the constraints and limitations. This is particularly so in the background of the rising crime against women and other similar sections of the society and the need to introduce required sophistication in the police organization to accept both criticism and resistance to traditional police methods.

Organizationally, the study has pointed out to certain deficiencies. Most important of this has been identified at the Police Station level, where the base of the Police structural pyramid—the constabulary—were being given the least amount of participation in police functions except mechanical, repetitive, drudgery. With the constabulary coming from comparatively well educated sections of the society, there is a duty on the part of the police department to make use of their talents and skills and also throw open to them some meaningful role in police functioning. Similarly, there is also the need for delegation and specialization at the levels of the Station House Officer (S.H.O), since a single S.H.O. in a heavy police station will not be able to meet the demands on his time. Therefore, the question of amending the required laws to provide for multiple S.H.Os independently handling areas requiring specialization is a suggestion that has to receive serious attention.

During the course of the study, an area that came up for serious criticism was the haphazard personnel management practices which make the organization at certain level blotted and obese. It has come out that posts are created to avoid stagnation at certain levels and to make available greater opportunities for promotion. It is evident that no work-study has preceded such creation of new posts. From among the samples of the police department, there was no female from the middle management level. It has also come out that when for sake of promotion, posts are created the incumbent does hardly get enough work to justify the post. Thus, it is obvious that, there are aberrations in the personnel management policy. This is an area that requires serious study for necessary reforms.

A recent study on police reforms had suggested that the police themselves may initiate reforms wherever possible and that changes at the police station level in treating the public with courtesy would be a good beginning. It was also suggested that police reform efforts should seek the support of the people without leaving it as an exclusive initiative of the political executive. It is axiomatic that police reforms should form part of a popular agenda, if it has to transcend the present attitude of indifference or negative response. Therefore, while the police should launch a reform agenda on their own, side by side there should also be serious efforts to enlist the cooperation of all concerned to launch police reform as a serious political and administrative agenda. This is an area where the police leadership should take the initiative and establish rapport with all concerned to canvass the case for police reform. It has been seen that all efforts, so far made at the State as well as at the national level were purely political and not borne out of a demand from the people to reform their police so that they get a quality of service which gives them satisfaction. The next phase of police reform, the present study reveals, is launching of police reform as a people's initiative with close public-police partnership.

The hypotheses projected for the study were:

1. In spite of the Reports of various Committees/ Commissions on police reform, no serious or well considered effort has been made to implement the recommendations.
2. Instead of reforming the police, what the State Government has attempted so far is piecemeal modernization; and,
3. As clientele, the people are not satisfied with the performance of the police.

As can be seen from the above discussions the study has substantiated the validity of all the three hypotheses.

Bibliography

Primary Sources

1. Government of Assam, *Report of the Assam Police Commission*, Tezpur, 1971.
2. Government of Great Britain, *Report of the Royal Commission on the Police*, London, 1962.
3. Government of India, *Crime in India*, New Delhi, National Crime Records Bureau, Ministry of Home Affairs, 2000.
4. Government of India, *Report of the Indian Police Commission, 1902-03*, Simla, Central Printing Press, 1903.
5. Government of India, *Report of the Padmanabhayya Committee*, New Delhi, 2000.
6. Government of India, *Report of the Police Performance and Accountability Committee*, New Delhi, 1999.
7. Government of India, *Reports of the National Police Commission*, New Delhi, 1979-1981.
8. Government of Kerala, Annual Administration Reports of the Police Department for various years, Thiruvananthapuram
9. Government of Kerala, *Final Report of the Kerala Police Re-organization Commission*, Thiruvananthapuram 1986.
10. Government of Kerala, *Report of the Administrative Reforms Committee*, Thiruvananthapuram, 1958.

11. Government of Kerala, *Report of the Administrative Reforms Committee*, Thiruvananthapuram, 1997.

12. Government of Kerala, *Report of the Administrative Re-organization and Economy Committee*, Thiruvananthapuram, 1967.

13. Government of Kerala, *Report of the Kerala Police Re-organization Committee*, Thiruvananthapuram, 1959.

14. Government of Kerala, *Report of the Kerala Police Re-organization Commission*, Thiruvananthapuram, 1984.

15. Government of Kerala, *Report of the Study Group* constituted to assist the National Police Commission, Thiruvananthapuram, 1978.

16. Government of Maharashtra, *Report of the Maharashtra Police Commission*, Bombay, 1964.

17. Government of Punjab, *Report of the Punjab Police Commission*, Chandigarh, 1961-62.

18. Government of Tamil Nadu, *Report of the Tamil Nadu Police Commission*, Madras, 1971.

19. Government of Uttar Pradesh, *Report of the Uttar Pradesh Police Commission*, Lucknow, 1970-71.

20. Government of West Bengal, *Report of the West Bengal Police Commission*, Calcutta, 1960-61.

Secondary Sources

A. Books and Articles

1. Ahorn, James. F., *Police in Trouble*, New York, Praeger, 1972.

2. Alexander, P.J., "Legal Framework of Police Process, Tortion and Distortion", (Mimeo), Bangalore, Ecumenical Christian Centre, 2003.

3. Alexander, P.J., "Police Reform Perspectives", (Mimeo), Thiruvananthapuram, Institute of Management in Government, 1988.

4. Alexander, P.J., "Role of the Civil Service in the Context of the New Economic Policy", Thiruvananthapuram, *Kerala Journal of Social Science*, Vol. I, No. 1, January-June, 1996.

5. Alexander, P.J., "Why We are Not Consulted? A Policeman's Dilemma", (Mimeo), Thiruvananthapuram, Institute of Management in Government, 1986.

6. Alexander, P.J.; (ed.), *Policing India in the New Millennium*, New Delhi, Allied Publishers, 2002.

7. Alexander, P.J., *Police and Elections in India*, Thiruvananthapuram, Indian Institute of Police Studies, 1989.

8. Alexander, P.J., *Sasthreeya Kuttanweshanam*, (Mal.), Trivandrum, D.C. Books, 1989.

9. Anil Bhatt, *Development and Justice*, New Delhi, Jaya Publications 1989.

10. Aravind.S., *Indian Administration*, Bombay, Himalaya Publishers, 1992.

11. Arnold David, *Police Power and Colonial Rule, 1859-1947*, Madras, B.N.K. Press, 1992.

12. Arora, Ramesh, K., *Indian Administration: Perceptions and Perspectives*, Jaipur, Aalekh Publishers, 1999.

13. Baruah, Arunima, *Crime Against Children*, New Delhi, Gyan Books, 2003.

14. Bayley, David. H., *Police and Political Development in India*, New Jersey, Princeton University Press, 1969.

15. Belson, W., *The Public and the Police*, Boston, Harper and Row, 1975.

16. Berkley, George. E, *The Democratic Policeman*, Boston, Beacon Press, 1969.

17. Bharadwaj. A., "Police Modernization in India: A Study of Women Police in Delhi", New Delhi, *The Indian Journal of Social Work*, Vol. 37, No. 1. 1976.

18. Bhattacharya, Mohit, *Organization and System of Policing of Medium Size Cities*, New Delhi, Indian Institute of Public Administration, 1976.

19. Bhattacharyya, D.G., *Random Reminiscences of a Police Officer Under Two Flags*, New Delhi, Gyan Books, 2003.

20. Black, Algernon, D., *The People and the Police*, New York, Mc-Graw Hill Book Co., 1968.

21. Bopp, W.J., *The Police Rebellion*, Spring Field, Charles C. Thomas, Illinois, 1971.

22. Bopp, W.J., *Police Administration, Selected Readings*, Boston, Helbrook Press, 1975.

23. Bouza, Anthony V., *Police Administration, Organization and Performance*, U.S.A., Pergamon Press, 1978.

24. Brown, John and Grahan Howse, (eds.), *Police in the Community*, Lexington, Lexington Books, 1975.

25. Bunyard, R.S., *Police, Organisation and Command*, London, ELBS, 1978.

26. Butter, A.J.P., *Police Management*, Aldershot, Gower Publishing Company, 1984.

27. Cain, M.E., *Society and the Policeman's Role*, London, Rouledge and Kegan Paul, 1973.

28. Chandra, Ramesh, *Global Terrorism: A Threat to Humanity*, New Delhi, Gyan Books, 2003.

29. Chapman, Brain, *Police State*, New York, Praegar, 1970.

30. Chaturvedi, T.N. and Rao. S, Venugopal, (eds), "*Police Administration*", New Delhi, Indian Institute of Public Administration, 1982.

31. Chaurvedi, T.N. (ed.), "*Police Administration*", New Delhi, Indian Institute of Public Administration, 1978.

32. Chevigny, Paul, *Corps and Rebels*, New York, Pantheon Books, 1972.

33. Coatman John, *Police*, London, Oxford University Press, 1959.

34. Coffey Atan, et.al., *Police Community Relations*, New Jersey, Engle Wood Cliffs, Prentice Hall, 1971.

35. Cox, Edmund, C., *Police and Crime in India*, London, Stanley Paul and Company, 1961.

36. Cramer, James, *The World's Police*, London, Cassell, 1964.

37. Curry, J.C., *The Indian Police*, London, Faber and Faber, 1932.

38. Das, S.T., *National Security in Perspective*, New Delhi, Gyan Books, 1987.

39. Das, D.K., *Understanding Police Human Relations*, London, The Scare Crow Press, 1987.

40. Dhameja, Nand and Singh, Rajesh, "Prison Administration Privatisation Practices, Issues and Prospects", New Delhi, *Indian Journal of Public Administration*, Vol. XLV, No. 1, January-March, 1999.

41. Dhawan, Rajeev, "Transferred Justice", *The Hindu*, 28, November, 2003.

42. Diaz, S.M., *Police and Correctional Services in Crime and Correction in India*, Bombay, Tata Institute of Social Sciences, 1983.

43. Dikshit, R.C, *Police, The Human Face*, New Delhi, Gyan Publishing House, 2000.

44. Duverger, Maurice, *Ideas of Politics, The Use of Power in Society*, London, Mathaen Commissioner Limited, 1964.

45. Earle, Howard. H., *Police Community Relations, Crisis in Our Times* 2nd Edition, Spring Field, Illinois, Charles C. Thomas, 1972.

46. Erayil, A.L. and Vadackumchery, James, *Police and the Society*, Thiruvananthapuram, Kairali Books International, 1985.

47. Erayil, A.L. and Vadackumchery, James, *Public Relations at the Cutting Edge Level*, New Delhi, National Publishing House, 1984.

48. Favrean, Donal F. and Joseph Gillespie, *Modern Police Administration*, New Jersey, Eagle Woodcliffs, 1978.

49. Fink Joseph and Seely, *The Community and the Police*, New York, 1979.

50. Fleisher, Leslie. A., *Police-Community Relations*, North Carolina, Chapel Hill, Institute of Government University, 1967.

51. Gaines, Lorry. K., *Policing in America*, 3rd ed., New Jersey, Anderson Publishing Company, 1999.

52. Gautam, B.N., "Police and Electoral Offences", *Sardar Vallabhai Patel National Police Academy Magazine*, January-June, 1990.

53. Geeller, A. William (ed.), *Police Leadership in America Crisis and Opportunity*, New York, Praeger, 1985.

54. Ghosh. S.K., *Indian Police at Cross Roads*, Allahabad, Eastern Law House, 1971.

55. Ghosh. S.K., *Law and Order from Police Point of View*, Calcutta, Eastern Law House, 1972.

56. Gibaldi, Joseph, *The Modern Language Association of America, Handbook for Writers of Research Papers*, 5th ed., New Delhi, East West Books Pvt. Ltd, 1999.

57. Gill, K.P.S., *Terror and Containment, Perspectives of India's Internal Security*, New Delhi, Gyan Books, 2001.

58. Goldsmith J. Andrew, (ed.), *Complaints Against the Police, The Trend to External Review*, Oxford, Clarendon Press, 1991.

59. Gourley, G.D., *Police and the Public*, Springfield, Illinois, Charles C. Thomas, 1953.

60. Griffiths, Percival, *To Guard My People: The History of the Indian Police*, London, Earnest Benn Ltd, 1971.

61. Grifflin, B.S. and Griffin, T.C., *Juvenile Delinquency in Perspective*, New York, Harper and Row Publishers, 1978.

62. Gupta, M.C., *Child Victims of Crime: Problems and Perspectives*, New Delhi, Gyan Books, 2001.

63. Hagan William, T., *Indian Police and Judges*, Yale, University Press, 1966.

64. Hale, Charles, D., *Fundamentals of Police Administration*, Boston, Hall Brook Press, 1971.

65. Hewitt, Cecil. R., *The Police and the Public*, London, Heinemann, 1962.

66. Hodge, Robert, W., *The Public the Police and the Administration*, Chicago, National Opinion Centre, 1965.

67. Holmgrem, Bruce, R., *Primary Police Function*, New York, William Capp, 1962.

68. Inspector General of Police, *The History of Madras Police Centenary, 1859-1959,* Madras, B.N.K. Press, 1959.

69. Iyer, Krishna, V.R., *Police in a Welfare State*, New Delhi, Asia Book Centre, 1958.

70. Jafa, Y.S., "Challenges for Police in the 21st Century", New Delhi, *Indian Journal of Public Administration*, Vol. XLVII, No. 1, Jan-March 2001.

71. Jenkins, Robert, *Keeping the Peace*, New York, Harper and Row, 1970.

72. Johnson, Buttolph Janet and Joslyn A. Richard, *Political Science Research Methods*, New Delhi, Prentice Hall of India, 1989.

73. Joseph, M.K., "A Brief History of the Kerala Police", Thiruvananthapuram, *Kerala Police Centenary Souvenir*, 1961.

74. Kamte, N.M. and Teelang, T.K., *The Police in India and Abroad*, Pune, M.J. Kanite House, 1980.

75. Kapoor, H.L., *Police Investigation, Law and Procedure*, New Delhi, ESS ESS Publications, 1989.

76. Kashyap, Subhash, C., (ed.), *Crime and Corruption to Good Governance*, New Delhi, Uppal, 1997.

77. Khobragade, Ram, *Indian Constitution Under Communal Attack*, New Delhi, Gyan Books, 2002.

78. Kooken, Don, L., *Ethics in Police Service*, Spring Field, Illinois, Charles. C. Thomas, 1957.

79. Krishnaswamy, O.R., *Methodology of Research in Social Sciences*, Mumbai, Himalaya Publishing House, 1999.

80. Laaurie Peter, *Scotland Yard: A Study of the Metropolitan Police*, England, Bengain Press, 1951.

81. Lakshmi Narayanan, V.R., "Issues in Policing", *The Hindu*, 29 October, 2002.

82. Lal A.K., *Neo Terrorism: An Indian Experience*, New Delhi, Gyan Books, 2003.

83. Logan, William, *Malabar*, Madras, Superintendent, Government Press, 1951.

84. Lynch, Ronald, G., *The Police Manager*, Boston, Holbrook Press, Inc. 1975.

85. Macnamara, E.J., and Riedel, M. (eds)., *Police Perspectives, Problems, Prospects*, New York, Praeger, 1974.

86. Madhurima, *Violence Against Women: Dynamics of Conjugal Relations*, New Delhi, Gyan Books, 1996.

87. *Malayala Manorama Year Book*, Kottayam, 2000.

88. *Malayala Manorama Year Book*, Kottayam, 2001.

89. *Malayala Manorama Year Book*, Kottayam, 2002.

90. *Malayala Manorama Year Book*, Kottayam, 2003.

91. Maltik, P.J., *The Criminal Court Hand Book*, Lucknow, Eastern Book Company, 1992.

92. Mark, Robert, *Policing a Perplexed Society*, London, George Allen and Unwin Publishers Limited, 1977.

93. Marwah, Ved, "Police and Good Governance", *Indian Journal of Public Administration*, New Delhi, Vol. XLIV, No. 3, July-September, 1998.

94. Mathur, K.M., *Administration of Police Training in India*, New Delhi, Gyan Books, 1987.

95. Mathur, K.M., *Indian Police: Role and Challenges*, New Delhi, Gyan Books, 1994.

96. Mathur, K.M., *Management of Internal Security and Related Issues*, New Delhi, Gyan Books, 1995.

97. Mathur, K.M., *Police Law and Internal Security*, New Delhi, Gyan Books, 1994.

98. Mathur, K.M., *Problems of Police in a Democratic Society*, Jaipur, R.B.S.A Publishers, 1987.

99. Mathur, Kuldeep and Bhattacharya, Mohit, "*Top Management in the Police Case Study of A State Police Organization*", New Delhi, Indian Institute of Public Administration, 1976.

100. Mathur, Kumar Pragya, *Stress in Police in India*, New Delhi, Gyan Books, 1999.

101. Matthai, John, *Village Government in British India*, London, T.Fisher Unwin, Ltd., 1915.

102. Menon, A. Sreedhara, *Triumph and Tragedy in Travancore*, Trivandrum, Current Books, 2001.
103. Menon, A., Sreedhara, *A Survey of Kerala History*, Kottayam, National Book Stall, 1976.
104. Menon, Achutha, C., *The Cochin State Manual*, Ernakulam, Cochin, Government Press, 1911.
105. Misra, S.C., *Police Administrations In India*, Mount Abu, National Police Academy, 1972.
106. Misra, S.C., *State Police Organization in India*, New Delhi, Gyan Books, 1975.
107. Mohan, V.K., *Crime Community and Police*, New Delhi, Gyan Books, 1987.
108. Murray, Joseph, A., *Police Administration and Criminal Investigation*, New York, 3rd ed., Arco, 1968.
109. Nair, A. Balakrishnan, "*Landmarks in the Administration of Kerala*", Thiruvananthapuram, Indian Institute of Public Administration, 1996.
110. Nair, Ramakrishnan, R., "Social Structure and Political Development in Kerala", Trivandrum, *The Kerala Academy of Political Science*, 1976.
111. Nair, Ramesan, K., *Kerala Police, Nootandukalilude*, (Mal.), Thiruvananthapuram, Valsa Printers, 1989.
112. Nair, Sankarankutty, T.P. (ed.), "*Society and Politics Issues and Perspectives*", Trivandrum, Indian Institute of Police Studies, 1998.
113. Nath, Trilok, *The Indian Police*, New Delhi, Sterling Publishers, 1978.
114. Nath, Trilok, *The Indian Police: A Case for a New Image*, New Delhi, Sterling Publishers, 1978.
115. Neiderhoffer, Arthur, and Smith, Alexander B, *New Directions in Police Community Relations*, New York, Rinehart Press, 1974.
116. Newell, Roberto and Wilson, Gregory A., "Premium for Good Governance", Illinois, *MCK Quarterly*, 2002.

117. Niederhoffer, A., *Behind the Shield, A Police in Urban Society*, New York, Routledge and Company, 1976.

118. Nigam, S.R., *Scotland Yard and the Indian Police*, Allahabad, Kitab Mahal Pvt. Ltd, 1963.

119. Norris, Donald F., *Police Community A Programme that Failed*, Lexington, Lexington Books, Mass, 1973.

120. Olimos R.A., *An Introduction to Police Community Relations*, Spring Field, Charles C. Thomas Publications.

121. Patrick, Clarence. H., *The Police, Crime and Society*, Spring Field, Charles C. Thomas, U.S.A., 1972.

122. Pell, Arthur, R., *Police Leadership*, Springfield Charles C. Thomas, U.S.A., 1967.

123. Peper, John, P., "Public Relations for the Law Enforcement Officer", *Bureau of Industrial Education*, California State, Department of Education, Sacramento, California, 1965.

124. Police Commissions, "The Gap Between Recommendations and Their Implementation" (Mimeo), *Sardar Vallabhai Patel National Police Academy Magazines*, Hyderabad, 1976.

125. Prabha, M., *Nammude Police*, (Mal.), Thiruvananthapuram, Samrdhi Media, 1983.

126. Prakasham, R., *Kaalathinotha Police: M. Gopalante Dauthyavum Darshanavum* (Mal.), Trivandrum, D.C. Books,.2003.

127. Prosser, Charles Wegg., *The Police and the Law*, London, Oyez Publishing Limited, 1973.

128. Pursuit G. Dan, et.al., *Police Programmes for Preventing Crime and Delinquency*, U.S.A., Charles C. Thomas, 1972.

129. Radelet, Louis, A., *The Police and The Community*, New York, MacMillan Company, 1986.

130. Raj, James, Lawrence, *The Making and Unmaking of British India*, London, Abacus, 1997.

131. Ramesan Nair. K. *Kerala Police Nootandukalilude* (Mal.), Trivandrum, Valsa Printers, 1985.

132. Rao, Venugopal, S. *Women in India, Police Research and Development*, New Delhi, 1975.

133. Regoli, R.M., *Police in America, A Study of Cynicism*, Washington DC, University Press of America, 1976.

134. Reith Charles, *A Short History of British Police*, London, Oxford University Press, 1948.

135. Reith, Charles, *British Police and Democratic Ideal*, London, Oxford University Press, 1943.

136. Riccio, L.C. and Colin A.W., *The Future of Policing*, London, Sage Publications, Beverley Hills, 1978.

137. Roy, J.G., *Prisons and Society: A Study of the Indian Jail System*, New Delhi, Gyan Books, 1989.

138. Ruchelman, L. (ed.), *Who Rules the Police*, New York, New York University Press, 1973.

139. Sabha, B.P., *Indian Police Legacy and Quest for Formative Role*, Delhi, Konark Publishers Private Limited, 1990.

140. Saha, B.P., *The Police in Free India*, Konark Publishers, 1989.

141. Sapru, R.K., *Civil Service Administration in India*, New Delhi, Deep and Deep Publications 1985.

142. Saxena, N.S., *Law and Order in India*, New Delhi, Abhinar Publications, 1987.

143. Sen, Sankar, and Saxena A.K. (ed.), *Police Training, Problems and Perspectives*, Jaipur, Rawat Publications, 1994.

144. Sharma P.G., *Police, Polity and People in India*, New Delhi, Uppal Publishing House, 1981.

145. Sharma, K.K., "The Police and the Corruption—An Empirical Exploration", New Delhi, *Indian Journal of Public Administration*, Vol. XLVII, No. 2, April-June, 2002.

146. Simpson, Antony, E., *The Literature of Police Corruption*, New York, John Jay Press, 1977.

147. Singh, Joginder, *Outside C.B.I.*, New Delhi, Gyan Books, 2001.

148. Sowle, C.R., (ed.), *Power and Individual Freedom*, Chicago, Aldini, 1962.

149. Steadman, Robert, F., (ed.), *The Police and the Community*, Bathmore, 1972.

150. Subramariam, C. *Indian Police*, Delhi, B.R. Publishing Corporation, 2000.

151. Tandon, O.P., "Law and Order: A Precondition for Good Governance", New Delhi, *Indian Journal of Public Administration,* Vol. XLIV, No. 3, July-September, 1998.

152. Thakur, R.N. *The All India Services*, Patna, Bharathy Bhavan, 1969.

153. Tiwari, R.S., "Good Governance: Populist Democracy to Quality Democracy"-*Indian Journal of Public Administration*, New Delhi, Vol. XLVIII, No.4, October, December 2002.

154. Vadackumchery, James, *Policing the Largest Democracy, 50 years and After*, New Delhi, A.P.H. Publishing Corporation, 1998.

155. Vadackumchery, James, *The Police, The People and Criminal Justice,* New Delhi, A.P.H. Publishing Corporation, 1997.

156. Vadackumchery, James, *Third Millennium Police, Take of Trends in India*, New Delhi, A.P.H. Publishing Corporation, 2000.

157. Vadakkumchery, James, *Police Criminology and Crimes*, New Delhi, Gyan Books, 2002.

158. Vadakkumchery, James, *Police Morality*, New Delhi, Gyan Books, 2001.

159. Vaddakkumcherry, James, *Indian Police and Nexus Crime*, New Delhi, Gyan Books, 2002.

160. Velupillai, T.K. *The Travancore State Manual*, Trivandrum Vol. 4, , 1940.

161. Venkiteswaran, K., "Kerala Must Press for Special Grants", *The Hindu*, 4 December, 2003.

162. Verma, Aravind, "Police Accountability—Lessons From Other Countries", New Delhi, *Indian Journal of Public Administration*, Vol. XLIV, No. 4, October-December, 1998.

163. Vittal, N., "Strategy for Better Governance", *The Hindu*, 31, March, 2002.

164. Walker, Samuel, *The Police in America, An Introduction*, New York, 2nd Edn., McGraw Hill, 1992.

165. Westly, William, *Violence and the Police*, Cambridge, Mass MIT Press, 1970.

166. Westom Paul, B., *The Police Traffic Control Function*, Illinois, Charles C. Thomas, Springfield, 1968.

167. Whisenand Paul, M., *Police Supervision Theory and Practice*, New Jersey, Englewood Chiffs, Prentice Hall, 1973.

168. Whitaker, Ben, *The Police*, Baltimore, Penguin Book, 1964.

169. Wilson, O.W., *Police Administration*, New York, McGraw Hill, 1950.

170. Wright R. Gene and Marlo, A. John, *The Police Officer and Criminal Justice*, New York, McGraw Hill, 1970.

B. Newspapers

1. *Deepika* (Mal.), Thiruvananthapuram.
2. *Desabhimani* (Mal.), Thiruvananthapuram.
3. *Kerala Kaumudi* (Mal.), Thiruvananthapuram.
4. *Malayala Manorama* (Mal.), Thiruvananthapuram.
5. *Mathrubhumi* (Mal.), Thiruvananthapuram.
6. *The Hindu*, Thiruvananthapuram.
7. *The New Indian Express*, Thiruvananthapuram.

Index

O

P

❑❑❑